Get to know and understand your

Financial Instruments

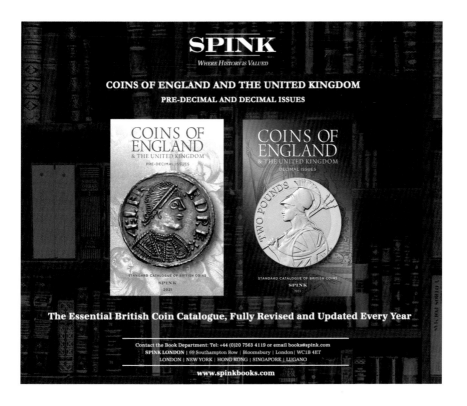

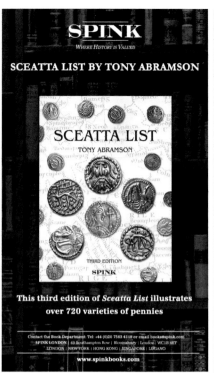
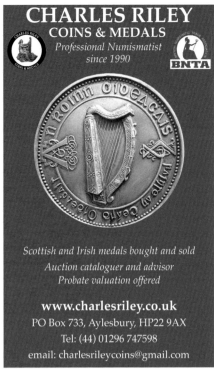

BY APPOINTMENT TO
HER MAJESTY THE QUEEN
MEDALLISTS & PHILATELISTS
SPINK & SON LTD. LONDON

BY APPOINTMENT TO
H.R.H. THE DUKE OF EDINBURGH
MEDALLISTS
SPINK & SON LTD. LONDON

SPINK

LONDON
1666

THE COINS OF ENGLAND COLOURING BOOK

SPINK BOOKS ARE PROUD TO PRESENT THE FIRST EVER
COINS OF ENGLAND COLOURING BOOK
A COLOURING BOOK FOR ALL AGES

22 FULL PAGE ILLUSTRATIONS
FILLED WITH A SELECTION OF OUR NATION'S MOST BEAUTIFUL COIN DESIGNS
EACH COLOURING DESIGN IS ACCOMPANIED BY A SHORT PAGE OF HISTORICAL CONTEXT

ISBN: 978-1-912667-40-6
RRP: £6.99

Standard Catalogue of British Coins, volume 2

COINS OF SCOTLAND, IRELAND AND THE ISLANDS

(Jersey, Guernsey, Man & Lundy)

and

Anglo-Gallic coins

PRE-DECIMAL ISSUES

Fourth Edition

SPINK

LONDON

A Catalogue of the Coins of Great Britain
and Ireland
first published 1929

Standard Catalogue of British Coins
Coins of Scotland, Ireland and the Islands
first published 1984
2nd revised edition 2003
3rd revised edition 2015
4th revised edition 2020

© 2020 Spink & Son Ltd.
69 Southampton Row, Bloomsbury
London WC1B 4ET

ISBN 978-1-912667-48-2

Typeset by Galata Print Ltd, Llanfyllin

Printed and bound in Malta by Gutenberg Press Ltd

CONTENTS

PREFACE TO THE FIRST EDITION (1984)

Seaby's first catalogue, *A Catalogue of the Coins of Great Britain and Ireland*, published in 1929 was a list of coins in stock offered for sale. Our *Standard catalogue of the Coins of Great Britain and Ireland*, first published in 1945, was a general guide to values for the collector. In 1962 the first volume of a revised edition was published under the title *Standard Catalogue of British Coins* – Parts 1 and 2 being 'Coins of England and the United Kingdom', followed by Part 3, being, 'Coins and Tokens of Ireland' by P J Seaby (1970), and Part 4, "Coins and Tokens of Scotland' by P F Purvey (1972). A further major revision in 1978 saw 'Coins of England and the United Kingdom' issued in a larger format as 'Volume 1' of the *Standard Catalogue of British Coins*.

'Volume 2 – Coins of Scotland, Ireland and the Islands' incorporates not only the previous Parts 3 and 4, suitably revised, but also the coinages of the Isle of Man, Guernsey, Jersey and Lundy Island. The catalogue has been compiled with the collector principally in mind, but it is hoped that the volume will also be a compact general handbook for the archaeologist, museum curator, history student and amateur coin finder, and, for that matter, any person who has a coin to identify and perhaps wishes to know its approximate value. We have endeavoured to incorporate new information that has come to our notice since the earlier catalogues were published and, of course, values have been amended in the light of current market conditions. If we omit all the personal acknowledgements made in the earlier editions it is no indication that the editors underestimate the value of the help they have received from many sources over the years. Collectors, students of numismatics and museum keepers have made a major contribution by their willingness to share their knowledge and expertise. However, they would like to record their thanks to Robert Sharman for his valuable advice in repricing the catalogue and to Alan Miles for providing the two new mint maps. All the photographs in this volume have been taken by Frank Purvey with the co-operation of the British Museum, the Ashmolean Museum, Oxford, the National Museum of Ireland, Dublin, the Ulster Museum, Belfast, and the owners of several private collections.

We have appended to this preface notes on coin values and grades of condition, i.e., state of preservation, as this is a major factor in determining the value of a coin, and a list of numismatic terms. Under each of the three main sections of this catalogue we have given a brief introduction to the coinage, a list of Latin legends with their translations and a select bibliography. The arrangement of the list of coins is not completely uniform but generally, under each reign, it is divided into metals (gold, silver, copper, etc.), then into distinctive coinages or directly into denominations and varieties, every date of coin being listed. The token coinage of Scotland, Ireland and the Islands will be included in the forthcoming edition of Seaby's *British Token Coinage*. For the new collector we would recommend a reference to 'A Beginner's Guide to Coin Collecting', to be found on pages viii-xii in Volume 1.

PREFACE TO THE SECOND EDITION (2003)

This new edition has been totally re-priced and brought up to date throughout. It incorporates recently published research, particularly in Alexander III, with a re-classification of the second coinage, Sterlings, based on the works of North and Stewart.

Many new varieties of Scottish Milled silver are now listed with prices, and the proof issues in the Irish section have been incorporated within the main body of the text. Many new varieties of Gunmoney have been discovered since 1984, and these have now been included. All the Free State and Republic issue proofs have been included and priced in the main body of the catalogue.

Mintage figures have been included in the Modern Irish and Channel Island sections, whilst many of the more unusual proofs are now included with prices in the Isle of Man section.

We hope to publish revised editions of this catalogue on a more regular basis, and with this in mind, we would be grateful to hear from anyone with unpublished material with a view to including it in subsequent editions.

PREFACE TO THE THIRD EDITION (2015)

After ending the preface to the second edition by stating that we intended to publish revised editions of this catalogue on a more regular basis, 12 years have somehow passed, but what you have in your hands is the fruit of the labours of at least the last five years work.

The first of the major changes in this edition is the obvious move from black and white images to full colour, a task that seemed at first to be relatively straightforward, but which proved to be the most time-consuming and difficult of all. The second major update is the introduction of a completely new section covering the Anglo-Gallic coinage, namely those coins struck in France by the kings and princes of England between 1154 and 1453. No attempt has previously been made to produce a priced catalogue of this coinage and it seemed an appropriate place to publish this for the first time. The third major update is the re-pricing of the entire catalogue, another task which appears simple at first but when 12 years have passed since the last edition of this work, the amount of data which requires attention is both broad and sparse at the same time. There have been some excellent collections sold on the market in that time, those of Lucien LaRiviere in 2006 being the largest offerings of both Scottish and Irish coins but, in some areas, there has been such a small amount of material that it makes the job of putting forward meaningful prices somewhat more difficult.

Major updates of standard references such as this don't happen without the collaboration of numerous individuals who give of their time and resources to assist in achieving the most complete and accurate catalogue available on the market. We would like to single out a number of these individuals without whose help this catalogue simply would not have been possible.

Bente Withers completely re-typed the entire text from the previous edition, correcting it as she went along, and has patiently and conscientiously worked through several drafts of the text.

Paul Withers remains one of the best numismatic photographers in the business and has travelled far and wide to museums and private collections to source the best possible images for this edition. Together they have edited thousands of images ready for publication. The new section on the Anglo-Gallic coins was created by them together with Steve Ford, a simplified version of a book which they have been working on for many years.

In mentioning museums, one cannot stress too heavily the role they play in preserving national treasures for future generations and coins fall very heavily into that category. Michael Kenny, retired keeper of coins in the National Museum of Ireland, literally came out of retirement for several days in order to assist with the inspection and photography of the wonderful collection of Irish coins now housed at Collins Barracks in Dublin. A similar favour was afforded by Nicholas Holmes, Research Associate in Numismatics at the National Museum of Scotland, who not only sourced numerous images for this edition but corrected and updated the text where necessary to reflect current research. In the Irish section, the expertise of John Stafford-Langan cannot go unmentioned in contributing to the updating of the hammered coinage; primarily that of Edward I to Edward IV. Users will notice significant changes in this section and should pay attention to the renumbering.

For reference the numbers from the previous edition have also been included. Last, but not least, Alan Kelly of Mannin Collections Ltd. offered his expertise in updating the Isle of Man coinage, a small but not insignificant part of this book.

ACKNOWLEDGEMENTS
We thank the following institutions for permission to reproduce images of their coins:

Ashmolean Museum, Oxford (AM), Bibliothèque nationale de France (BnF) Fitzwilliam Museum, Cambridge (FM), National Museum of Ireland, Dublin (NMI) National Museums of Scotland, Edinburgh (NMS), Trustees of the British Museum, London (BM). Some images are reproduced courtesy of Dix Noonan Webb.

We thank the following individuals for their contributions:

Martin Allen (FM)	Heritage Auctions	Bill Pugsley
Michael Anderson	Philip Higginson	John Rainey
Jasper Burns	Steve Hill	Brad Shepherd
Garry Byrne	Nicholas Holmes (NMS)	May Sinclair
Peter Cherry	Ian Jones	Andy Singer
David Collins	Alan Kelly	Tom Smith
Geoffrey Cope	Michael Kenny (NMI)	Peter Spencer
Allan Davisson	Michael E. Kenny	David Stuart
Valerie Dowling (NMI)	John Mattinson	Richard Walsh
Tim Everson	Sarah Nolan (NMI)	Tim Webb Ware
Steve Ford	Raghnall O'Floinn (NMI)	Maggie Wilson (NMS)
David Guest	Del Parker	Andrew Woods
David Headon	William Prentice	

PREFACE TO THE FOURTH EDITION

In a bid to keep our promise of publishing revised editions of this catalogue on a more regular basis, we are pleased to be releasing this fourth edition only five years after its last major overhaul. Again, Paul and Bente Withers of Galata have been an indispensable help in co-ordinating and assimilating the many new additions, illustrations and price changes, and we are indebted to Bente for overseeing the whole project in such a calm and knowledgeable manner. Their huge amount of work on the previous edition has certainly stood the test of time. This new edition contains Alan Kelly's write up of the 1721-1725 Isle of Man coinage, which has never been done before, plus Oisín Mac Conamhna's complete overhaul of the coinages of Edward IV. We are grateful to them both for giving so generously of their time. Thanks also to Vincent Morley for the Saorchló font for the modern Irish coin inscriptions. We have relied on the contribution of many experts who have kindly given their time and knowledge to achieve the most up-to-date and accurate catalogue of this coinage on the market, and are truly indebted to you all.

ACKNOWLEDGEMENTS

We would like to thank the institutions listed above who provided images of their coins for the Third Edition for their continued use in this catalogue, and the following individuals for their invaluable input:

Martin Allen	David Guest	Andy Singer
Garry Byrne	Nick Holmes	John Stafford-Langan
David Collins	Alan Kelly	David Stuart
Gillian Davies	Oisín Mac Conamhna	Tim Webb Ware
David Dykes	John Rainey	Paul Withers
Steve Ford	Mark Rasmussen	Andrew Woods

THE VALUE OF A COIN

Except in a very few instances this catalogue will not give the exact value of any coin. Its purpose is to give a general value for a particular class of coin in the states of preservation noted at the head of each column of prices, and also to give the collector an idea of the range and value of coins. The value of any particular piece depends on three things:

Its exact design, legend, mintmark or date.
Its exact state of preservation; this is of prime importance.
The demand for it in the market at any given time.

Some minor varieties are much scarcer than others, and, as the number of coins varies considerably from year to year, coins of certain dates and mintmarks are rarer and of more value than other pieces of a similar type. The prices given for any type are for the commonest variety, mintmark or date of that type. Values given are typical selling prices at the time of going to press and *not* the price we would pay.

NUMBERING USED. The numbering used in the Scottish section is the same as in *Scottish Coins and Tokens*. In the Irish section, however, the first digit 4 has been changed to a 6, this retaining the essential reference number as used in *Irish Coins and Tokens*. The Islands section begins at 7000 and numerous gaps occur to facilitate the addition of new types, etc. The new section for Anglo-Gallic coins begins at 8000.

CONDITION GRADING

Proof. See page viii.

FDC = *Fleur-de-coin.* Mint state, unused, flawless, without any wear, scratches or marks.

Unc. = *Uncirculated.* A coin in new condition as issued by the Royal Mint, but, owing to modern mass-production methods of manufacture, not necessarily perfect.

EF = *Extremely Fine.* A coin that shows little sign of having been in circulation, but which may exhibit slight surface marks on very close inspection.

VF = *Very Fine.* Only slight traces of wear on the raised surfaces; a coin that has had only slight circulation.

F = *Fine.* Considerable signs of wear on the raised surfaces, or design weak through faulty striking.

Fair. A coin that is worn, but which has the inscriptions and main features of the design still distinguishable, or a piece that is very weakly struck.

Poor. A very worn coin, of no value as a collector's piece unless extremely rare.

SOME NUMISMATIC TERMS AND ABBREVIATIONS

Blank	The coin as a blank piece of metal, i.e. before it is struck.
Cuirassed (cuir.)	Protected by armour on breast and shoulder.
Die	The block of metal, with design cut into it, which impresses the blank with the design.
Die variety	A coin of the same type but with slight variation of the design through having been struck by another die.
Draped (dr.)	Drapery around the bust.
Exergue (ex.)	That part of the coin below the main design, normally separated by a horizontal line, and frequently occupied by the date.
Field	The flat part of the coin between the main design and the inscription or edge of the coin.
Flan	The piece of metal as distinct from the design of the coin (one speaks of 'a cracked flan', 'a flaw in the flan', etc.). In the USA 'planchet'.
Graining	The crenellations round the edge of the coin, commonly known as 'milling'.
Hammered	Refers to the old craft method of striking a coin between dies hammered by hand.
Laureate (laur.)	Head with laurel wreath.
Left, or Right (l., or r.)	Coin descriptions normally refer to the *viewer's* left or right.
Milled	Coins struck by dies worked in a coining press.
Mintmark (*Mm.*)	A special mark, usually at the beginning of the inscription, indicating period of issue.
Mule	A coin with the current type on one side and a previous (and sometimes obsolete) type on the other, or a piece struck from two dies not normally used together.
Obverse (O., *obv.*)	That side of the coin which normally shows the monarch's head, gives the name of the country or shows the main type.
Pattern	A number of pattern pieces exist for coins, the designs of which were not adopted for currency. These are not included in this catalogue.
Penny ('d', i.e., from *denarius*)	
Proof	A coin struck as a specimen of the coinage from specially prepared dies with polished surfaces that give the coin a high brilliance (though a few non-Irish proofs have a matt surface).
Reverse (R, *rev.*)	The opposite to the obverse.
Seated (std.)	
Shilling ('s')	
Standing (stg.)	

N gold (*aurum*)   *R* silver (*argentum*)   Æ base metal (*aes*)

SCOTLAND

INTRODUCTION TO SCOTTISH COINS

Scotland did not have a native coinage for well over a millenium after a coinage system had been adopted in Southern Britain and for over a century after the Norsemen first minted pennies in Ireland. This does not mean that coinage was unknown in ancient Alban: far from it, for the occasional Celtic coin from the South has been discovered north of the Border and, of course, many hoards and individual specimens of Roman coins have been found in the areas of Roman military occupation between the Hadrianic and Antonine fortification systems, and even north of these along the route to the North-East coast. But in the Celtic lands of Ireland, Wales, Strathclyde and Scotland, where the socio-economic system did not favour large urban settlements, there was not the same need for coin as there was in the more commercially developed South.

The few finds of 9th century Northumbrian *stycas* north of the Border are numismatic records of the Anglian hegemony imposed upon the natives of Lothian and the Strathclyde Britons, though there is insufficient evidence to warrant any assumption that there might have been a Northumbrian mint on Scottish soil. More spectacular are the substantial treasure hoards of the Viking period scattered along the western seaboard from Man to Islay, Iona, Tiree, Skye, N. Uist, Cromarty, Orkney and Shetland, reminding us that the Norsemen held the Western and Northern Isles, Caithness and other points on the mainland, and brought their own contribution to Scottish culture and character. These hoards represent both trade and plunder, comprising principally English silver pence but sometimes including *deniers* from continental Christian Europe and *dirhems* from the Moslem East. Though local tradition has it that the Vikings were the first to exploit the silver mines of Islay there has been no evidence presented for a Viking mint on the island.

Following the Norman conquest of England, after which many of the Anglo-Saxon aristocracy took refuge in Scotland and brought with them the techniques of a sophisticated central administration, the way was prepared for the first native Scottish coinage in the 12th century.

For over two centuries the Scottish coinage followed a course parallel to that of England both as regards general design and quality of metal. At one time in the reign of Alexander III at least sixteen separate mints were in operation. A distinctive Scots gold coinage appeared at the end of the 14th century and the 15th century saw the first debasement of the silver coinage and the establishment of a base metal coinage. Two essays at genuine portraiture under James III ante-date the earliest English portrait pieces of Henry VII, and during the 16th and 17th century a great variety of interesting types were produced, especially under James VI. The Edinburgh mint was finally closed down shortly after the Act of Union in the reign of Queen Anne.

LATIN LEGENDS ON SCOTTISH COINS

CHRISTO AUSPICE REGNO (I reign under the auspices of Christ). Æ half-merk of Charles I.

CRUCIS ARMA SEQUAMUR (Let us follow the arms of the cross). N crowns of James V and Mary.

CRVX PELLIT OMNE CRIMEN (The cross drives away all sin). From a fourth-century hymn by Prudentius. Æ penny of Bp. Kennedy, c.1452-1480.

DA PACEM DOMINE (Give peace, O Lord). Æ testoons and half-testoons of Mary.

DAT GLORIA VIRES (Glory gives strength). Æ ryal, two-thirds ryal and one-third ryal of Mary and Henry Darnley and Mary alone.

DECUS ET TUTAMEN (An ornament and a safeguard: *Virg. Aen.* v. 262). Edge reading for William and Mary, William III, and Anne.

DEUS JUDICIUM TUUM REGI DA (Give the king Thy judgments, O God: *Psalm* lxxii. 1). N lion noble, two-thirds lion noble and one-third lion-noble of James VI.

DILICIÆ DOMINI COR HUMILE (An humble heart is the delight of the Lord). Æ testoons and half-testoons of Mary.

DILIGITE IUSTICIAM (Observe justice). N forty-four shillings of Mary.

DOMINUS PROTECTOR MEUS ET LIBERATOR MEUS (God is my Defender and my Redeemer: *comp. Psalm* lxx.6). Æ groats and half-groats from David II; N lions and demis of Robert III.

ECCE ANCILLA DOMINI (Behold the handmaid of the Lord: *Luke* i. 38). N twenty shillings of Mary.

EXURGAT DEUS ET DISSIPENTUR INIMICI EIUS (Let God arise and let His enemies be scattered: *Psalm* lxviii. 1). N unicorns and half unicorns from James III; N crown of Mary, dated 1561; Æ ryal, two-thirds ryal and one-third ryal of Mary and Henry and Mary alone; N ducat of James VI.

FACIAM EOS IN GENTEM UNAM (I will make them one nation: *Ezek.* xxxvii. 22). N unit of James VI.

FECIT UTRAQUE UNUM (He has made both one). Æ testoon of Mary and Francis.

FLORENT SCEPTRE PIIS REGNA HIS IOVA DAT NUMERATQUE (Sceptres flourish with the pious, Jehova gives them kingdoms and numbers them). N thistle noble of James VI.

HENRICUS ROSAS REGNA IACOBUS (Henry (united) the roses, James the kingdoms). N double crown and Britain crown of James VI.

HIS DIFFERT REGE TYRANNUS (In these a tyrant differs from a king). Æ balance half merk and quarter merk of James VI.

HIS PRÆSUM UP PROSIM (I am set over them, that I may be profitable to them). N unit of Charles I.

HONOR REGIS IUDICIUM DILIGIT (The King's power loveth judgment: *Psalm* xcix. 4). N ducat, two-thirds ducat and one-third ducat of James V; Æ 40s., 30s., 20s. and 10s. of James VI.

HORUM TUTA FIDES (The faith of these is whole). N ducat of Mary.

IN IUSTITIA TUA LIBERA NOS DOMINE (Deliver us, O Lord, in Thy righteousness: *com. Psalm* xxxi. 1). Æ pattern half testoon of Mary and Francis.

IN UTRUNQUE PARATUS (Prepare for either, *i.e.* peace or war). N twenty pound piece of James VI.

IN VIRTUTE TUA LIBERA ME (In Thy strength deliver me). Æ testoons and half testoons of Mary.

IAM NON SUNT DUO SED UNA CARO (They are no more twain, but one flesh: *Matt.* xix. 6). Billon groat or 'nonsunt' of Mary and Francis.

IESUS AUTEM TRANSIENS PER MEDIUM ILLORUM IBAT (But Jesus, passing through the midst of them, went His way: *Luke* iv. 30). N noble of David II.

IUSTITIA THRONUM FIRMAT (Justice strengthens the throne). Æ twenty pence and two shillings of Charles I.

IUSTUS FIDE VIVIT (The just man lives by faith: *comp. Rom*. i. 17). Nʹ three pounds and thirty shillings of Mary.

MONETA PAUPERUM (Money of the poor). Æ farthing of *c.*1452-1480.

NEMO ME IMPUNE LACESSET (or LACESSIT) (No one shall hurt me with impunity). Æ two merk and one merk; 16s., 8s., 4s., 2s.; 10s., 5s., 30d., and 10d. of James VI; Æ 2d of Charles I; Æ 60s. and Æ bawbee and bodle of William and Mary.

PARCERE SUBJECTIS ET DEBELLARE SUPERBOS (To spare the humbled and subdue the proud: *Virg. Aen*. vi. 854). Nʹ twenty pound piece of James VI.

PER LIGNUM CRUCIS SALVI SUMUS (By the wood of the Cross are we saved). Nʹ crown of James V.

POST 5 & 100 PROAVOS INVICTA MANENT HÆC (After one hundred and five ancestors these remain unconquered). Nʹ lion noble, two-thirds lion noble and one-third lion noble of James VI.

PRO ME SI MEREOR IN ME (For me; but against me if I deserve). Æ ryal, two-thirds ryal and one-third ryal of James VI.

PROTEGIT ET ORNAT (It protects and adorns). Æ 60s. and 40s. of William and Mary.

QUÆ DEUS CONIUNXIT NEMO SEPARET (What God hath joined together, let no man put asunder: *Matt*. xix. 6). Æ 60s., 30s., 12s., and 6s. of James VI and Charles I, and Æ half merk of Charles I.

QUOS DEUS CONIUNXIT HOMO NON SEPARET (Those whom God hath joined together, let not man put asunder). Æ ryal of Mary and Henry.

REGEM IOVA PROTEGIT (Jehovah protects the king). Æ thistle merk, half thistle merk, quarter thistle merk and one-eighth thistle merk of James VI.

SALUS POPULI SUPREMA LEX (The safety of the People is the supreme law). Nʹ sword and sceptre and half sword and sceptre pieces of James VI.

SALUS REIPUBLICÆ SUPREMA LEX (The safety of the State is the supreme law). Æ forty pence and 3s. of Charles I.

SALVATOR IN HOC SIGNO VICISTI (O Saviour, in this sign hast Thou conquered). Nʹ pattern angel of James III.

SALVUM FAC POPULUM TUUM DOMINE (O Lord, save Thy people: *Psalm* xxviii. 10). Nʹ demy and half demy of James I; lions and half lions from James II; rider, half rider and quarter rider of James III; Æ groat, 2d and 1d of James IV; testoon and half testoon of Mary; noble and half noble of James VI.

SERVIO ET USU TEROR (I serve and am worn by use). Billon plack of Mary.

SPERO MELIORA (I hope for better things). Nʹ rider and half rider of James VI.

TE SOLUM VEREOR (Thee alone do I fear). Nʹ hat-piece of James VI.

TUEATUR UNITA DEUS (May God guard these united, i.e. kingdoms). Nʹ halfcrown and thistle crown of James VI; Æ 2s. and 1s. of James VI.

UNITA TUEMUR (These united we guard). Nʹ half-unit, Britain crown and halfcrown of Charles I.

VICIT LEO DE TRIBU IUDA (The Lion of the tribe of Judah hath prevailed: *Rev*. v. 5). Æ testoon of Mary and Francis.

VICIT VERITAS (Truth has conquered). Æ lion or hardhead of mary, Francis and mary, and James VI.

VINCIT VERITAS (Truth conquers). Æ hardhead of James VI.

XPC. REGNAT XPC. VINCIT XPC. IMPERAT (Christ reigns, Christ conquers, Christ commands). Nʹ lions and demis from Robert III.

SOME SCOTTISH DENOMINATIONS

Not all multiples and fractions are included in this list.

Gold
Crown (or écu). 20 shillings Scots, James V; 22s. Mary.
Britain Crown. £3 Scots, James I and Charles I.
Thistle Crown. 48s. Scots, James VI.
Demy. 9s., James I and II.
Ducat. 40s., James V; 60s., Mary; 80s., James VI.
Hat piece. 80s., James VI, 1591-3.
Lion. 5s., Robert III; 10s., James II; 13s. 4d., James IV.
Lion Noble. 75s., James VI, 1584-8.
Noble (half merk). 6s. 8d, David II.
Thistle Noble. 146s. 8d (11 merks), James VI.
Pistole. £12 Scots, William II (III), 1701.
Twenty Pounds. James VI, 1575-6.
Three Pounds. Mary, 1555-8.
Rider. 23s., James III; £5 Scots, James VI.
Sword-and-Sceptre piece. £6 Scots, James VI.
Unicorn. 18s., James III & IV; 20s., James V.
Unit. £12 Scots, James VI and Charles I.

Silver
Penny. Standard unit of currency from *c.*1136 until 1513.
Halfpenny. From 1280 to *c.*1406.
Farthing. From 1280 to *c.*1333.
Groat. Fourpence from 1357; later rated at 6d, 12d, 14d and 18d Scots.
One-third groat. James V, 1526-39.
Testoon. Mary, 4 shillings Scots in 1553; 5s. from 1555.
Ryal. 30s. Scots, 1565-71.
Merk (*i.e.* mark). 13s. 4d Scots, 1579-1675.
Noble (half merk). 6s. 8d Scots, 1572-1675.
Sixty Shillings. James VI, from 1603; Charles I and William and Mary, 1691-2.
Forty Shillings. 1582 and 1687-1700. 30, 20, 16, 12, 10, 6, 5, 3, 2 and 1 shilling (equivalent to English penny) were also issued.
Dollar. Charles II, 1676-82.

Billon
Penny. James I-IV & Mary.
Halfpenny. James I, III & IV.
Plack. 4d Scots, James III-V & Mary; 8d, James VI.
Bawbee. 6d, James V.
Lion ('hardhead'). 1½d, Mary, 1558-60; 2d, James VI.
Groat ('nonsunt'). 4d, Mary & Francis, 1558-9.
Saltire Plack. 4d, James VI.

Copper
Farthing. James III.
Penny. James III & VI, Charles I.
Turner ('bodle'). 2d, James VI to William III.
Bawbee. 6d, Charles II to William & Mary.

SELECT BIBLIOGRAPHY OF SCOTTISH COINS

Included in this list are books which although not specifically on Scottish coins or tokens contain useful information.

ANDERSON, J. *Diplomatum et Numismatum Scotiae Thesaurus.* 1739.

BATESON, J.D. *Coinage in Scotland.* 1997.

BATESON, J.D. and MAYHEW, N.J. *Scottish coins in the Ashmolean Museum, Oxford and the Hunterian Museum, Glasgow. SCBI* 35, 1987.

BURNS, E. *The Coinage of Scotland.* 1887. The standard work of reference.

CARDONNEL, A.De, *Numismata Scotiae.* 1786.

COCHRAN-PATRICK, R.W. *Records of the Scottish Coinage.* 1876.

DAVIS, W.J. *The Nineteenth Century Token Coinage.* 1904. (Reprinted with addenda 1969). One of the principal sources of reference to the countermarked Spanish dollars used in Scotland.

GRUEBER, H.A. *Handbook of the Coinage of Great Britain and Ireland in the British Museum.* 1899.

HOLMES, N.M.McQ. *Scottish Coins. A history of small change in Scotland.* 1998.

HOLMES, N.M.McQ. and LORD STEWARTBY. 'Scottish Coinage in the first half of the Fourteenth Century' *BNJ* Vol. 70, 2000.

HOLMES, N.M.McQ. *National Museums of Scotland, Edinburgh. Scottish Coins, Part 1. 1526-1603. SCBI* 58, 2006.

LINDSAY, J. *View of the Coinage of Scotland.* 1845. (Supplements in 1859 and 1868).

METCALF, D.M. (ed.), ed.). *Coinage in Medieval Scotland. The Second Oxford Symposium on Coinage and Monetary History,* British Archaeological Reports 45 (Oxford, 1977).

RICHARDSON, A.B. *Catalogue of Scottish Coins in the National Museum, Edinburgh.* 1901. A useful catalogue in the style of Burns.

ROBERTSON, J.D. *Handbook to the Coinage of Scotland.* 1878.

RUDDIMAN, T. *An Introduction to Mr. James Anderson's Diplomata Scotiae.* 1773.

SNELLING, T. *A View of the Silver Coin and Coinage of Scotland.* 1774.

STEWART, I.H. *The Scottish Coinage.* 2nd edition with supplement. 1967. The best and most up-to-date synopsis of the coinage.

STEWART, I.H. 'Scottish Mints' in *Mints, Dies and Currency*, the memorial volume of essays for Albert Baldwin, edited by R.A.G. Carson. A masterly treatise on the medieval coinage.

WINGATE, J. *Illustrations of the Coinage of Scotland.* 1868.

In addition to the foregoing the following list of articles on specific subjects may be of use:

DAVID I and PRINCE HENRY

ALLEN, M. 'A probable addition to the coinage of Henry, Earl of Northumberland (d. 1152)', *NC* 177, 2017.

ASKEW, G. 'The Mint of Bamburgh Castle'. *NC* 1940.

HOLMES, N.M.McQ. 'A 'mule' sterling of David I of Scotland from the Carlisle mint', *BNJ* 87, 2017.

MACK, R.P. 'Stephen and the anarchy, 1135-54'. *BNJ* 35, 1966.

MATTINSON, J. and CHERRY, P. 'The Carlisle mint coinages of Henry I, Stephen, David I and Earl Henry', *BNJ* 83, 2013.

SAVAGE, C. and ALLEN, M. 'A coin of David I of Scotland from Nottinghamshire', *BNJ* 89, 2019.

STEWART, I.H. 'An eighteenth century Manx find of early Scottish Sterlings'. *BNJ* 33, 1964.

— 'An uncertain mint of David I'. *BNJ* 29, 1959.

WILLIAM THE LION

ALLEN, M. and HOLMES, N.M.McQ. 'An Intermediate Issue of William the Lion of Scotland', *BNJ* 87, 2017.

JONES, I. and SUGDEN, K. 'Dies of Henri le Rus', *BNJ* 81, 2011.

JONES, I. and SUGDEN, K. 'The later posthumous coinage of William the Lion', *BNJ* 83, 2013.

ALEXANDER II and ALEXANDER III

ALLEN, M., HIGGINSON, P. and PENRICE, R. 'The Short Cross and Stars coinage in the names of Alexander II and Alexander III of Scotland', *BNJ* 90, 2020.

HOLMES, N.M.McQ. 'A corpus of dies used in the Long Voided Cross coinage of Alexander III: the minor mints', *BNJ* 86, 2016.

ALEXANDER III

HOLMES, N.M.McQ. 'Unpublished Scottish Fractions from the David Rogers Collection' *BNJ* 71, 2001. (Alexander III and David II)

KIRTON, R.W. and STEWARTBY, Lord. 'The Long Voided Cross Sterlings of Kinghorn'. *NC* 2000.

STEWART, I.H. 'The Brussels hoard: Mr. Baldwin's arrangement of the Scottish coins'. *BNJ* 29, 1958-9.

— 'The Long Voided Cross sterlings of Alexander III illustrated by Burns'. *BNJ* 39, 1970.

STEWART, I.H. and NORTH, J.J. 'Classification of the Single-Cross sterlings of Alexander III'. *BNJ* 60, 1990.

JOHN BALIOL

HOLMES, N.M.McQ. and STEWARTBY, Lord. 'The Coinage of John Baliol'. *BNJ* 80, 2010.

DAVID II

DAKERS, C.H. 'The Rex Scottorum pennies of David II'. *PSAS* LXXII.

DAKERS, H.J. 'The first issue of David II'. *BNJ* 23, 1941.

DAVIDSON, J. 'Some distinguishing marks on the later issues of David II'. *BNJ* 26, 1950.

HOLMES, N.M.McQ. 'An unrecorded farthing type of David II of Scotland'. *BNJ* 66, 1996.

ROBERT III

DAKERS, C.H. 'Edinburgh light groats of Robert III'. *PSAS* LXXII.

JAMES I

DAKERS, C.H. 'Two unpublished groats of James I'. *PSAS* LXXI.

JAMES II-III

HOLMES, N.M.McQ. 'A Fifteenth-Century Coin Hoard from Leith'. *BNJ* 53, 1983.

JAMES III

HOLMES, N.M.McQ. 'The Scottish Copper *Crux Pellit* Coinage: a typological analysis'. *BNJ* 78, 2008.

— ' "Abject orts and imitations": some variants of the "Black Farthing" coinage of James III. *BNJ* 78, 2008.

MACDONALD, Sir G. 'The Mint of Crossraguel Abbey'. *NC* 1919.

MURRAY, Mrs. J.E.L. 'The Black Money of James III' in D.M. Metcalf (ed.), *Coinage in Medieval Scotland* (*BAR* British Series 45) Oxford, 1977.

MURRAY, Mrs. J.E.L. and STEWART, I.H. 'Unpublished Scottish coins'. Part IV, *NC* 1967 and Part V, 1970.

STEVENSON, R.B.K. 'Crossraguel Pennies – Re-attribution to Bishop Kennedy'. *PSAS* LXXXIV.

STEWART, I.H. 'The attribution of the Thistle-Head and Mullet Groats'. *BNJ* 27, 1952.
— 'The heavy silver coinage of James III and IV'. *BNJ* 27, 1953.
— 'The Glenluce and Rhoneston Hoards of 15th century coins'. *PSAS* XCIII.

JAMES IV
MURRAY, Mrs. J.E.L. 'The early unicorns and the heavy groats of James III & IV'. *BNJ* 40, 1971
STEWART, I.H. 'The Maundy Groat of 1512'. *PSAS* XCVII.

JAMES V
GRIERSON, P. 'The Eagle Crown'. *BNJ* 28, 1957.
HOLMES, N.M.McQ. and STEWARTBY, Lord. 'The 1533 issue of James V placks'. *BNJ* 78, 2008.
STEVENSON, R.B.K. 'The groat coinage of James V, 1526-38'. *BNJ* 61, 1991.
— 'The bawbee issues of James V and Mary'. *BNJ* 59, 1989.

MARY
MURRAY, Mrs. J.E.L. 'The First Gold Coinage of Mary Queen of Scots'. *BNJ* 49, 1979.
MURRAY, J.E.L & J.K.R. 'Notes on the VICIT LEO Testoons of Mary, Queen of Scots'. *BNJ* 50, 1980.
MURRAY, J.K.R. 'The Stirling bawbees of Mary, Queen of Scots'. *Num. Circ.*, Dec. 1966 and Sept. 1968.
— 'The Scottish Coinage of 1560-1561'. *Num. Circ.*, April 1967.
— 'The Scottish Coinage of 1553'. *BNJ* 37, 1968.

JAMES VI
KERR, R. 'The Forty shilling piece of James VI of Scotland'. *NC* 1948.
MURRAY, J.K.R. 'The gold forty shilling piece of James VI'. *BNJ* 38, 1969.
— 'Some notes on the small silver money of James I and VI'. *NC* 1968.

CHARLES I
MURRAY, J.K.R. 'The Scottish gold and silver coinage of Charles I'. *BNJ* 39, 1970.
MURRAY, J.K.R. and STEWART, B.H.I.H. 'The Scottish Copper Coinages, 1642-1697'. *BNJ* 41, 1972, and 48, 1978.
STEVENSON, R.B.K. 'The "Stirling" turners of Charles I, 1632-9'. *BNJ* 29, 1959.

CHARLES II
MURRAY, J.K.R. 'The Scottish Silver Coinage of Charles II'. *BNJ* 38, 1969.

JAMES VIII
FARQUHAR, H. 'Patterns and medals bearing the legend IACOBVS III or VIII'. *BNJ* 3, 1906.

ANNE
HOBLYN, R.A. 'The Edinburgh coinage of Queen Anne, 1707-1709'. *NC* new series XIX.
MURRAY, A.L. 'The Scottish Recoinage of 1707-1709 and its Aftermath'. *BNJ* 72, 2002.
PREVOST, N., HOWIE, J. and FAREY, R., 'Guide to the Die Varieties of Edinburgh Shillings, 1707 to 1709'. *Num. Circ.* Sept. 2013.

There are, in addition, numerous other notes on Scottish coins and these will be chiefly found in the following publications:

Numismatic Chronicle (NC)
British Numismatic Journal (BNJ)
Proceedings of the Society of Antiquaries of Scotland (PSAS)
Spink's Numismatic Circular (Num. Circ.)

8

SCOTTISH MINTS

N

Moray Firth

Forres

Inverness

Aberdeen

NORTH

Montrose

Forfar

SEA

Dundee

Perth

St. Andrews

Stirling

Dunfermline

Firth of Forth

Dumbarton

Kinghorn

Dunbar

Linlithgow

Glasgow

Edinburgh

Berwick

Lanark

Bamborough

Kelso

Ayr

Roxburgh

Firth of Clyde

Jedburgh

Corbridge

Carlisle

0   Scale   50 Miles

The location of Fres and Wilanerter is not known.

Between 1139–1157 Northumberland was in Scottish hands.

Map drawn by Alan Miles

DAVID I 1124-1153

David I appears to have been the first independent Scottish king to issue coins, an event no doubt allied to the capture of Carlisle by the Scots under David and his son prince Henry in 1136, which gave them an established mint and nearby silver mines. The moneyer of Henry I's last type at Carlisle (Erebald) is the moneyer on an extremely rare coin of similar type but struck in David's name.

David was the ninth and youngest son of Malcolm 'Ceanmor', and he succeeded his brother Alexander I. His mother was an Anglo-Saxon princess, Margaret, the daughter of Eadward Aethling, so David was the great-grandson of Aethelred II of England. He received Cumbria and Lothian from his uncle King Eadgar in 1107 and the Earldom of Northumberland on his marriage to the heiress of Earl Waltheof, thus making him an English baron in his own right.

Although the Scots under David were defeated at the battle of the Standard near Northallerton he concluded a peace treaty with Stephen in 1139 which gave to Prince Henry, his son, the Earldom of Northumberland. For the remainder of his reign Northumberland, Cumberland and Westmorland were in Scottish hands.

Approximate chronology of the early pennies, 1136-65:

Period A. 1136 to the beginning of the 1140s
Period B. The middle and later 1140s
Period C. Later civil war years to 1153 and David's death
Period D. After the death of David and Earl Henry
  Pennies only: Weight 22.5 grains; 0.925 silver.

Mints: *Carlisle, Edinburgh, Berwick, Roxburgh.*

Period A

		F £	VF £

5001   5003

5001	As Henry I type 15, but in the name of David. Facing bust. ℞ Cross moline-fleury. *Carlisle.*	5750	15000
5001A	As Henry I type 15, but in the name of David. Bust r. ℞ Cross moline, lis in angles, as Stephen type 1. *Edinburgh ?*	1750	5750
5002	As Stephen (type I) in Stephen's name. Bust r., with sceptre. ℞ Cross moline, lis in angles. *Carlisle. (Stewart,* fig. 290)	575	2250
5003	As last, but in David's name. *Edinburgh*	1750	5250
5003A	As last, but in the name of Henry. Bust l. ℞ Cross moline-fleury, as Henry I type 15. *Carlisle.*	375	1250

Period B

| 5004 | Derivative coins of Stephen's type. Blundered legends, sometimes retrograde. Mint names often illegible. *Edinburgh, Roxburgh.* (*Stewart,* fig. 5) | 575 | 2250 |

	F	VF
	£	£

5005

5005 Cross and Pellets in Annulets Coinage, in David's name. Bust r.
R Cross pattée, an annulet enclosing a pellet in each angle.
Carlisle, Roxburgh, Perth. 750 3250

5005A Cross and Pellets in Annulets Coinage, Crescents variant, in David's name.
Bust r. R Cross pattée, a crescent enclosing a pellet in each angle.
Berwick. 1000 4500

5006 Crowned bust r., palm branch instead of sceptre. R Cross fleury,
three annulets in each angle (cf. Stephen type 6). *Carlisle.*
(*Stewart*, fig. 291) .... *Extremely rare*

Period C

5007

5007 Coins of good workmanship, **DAVIT REX**, etc. Crowned bust r.,
with sceptre. R Cross fleury, single pellets in angles. *Carlisle* (moneyers
Richard and Willelm); *Berwick* (Folbold); *Roxburgh* (Folbold and Hugo);
St Andrews (Meinard) 750 3250

5008 Similar, but with other symbols in angles. *Berwick, Roxburgh* .. 900 3500

Period D

5009

5009 Coins of lesser workmanship, legends blundered, sometimes
retrograde, **AVIT**, etc. R Blundered legends. (*Stewart*, fig. 3).... 525 2000

5010 Better workmanship, legends meaningless but composed of properly
formed letters. R Cross fleury and pellets. (Stewart, fig. 4) 575 2500

PRINCE HENRY 1139-1152
Earl of Northumberland and Huntingdon

Mints: *Bamborough (?), Carlisle, Corbridge.*
Pennies only. *(Struck during lifetime of David I)*

	F £	VF £

Period A

5011

| 5011 | Crowned bust r. with sceptre (as Stephen, type I). hENRICVS, hENRIC ERL, or NENCON. ℞ Cross moline and lis in angles. *Corbridge* (moneyer Erebald). (*Stewart*, fig. 8) .... | 1750 | 5750 |

Period B

| 5011A | Cross and Pellets in Annulets Coinage, Long Voided Cross variant. Diademed bust r. ℞ Long voided cross, an annulet enclosing a pellet in each angle. *Newcastle?* .... | 1500 | 5250 |

Period B or C

5012

| 5012 | Similar to last but N: ENCI: CON, etc. ℞ Cross fleury without pellets in angles. *Carlisle* (moneyers Ricard, Wilelm). (*Stewart*, fig. 9) .... | 1700 | 5750 |

Period D

5013    5014

| 5013 | Similar to last. ℞ Cross-crosslet with a cross in each angle. *Bamborough* (?) (moneyer Wilelm) .... | 2000 | 6500 |
| 5014 | Style of *obv.* as last but reading **STIFENE REX**. ℞ Similar die ...... | 1850 | 6000 |

MALCOLM IV 1153-1165

Prince Henry's premature death in 1152 and David's the following year placed the latter's twelve year old grandson on the throne. He was known as the 'Maiden' on account of his tender years.

The coins of this reign are all extremely rare and it is likely that blundered coins in David's name continued to be struck (see Period D above).

In 1157 Northumberland and Cumberland were surrendered to the English and a stable Anglo-Scottish relationship was maintained until the end of the reign, although several rebellions in Scotland were suppressed in 1160-64.

Mints: *Roxburgh and Berwick.*
Pennies only.

	F £	VF £

5016   5017

5015 I. As David I (5006). Bust r, with sceptre, MALCOLM REX.
℞ Cross fleury, pellets, or pellets and rosettes in alternate angles.
Roxburgh. (*Stewart*, fig. 11) 3650 12500
5016 IIa. Facing bust with two sceptres. ℞ As last. *Roxburgh.*
(*Stewart*, fig. 12) 4250 13500
5017 IIb. As last. ℞ Cross fleury over lozenge fleury. *Roxburgh* ...... *Extremely rare*

5018    5019

5018 III. Bust r. ℞ Cross fleury, pellets in angles, two with stalks.
Roxburgh (?), *Berwick* (?). (*Stewart*, fig 13) 3250 10000
5019 IV. Bust l., retrograde legend. ℞ Cross fleury, pellet in each angle.
Roxburgh (?) 3500 11000

WILLIAM I 'The Lion' 1165-1214

William I, the younger brother of Malcolm, succeeded to the throne in 1165, the title 'Lion' being given him not for his valour, but for replacing the dragon on the arms of Scotland by the lion rampant. In July 1174 he was captured by the English and under the terms of the Treaty of Falaise in December, he was forced to do homage for the whole of Scotland and also to hand over the castles of Roxburgh, Berwick and Edinburgh. The latter, however, was restored as part of the dowry of Ermengarde, a cousin of Henry II, whom he married in 1186.

Richard Coeur de Lion, in need of funds for the Crusades, eventually sold back the independence of Scotland to William for 10,000 merks, an amount equivalent to 1,600,000 silver pence. Probably most of this sum was paid in bullion.

Mints: *Roxburgh, Berwick, Edinburgh, Dun (Dunfermline ?), Perth.*
Pennies only.

	F	VF
	£	£

Early issues, *c*.1165-74

5021   5022

5021 Crowned bust r. with sceptre, similar to David I (5007), but **+WILELMVS**. ℞ Cross
          pattée, lis in angles. Folpold of *Roxburgh*. (*Stewart*, fig. 16)   950   4000
5022 Bust l. or r. ℞ Cross pattée, crosslet of four or fivepellets in angles.
          Berwick, Roxburgh. (*Stewart*, fig. 17)   1250   5000

Crescent and Pellet coinage, *c*.1174-95
[The distinctive sceptres on the two groups correspond to those on the English 'Tealby' coinage (1158-80) and the 'Short Cross' coinage from 1180]

5024   5025

5023 I. (*c*.1174-80). Crowned bust l., with cross pattée sceptre-head.
          ℞ Cross pattée, pellet in crescent in angles, colons between the letters.
          No mint name..   175   675
5024 With mint name: *Edinburgh, Dun* (? *Dunfermline*)   150   650
5025 II. (*c*.1180-95). Similar, but cross pommée sceptre-head. *Berwick,*
          Edinburgh, Roxburgh, Perth   135   525
5026 Without mint name, moneyers Radulfus and Raul Derlig (? *Berwick*
          and *Roxburgh*); Ailbode (*Perth*).   125   500

	F	VF
	£	£

Short Cross and Stars coinage, 1195-1214

Phase A (1195-*c*.1205)

5027   5028

5027	Head l. with sceptre, crown of pellets, WILLELMVS REX. R Voided		
	short cross, stars in angles; large coins. *Edinburgh, Perth, Roxburgh*	110	475
5028	— Similar, but head r. *Roxburgh*	175	675

Late William I and posthumous issue

Short Cross, Phase B, *c*.1205-*c*.1230

Examples showing the variety of portait styles of 5029

5029	Coins without mint name (legends sometimes retrograde). As previous, head l. or r.; there are a number of different portrait styles, LE REI WILAM. R HVE WALTER or HVE WALTER O (The Edinburgh and Perth moneyers working jointly)	90	350
5030	— R WALTER ADAM (Adam replacing Hue at Edinburgh)	125	475
5031	— R hENRI LE RVS or retrograde SVRELIRNEh.	135	525
5032	— With mint name R hVE WALTER ON RO (*Roxburgh*)	150	575
5033	— — R hENRI LE RVS (DE) PERT (*Perth*)	175	650

ALEXANDER II 1214-1249

Alexander II was sixteen years old on the death of his father, William the Lion. He joined the barons against John in 1214 and much of his reign is one of insurrection, invasion and intrigue. He repelled the Norse invasion of 1230 and died from a fever while trying to regain the Hebrides from Norway.

His first marriage in 1221, was to Joan, daughter of King John, and his second in 1239 was to Mary, daughter of Ingelram de Courci.

It would appear that for some twenty years after William's death coins were still being struck in his name. These are divided into two groups. The first is a continuation of the last substantive type of William with double moneyers' names and, rarely, a mint name (see 5029-33). The second group is allied to the style of coins in the name of Alexander, the issue being apparently confined almost entirely to the mint of Roxburgh.

It was not until quite late in the reign that coins were struck in the name of Alexander.

Alexander II in the name of William, issue commencing *c.*1230
(Short Cross, Phase C)

	F £	VF £

5034

		F	VF
5034	Bearded portraits similar to Alexander II. ℞ Moneyers: Adam, Aimer and Peris either singly or in combination. *Roxburgh*	225	800

Alexander II in his own name, from *c.*1235
(Short Cross, Phase D)

Mints: *Berwick* (v. rare) and *Roxburgh.*

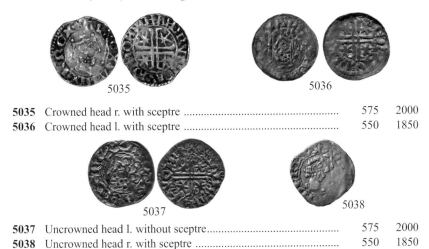

5035   5036

		F	VF
5035	Crowned head r. with sceptre	575	2000
5036	Crowned head l. with sceptre	550	1850

5037   5038

		F	VF
5037	Uncrowned head l. without sceptre.............................	575	2000
5038	Uncrowned head r. with sceptre	550	1850

ALEXANDER III 1249-1286

Alexander III succeeded his father at the age of seven. His reign produced the most extensive of all Scottish medieval coin issues and included the introduction of the round halfpenny and farthing. The first coinage, so largely represented in the Brussels hoard, shows a profusion of mints bursting in to life during the substantive class III which is represented in all the eighteen mints. A curious feature (although not unknown in previous reigns) is the interlinking of certain mints through obverse dies and it is likely that some moneyers coined at more than one mint. The identity of some mints is open to speculation.

Closely following the 1279 English recoinage of Edward I, a new style long cross coinage was introduced *c*.1280 but without mint names.

This was a prosperous reign, but short by Alexander riding his horse over a cliff during darkness at the age of forty-four. With all his children dead, his only heir was his grand-daughter Margaret, known as the Maid of Norway.

Transitional Coinage, *c.*1248-50
(Short Cross, Phase E, beginning under Alexander II, *c.*1248-1249)

	F £	VF £

5039

5039 Penny. IA. Beardless head l. or r. ℞ Short voided cross as previous reign.
 Berwick, Glasgow, Perth (unique), *Roxburgh* 750 2500

5040   5041

5040 — IB. Similar. ℞ Voided long cross with large hooked ends.
 Berwick 375 1250
5041 — IC. Similar. ℞ Normal voided long cross with stars 250 850
 (IB and IC are mules between IA and II).

| | F | VF |
| | £ | £ |

First coinage. Long Cross and Stars, 1250-c.1280
Obv. ALEXANDER REX R Mint and moneyer

5042

5042 Penny. Type II. Youthful filleted head, usually to r.	75	275

5043

5043 — Type III. Small head l. with neat crown.	45	175
5044 — Type IV. Similar, but moulded bust and tall fleured crown with large jewels.	150	525

5045

5046

5045 — Type V. Tall thin head l.	65	250
5046 — Type VI. Tall crowned head r.	150	525

5047

5048

5047 — Type VII. Similar but zig-zag profile, thick jewelled crown, head to r. or l.	75	275
5048 — Type VIII. Usually a squarish face with low crown, bust to r. or l.	70	250

The prices of nos. 5042-5048 are for the commonest mint of each type. A complete list of mints and moneyers with a value for the commonest type of each mint is given below.

List of mints, moneyers and types	F	VF
	£	£

Aberdeen: Alexander, II, III; Andreas, —, II, III; Ion, II, III;
  Rainald, VII ....*from* 110 350
Ayr: Simon, II, III, IV, VII ....*from* 150 475
Berwick: Arnald, VII, VIII; Iohan, VII, VIII; Robert, II, III, VI, VII;
  Wales, I, II, III; Robert and Wales jointly, II; Walter, III, VII, VIII;
  Willem, III, VII, VIII ....*from* 50 175
'Dun': Walter, III, IV; Wilam, III ....*from* 150 450
Edinburgh: Alexander, III, IV, V, VII; Nicol, III, VI; Wilam, III, V *from* 60 225
Forfar: Simond, III, Wilam, III ....*from* 225 700
'Fres': Walter, III, VII, VIII; Wilam (?), III ....*from* 250 750
Glasgow: Walter, II, III, IV, VII ....*from* 150 450
Inverness: Gefrai, III ....*from* 250 800
Kinghorn: Walter, III, VI; Wilam, III, VI ....*from* 275 850
Lanark: Wilam, II, III, V ....*from* 250 800
Montrose: Walter, III ....*from* 575 1750
Perth: Ion Cokin, II, III, VII; Ion or Iohan, III, VII, VIII; Martin, VII,
  Rainald, VII, VIII ....*from* 60 225
Roxburgh: Adam, III, VII, VIII; Andrews, II, III, VI, VII, VIII; Michel,
  II, III, VI; Wilam, II ....*from* 60 225
St Andrews: Thomas, III, IV ....*from* 250 800
Stirling: Henri, III, IV ....*from* 135 425
'Wilanerter': III, VI ....*from* 375 1250

Second coinage, *c.*1280-86

5049   5050

5049 Penny. A. Crowned head l. of new style, small neat portrait,
ALEXSANDER DEI GTA (G'SIA G'CIA or G'RA). R ESCOSSIE REX,
four mullets of 6 points each (24 points). Small lettering with closed
C and E, thick waisted S, A usually unbarred................................ 150 575
5050 — Similar, but REX SCOTTORVM 50 150

5051   5052

5051 B. Varied portraits, with ALEXANDER DEI GRA (or G'RA).
R ESCOSSIE REX, 24 points. Larger lettering with open C and E,
thin-waisted composite S, A usually barred 175 575
5052 — Similar, but REX SCOTORVM 40 135

5053

		F	VF
		£	£
5053	Ma. Portrait as class A, ALEXANDER DEI GRA, composite crown. R REX SCOTORVM 24 points. Straight-sided lettering, open C and E, thick-waisted S, A usually unbarred	40	125

5054    5055

5054	Mb. Similar but larger face with wider hair. R 24-25 points.	45	135
5055	Mc. Similar, but crown from single punch. R 21, 23, 24, 26 or 28 points	30	120
5055A	R. Similar. Unusual letter R with circular loop and curved tail, A barred. R 24 points	110	350

5056    5057

5056	E. New lettering with incurved uprights. Wedge-tailed R, thin-waisted S, A unbarred. R 20, 22-28 points	30	120
5057	D. Straight-sided letters, usually with serifs, A barred, C with peaked waist and fishtail wedges, usually *mm.* cross potent. R 24-26 points	40	135

5058    5059

5058	H. Obverse of cruder style, gaunt face and crude crown, A unbarred. R 24-26 points (mules only, with reverses of other classes)........	50	175
5059	J. Rough surface as John Baliol's first issue, crude plain lettering, reads GR. R reads RE XSC, 24 points	110	350

	F £	VF £

5060   5061

5060   **Halfpenny.** Crowned bust l. with sceptre, ALEXANDER DEI GRA.
R Two mullets of 5 points each in alternate angles of cross, REX

SCOTORVM 135   425

5061   — Similar but two (or rarely four) mullets of 6 points 85   275

5062   — As last, but one is a star 150   525

5063   5064

5063   **Farthing.** Similar, reads ALEXANDER REX. R SCOTORVM, four

mullets of 6 (rarely 5) points. 150   450

5064   — Similar, but *obv.* reads ALEXANDER DEI GRA 175   550

In the absence of mint names on the new style coinage long cross pennies of *c*.1280, mint identity may be linked to the number of points to the mullets and stars on the reverse. Coins with a total of 24 points (*Berwick?*) account for 56% of the total output and represent every class including the entire output of classes A, B, Ma and early Mb. Those the 26 points (*Perth?*) account for 23% of output spanning late class Mb through to class H, those with 25 points for 9%, 23 points for 5.5%, 20 points for 4% and 28 points for 1.5%, with trace outputs of 21, 22 and 27 points. A value for each combination of points and the classes for which they are known is given below.

20 points; class E	40	135
21 points; classes Mc, E	125	350
22 points; classes E, D	125	350
23 points; classes Mc, E	40	135
24 points; classes A, B, Ma, Mb, Mc, R, E, D, H, J	30	120
25 points; classes Mb, Mc, E, D, H	35	125
26 points; classes Mb, Mc, E, D, H	30	120
27 points; class E	125	350
28 points; classes Mc, E, D	55	225

MARGARET 1286-1290

Margaret, the 'Maid of Norway', daughter of King Eric II of Norway, succeeded to the throne of Scotland at the age of three following the death of her grandfather in 1286.

Her projected marriage to the future Edward II would supposedly achieve a union of England and Scotland and a cessation of all antagonism between the two countries. Margaret sailed for Scotland in 1290 but unfortunately died in the Orkneys, never having set foot in her kingdom.

No coins are known bearing her name, but it is likely that coins in Alexander's name continued to be struck during her reign and in all probability during the interregnum and for the first few years following the placing of John Baliol on the throne by Edward I.

JOHN BALIOL 1292-1296

John Baliol, a descendant of David I, was chosen as king from thirteen 'Competitors' for the Scottish throne who agreed to abide by the arbitration of Edward I of England in 1291.

His coins are of the same type as Alexander's but of coarser workmanship at first. Apart from the pence and halfpence of the St Andrews mint no mint name is given, but Berwick is likely to have been the main mint as it was under Alexander.

In all likelihood the system of mint-identity based on the number of points to the mullets on the reverse had broken down by this time, although the principal mint is again likely to be Berwick.

The loss to the Scots of Berwick, Edinburgh, Perth, Roxburgh and Stirling in 1296 was followed by John's abdication in July of that year. He was a prisoner of the English for three years before being allowed to return to his estates in France, where he died in 1313.

First coinage. Rough surface issue.

		F £	*VF* £
5065	**Penny.** As issue I (5059) of Alexander III, but reading IOhANNES DEI GRA. R + REX SCOTORVM Cross with four mullets, or stars, of 6 points. *? Berwick*	125	400
5066	— Similar, but two mullets of 6 points and two of 5. *? St. Andrews*	150	500

5067   5069   5070

5067	— — R CIVITAS SANDRE. *St Andrews*	135	475
5068	— — — As last but three mullets of 6 points and one of 5	175	525
5069	**Halfpenny.** As 5065. *? Berwick*	275	750
5069A	— As last, but only two mullets of 6 points	400	950
5070	— As 5069A, but CIVITAS SANDRE	750	1750

Second coinage. Smooth surface issue.

5071   5074

5071	**Penny.** As 5065 above, but smoother, neater style. R REX SCOTORVM + Four mullets of 5 points.	135	425
5072	— Similar, but CIVITAS SANDREE *St Andrews*	175	525
5073	— As last, but *obv.* reads I: DI: GRA: SCOTORVM: RX	325	900
5074	**Halfpenny.** Similar to 5071, but mullets in two quarters only	175	575
5075	— Similar. R CIVITAS SANDRE *St Andrews*	525	1500
5075A	**Farthing.** Similar to 5071, mullets in four quarters.	750	2250

ROBERT BRUCE 1306-1329

After ten turbulent years with armies moving backwards and forwards across Scotland, Robert Bruce, another descendant of David I, was crowned king at Scone in 1306. Edinburgh was not recaptured by the Scots until 1313, the year before victory over Edward at Bannockburn. Hoard evidence would seem to indicate that no coins were issued until shortly before 1320 and may have been connected with the recovery of Berwick.

In 1318, Bruce's reign saw the gradual repossession of the kingdom partly from the English and partly from Scottish rivals. In 1328, Bruce's infant son David was married to the English princess Joanna, sister of Edward III.

All Robert's coins are rare, the farthings particularly so. The weight of the penny was reduced to $21^3/_7$ grains.

		F £	VF £

5076

| 5076 | **Penny.** As 5071 above, but ROBERTVS DEI GRA. R Four mullets of 5 points .... | 475 | 1500 |

5077    5078

| 5077 | **Halfpenny.** Similar. R Two (or rarely four) mullets of 5 points. | 525 | 1500 |
| 5078 | **Farthing.** Similar. R Four mullets of 5 points. .... | 750 | 2500 |

EDWARD BALIOL 1332-1338

Son of John Baliol and a claimant to the Scottish throne backed by Edward III of England. Edward Baliol landed in Scotland supported by an English army and was crowned at Scone in September 1332. In 1334 he was forced to flee the country by the barons loyal to Robert Bruce's infant son David, and though later restored by Edward III he finally retired again to England in 1338, surrendering his titles to Edward in 1356 in return for a pension.

No coins are known bearing his name.

DAVID II 1329-1371

In 1329, David Bruce succeeded his father at the age of five, and was crowned in 1331. He had been married to Joanna, sister of Edward III, when he was four and she was six. Following the invasion of Edward Baliol he took refuge with his child bride in France and for seven years various guardians governed in his name. He returned to Scotland in 1341 to take administration into his own hands, invaded England in 1346 and was captured at the Battle of Neville's Cross near Durham, remaining a prisoner of Edward III for eleven years. His release in 1357 was on promise of payment of 100,000 marks over ten years.

His earliest coins have the unusual inscription MONETA REGIS DAVID SCOTOR (Money of King David of the Scots) and were probably struck at the same weight standard as those of his father ($21^3/_7$ grs.) although a reduction in weight took place c.1351.

The influence of Edward III's new gold and silver coinage on David is clearly seen as on his release he instituted Scotland's first, though shortlived gold coinage, a noble, closely resembling those of Edward III, also a silver groat (4d) and halfgroat all struck to the size and weight of the English coins. It is interesting to note that on the new silver coins David used the inscription DEVS PROTECTOR MEVS ET LIBERATOR MEVS (God is my Protector and Liberator) which matches POSVI DEVM ADIVTOREM MEVM (I have made God my Helper) on the English coinage.

The Aberdeen mint was re-opened for a time and as on the contemporary English coins extensive 'privy' marking was used to differentiate the various issues and act as a security control. In 1367 a new coinage of silver was issued at a lighter weight with Edinburgh as the sole mint.

Mint master's initials: I = James Mulekin; D = Donatus Mulekin.

Mints: *Aberdeen, Berwick* (?), *Edinburgh.*

	F	VF
	£	£

GOLD

5079

5079   **Noble**, or half-merk (= 6s 8d, wt. 120 grs.), c.1357. King in ship, holding sword and shield charged with the lion rampant, five or six lions on ship. ℞ Ornate floriate cross with crowns and lions around, saltire crosses or trefoils in tressures, IhC AVTEM TRANCIENS P MEDIVM ILLORVM IBAT 37500 135000

	F £	VF £

SILVER

First coinage
Mint: Berwick (?)
First issue (? early 1330s), wt. per penny 21^3/$_7$ grs (?).

	5080	5081	5084

		F	VF
5080	**Halfpenny.** Crowned head l., MONETA REGIS D R +AVID SCOTOR Mullets of 5 points in two quarters.	425	1200
5081	— Similar, but *obv.* legend reads DAVID DEI GRA REX R As last.	450	1250
5082	— — R REX SCOTORVM	400	1100
5083	— DAVID DEI GRACIA R REX SCOTORVM	350	950
5084	**Farthing.** As 5080 above, but mullets of 5 points in four quarters	450	1250
5085	— DAVID DEI GRACIA R AVID SCOTTOR	425	1200
5086	— As last. R REX SCOTORVM	400	1100

Second issue (probably *c*.1351-7)
Mint: *Edinburgh* (?)

5088

		F	VF
5087	**Penny.** Wt. 18 grs. Crowned head l. DAVID DEI GRA REX (or GRACIA) R REX SCOTORVM, large lettering, four mullets of 6 points	50	175
5088	— Similar, REX SCOTTORVM, small letters	45	160

	5090	 5090A

		F	VF
5089	**Halfpenny.** As last, but DAVID DEI GRACIA R REX SCOTORVM, mullets of 6 points in three quarters	325	950
5090	— As 5089, but I behind bust. R I and mullets of 6 points in alternate angles	450	1350
5090A	**Farthing.** Crowned head l., DAVID DEI GRACI R REX SCOTORVM Mullets of 6 points in alternate angles	575	1750

	F	*VF*
	£	£

Second coinage, 1357-67.

5091

5091 **Groat** (72 grs.) *Edinburgh.* A. Small young bust l. breaking plain
tressure. ℞ Cross and mullets, **DNS PTECTOR MS**, etc., in outer circle,
VILLA EDINBVRGh in inner circle 100 325

5092 — — Trefoils in arcs of tressure, rosette or saltire stops 110 375

5093 — — Rosettes in arcs of tressure 150 500

5094

5094 — — Pellets in arcs of tressure 125 425

5095

5095 — B. Large young bust l. ℞ Mullets only in quarters of cross 110 350

5096 — — Cross added in one quarter 135 450

5098

5097 — — D added in one quarter 125 425

5098 — C. Older head l. with aquiline nose, pierced pellet eyes 110 350

5099 — — D added in one quarter 125 425

	F	*VF*
	£	£

5100

5100	— D. Similar to Robert II, head large and ugly, pellet eyes	110	375
5101	— — Pellet behind crown and in one quarter	135	450

5103

5102	— — Pellet on sceptre handle	135	475
5103	*Aberdeen.* A. Small young bust. ℞ As 5091 but VILLA ABERDON	375	1250
5104	— B. Large young bust.	4275	1350

5105　　　　　5111

5105	**Halfgroat.** *Edinburgh.* A. Small young bust	100	275
5106	— B. Large young bust. ℞ No extra marks	110	350
5107	— — Cross added in one quarter of *rev.*	135	425
5108	— — D added in one quarter	150	475
5109	— C. Older head. ℞ No extra marks	110	325
5110	— — D added in one quarter	135	425
5111	— — Pellet behind crown and in first quarter of *rev.*	150	475

5111A　　　　　5113

5111A	— D. Head similar to Robert II	135	425
5112	*Aberdeen.* A. Small young bust	375	1250
5113	— B. Large young bust	425	1350

		F £	VF £

5115   5118   5120

5114	**Penny.** *Edinburgh.* A. Small young bust	75	225
5115	— B. Large young bust. ℞ No extra marks	85	250
5116	— — Cross added in one quarter	100	300
5117	— — Ð added in one quarter	110	350
5118	— C. Older head	100	300
5119	— D. 'Robert II' style head	85	250
5120	— — Pellet behind crown and in first quarter	135	425
5121	*Aberdeen.* A. Small young bust	350	1100
5122	— B. Large young bust	425	1250
5122A	**Halfpenny.** *Edinburgh.* As 5114	475	1500

Third (Light) coinage, 1367-71

The distinguishing mark of this coinage is the star behind the king's head or at the base of the king's sceptre.

5125   5127

5123	**Groat** (61½ grs.) *Edinburgh.* As class C, 5098 above; but with star behind head	250	750
5124	— As class D, 5100 above, with star on sceptre handle	125	375
5125	— As last, trefoils within tressure	110	350
5126	**Halfgroat.** *Edinburgh.* As 5098 above, with star behind head ..	175	575
5127	— — Star on sceptre handle	100	325
5128	— 'Robert II' style head, star on sceptre handle	110	325

5129   5130

| 5129 | **Penny.** *Edinburgh.* 'Robert II' style head, star behind | 150 | 525 |
| 5130 | — — Star on sceptre handle | 90 | 250 |

ROBERT II 1371-1390

Robert, the first Scottish king of the Stewart line, was the son of Walter, the sixth hereditary High Steward of Scotland, and of Marjorie Bruce, daughter of Robert Bruce.

He acted as regent during part of the period of imprisonment in England of David II and was himself imprisoned in England with his three sons for security reasons following the recognition of Edward III as David's successor. He was released in 1370 and peacefully succeeded to the throne on David's death.

The coinage was maintained at the same standard and in the same general style as that of David's last issue, but with coins being issued at Perth and Dundee in addition to those of Edinburgh mint.

Moneyer's initial: B = Bonagius.

Mints: *Dundee, Edinburgh, Perth.*

SILVER

		F	VF
		£	£

5132

5131	**Groat.** *Edinburgh.* Crowned bust l., usually star at base of sceptre, trefoils within tressure. ℞ Cross and mullets	90	275
5132	— Similar, but B behind head	200	650

5133

5133	— Saltire behind head	250	750
5134	— Saltires within tressure	250	750

5136

5135	*Dundee.* As 5132. ℞ VILLA DVNDE	525	1750
5136	*Perth.* As 5131. ℞ VILLA DE PERTh	100	325

		F	*VF*
		£	£

5137   5138

5137	— Similar but with B behind head	250	750
5138	**Halfgroat.** Edinburgh. As 5131	110	325

5139    5140

5139	— Similar, but B behind head	150	525
5140	— Saltire or pellet behind head, usually nothing in spandrils ...	175	550
5141	*Dundee.* As groat, B behind head, saltire on sceptre handle	525	1750
5142	— Similar, but saltire behind head, sceptre handle plain	475	1500

5143    5150

5143	*Perth.* As groat, 5136	110	350
5144	— B behind head, nothing in spandrils, cross on sceptre handle	250	750
5145	**Penny.** *Edinburgh.* Crowned bust l., star on sceptre handle	100	325
5146	— Similar, no star on sceptre handle	110	350
5147	— B behind head	200	650
5148	— Trefoil behind head	175	525
5149	*Dundee.* As 5147, but VILLA DVNDE	6750	2000
5150	*Perth.* As 5145-6. Star, saltire or nothing on sceptre handle. R VILLA DE PERTh	110	325
5151	— — B behind head, saltire on sceptre handle	175	475

5152

5152	**Halfpenny.** *Edinburgh.* As penny. VILA EDINRVR, EIDINBVG, etc.	100	325
5153	*Dundee.* As last, but VILLA DVNDE	425	1100
5153A	*Perth.* As last, but VILLA DE PERTh X	*Extremely rare*	

ROBERT III 1390-1406

John, Earl of Carrick, eldest son of Robert II, changed his name to Robert on succeeding to the throne. He was almost totally disabled by an accident which occurred before his father's death, and throughout his reign the administration was in the hands of his younger brother Robert Stewart, Duke of Albany.

During his reign a regular gold coinage was instituted, the lion and it half, the 'demy', being at first roughly equivalent to the English half and quarter noble.

The majority of the coins of his reign follow the regulations laid down in the Act of Parliament of 1393, but the coinage is divided by a reduction in the weights towards the end of the reign, the groat being reduced from 46½ grains to between 28 and 30 grains.

Most of the surviving coins of Robert III are of the heavy issue, although lack of silver being brought to the mint for recoinage (a current problem at the English mints) is not the only reason why the light coins are so scarce. The number of dies employed would indicate a considerable issue, their rarity, perhaps, due to lack of finds of the period.

Pennies and halfpennies were only struck in substantially debased silver.

Mints: Edinburgh, Aberdeen, Perth, Dumbarton.

	F £	VF £

Heavy coinage, 1390-c.1403

5154

5154	Lion (= 5s, wt. 61½ grains). First issue. Large crowned shield. R St Andrew crucified on long saltire cross, lis at sides, XPC REGNAT XPC VINCIT XPC IMPERAT	1500	4500

5155   5157

5155	Second issue. Small crowned shield. R St Andrew on short cross.	1650	5000
5156	**Demy-lion** (= 2s. 6d). First issue. Shield in tressure. R Long saltire cross, lis either side, large open trefoil above and below	2000	6500
5157	— Similar, but without tressure	1100	3250
5158	Second issue. Similar to last, but with small closed trefoils	1100	3250

	F £	VF £

Light coinage, *c.*1403-1406

5160

5161

5159	**Lion** (wt. c.38 grs.) I. Crowned arms. ℞ St Andrew, XPC legend	1750	5750
5160	II. ℞ St Andrew, often without cross visible, D Ո S PTECTOR Ո S legend	1650	5000
5161	**Demy-Lion** (wt. c.20 grs.) Ia. As 5158, but smaller	1350	4250
5162	Ib. King's name and titles both sides	*Extremely rare*	
5163	II. ℞ DՈS PTECTOR legend	1500	4750

SILVER

Heavy coinage, 1390-*c.*1403

5164

5164B

5164	**Groat** (wt. 46 grs.) *Edinburgh.* First issue. Rough tall facing bust, three large pellets at cusps of tressure of seven arcs. ℞ Long cross, pellets in angles	90	275
5164A	— — Fleur de lis in legend	100	300
5164B	— — Nine arcs to tressure	210	650

	F £	VF £

5165

5166

5165	— — As 5164, but no pellets at cusps, bust breaks tressure	225	675
5166	Second issue. Neat bust, with or without trefoils at cusps	100	325
5167	— — Similar, but annulets in spandrils	125	375
5168	*Aberdeen.* Second issue. As 5166	475	1350

5169

5170

5169	— As 5167	525	1500
5170	*Perth.* Second issue. As 5166	100	325
5171	— As 5167	135	450

5172

5175

5172	**Halfgroat.** *Edinburgh.* First issue. As 5164	150	525
5173	— — As 5165	225	675
5174	— Second issue. As 5166	175	625
5175	*Perth.* As 5166	175	625

Light coinage, *c.*1403-1406

5177

5178

5176	**Groat** (wt. *c.*28 grs.) *Edinburgh.* Smaller portrait, not well defined, single pellet on cusps of tressure	325	1000
5177	— Multiple pellets on cusps, or four pellets on head	425	1250

	F £	VF £

5179

5178	*Dumbarton.* Busts varied, three pellets, one pellet or nothing on cusps, R VILLA DVNBERTAN	1250	3000
5178A	— — Five arcs to tressure	1350	4000
5179	*Aberdeen.* Bust with small head (as James I coins), with or without pellets on cusps	750	2000

DEBASED SILVER

5180	5186	5188

5180	**Penny.** (wt. 17¼ grs.) *Edinburgh.* First issue. Rough facing bust with tall neck. R Cross and pellets	375	1250
5181	— Second issue. Neater bust, larger crown	350	1100
5182	— — R Omitting mint, REX SCOTORVM	425	1350
5183	— King's name repeated on *rev.*	525	1500
5184	*Perth.* Second issue. As 5181	425	1350
5185	*Aberdeen.* Similar	650	2000
5186	**Halfpenny.** *Edinburgh.* First issue. As 5180	175	600
5187	— Second issue. As 5181	200	650
5188	*Perth.* Second issue. Similar	300	850
5188A	*No mint name.* Low, wide crown and bust. R REX SCOTORVM	*Extremely rare*	

JAMES I 1406-1437

At Robert III's death, his son James was a prisoner of the English. A regency was formed first under Robert, Duke of Albany, and on his death in 1420, under his son Murdoch. In 1424 James married Janet Beaufort and returned to Scotland against a ransom of £40,000. James was murdered in 1437.

The practice of debasing the smaller denominations begun during the previous reign continued through the fifteenth century. As their intrinsic value became less, so the nominal value of the silver groat increased. Gold coins were reduced to a fineness of 22 cts.

Probably the billon pence and halfpenny of group A were struck during the period of the Regency. The fleur-de-lis groats (so called from the reverse which has fleurs-de-lis and three pellets in alternate angles) were the first substantial issue of James and probably resulted from the Act of Parliament of Perth in May 1424, just six weeks after his return to Scotland.

For the second and last time, Inverness is operative as a mint.

Mints: *Aberdeen, Edinburgh, Inverness, Linlithgow, Perth, Stirling.*

	F £	VF £

GOLD

5189   5192

		F	VF
5189	**Demy** (= 9s, wt. 54 grs.) I. Lion rampant on lozenge, mm. crown. R Saltire cross flanked by two lis in fleured tressure of six arcs. Small quatrefoils in arcs, **SALVVM FAC POPVLVM TVVM OnE**, or similar	1350	4000
5190	II. Similar, but large quatrefoils with open centre	1100	3250
5191	— As above, but chain pattern inner and outer circles	1500	4500
5192	III. Large quatrefoils with small pellet centres, normal circles ..	1050	3000

5193   5194

		F	VF
5193	**Half demy.** II. Similar to 5190	1500	4500
5194	— Tressure of seven arcs	1350	4000

	F £	VF £

SILVER

5195   5196

5195 Groat (= 6d, wt. c.36 grs.) First fleur-de-lis issue. *Edinburgh*. Small
neat bust, often with various ornaments, sceptre to l. ℞ Long cross,
fleur-de-lis and three pellets in alternate angles, many varieties .   150   575
5196 — Similar, sceptre to r.   200   675

5197   5200

5197 — Similar, but with chain circles   375   1000
5198 — *Perth*. As 5195. ℞ VILLA DE PERTh   350   950
5199 — *Linlithgow*. Similar. ℞ VILLA DE LINLITHGO   675   2000
5200 Second fleur-de-lis issue. *Edinburgh*. Bust of rougher work, large
crown with tall central fleur   175   625
5201 — *Perth*. Similar   375   1000
5202 — *Linlithgow*. Similar   750   2250

5203   5207

5203 — *Stirling*. Similar. ℞ VILLA STREVELIN etc.   625   1750
5204 Penny (wt. c.16 grs.) A. (Probably struck prior to 1424, during
the period of the Regency). *Edinburgh*. Bust as Robert III coins,
IACOBI etc. ℞ Cross and pellets, no initial cross   200   750
5205 — — Similar, but lis by neck   225   800
5206 — — large head with neck, IACOBVS. ℞ As above   225   800
5207 — *Aberdeen*. ℞ No initial cross.   525   1500
5208 — *Inverness*. ℞ Similar, VILLA INVERNIS   675   2000

| | | F £ | VF £ |

5210   5216

5209	**Penny.** B. *Edinburgh*. Bust as 1st issue groats, but without sceptre. ℞ Initial cross before VILLA	300	900
5210	— — Similar, but saltires by neck and crown	350	1000
5211	— Inverness. As 5209	750	2250
5212	C. *Edinburgh*. As 5209, but annulet stops and annulets and saltires by crown	375	1100
5213	— Bust from halfpenny punch	450	1350
5214	— *Aberdeen*. Bust as on 2nd issue groats, but without sceptre, annulet stops, sometimes annulets by bust	525	1500
5215	**Halfpenny.** A. *Edinburgh*. ℞ No initial cross	475	1350
5216	C. *Edinburgh*. Bust as on 2nd issue groats	525	1500

JAMES II 1437-1460

The murder of James I in 1437 left the Scottish throne to his seven year old son James.

No immediate changes were made to the coins, the first coinage of james II being merely a continuation of that of his father. For the sake of clarity the first and second issues of 'fleur-de-lis' groats are usually ascribed to James I and the third and fourth issues to james II, although the change of reign may well have occurred just prior to the end of the second issue.

The second coinage which began in 1451, in an attempt to bring it more into line with the English issues, sees the reappearance of the lion and half-lion, and also a heavier groat worth 12d. A revaluation making the groat 8d was proposed but apparently never carried out. This coinage was continued in the next reign, until *c*.1467, but all varieties are listed under this reign.

James was crowned at Holyrood in 1437 and married Mary of Gueldres in 1449. Much of his reign was marred by his quarrel with the Douglas family, and in 1455/6 he proposed joint action with the French against England. The substantial support he sought never materialised and after ravaging Northumberland he concluded a peace treaty with Henry VI in 1457. James established annual circuits of the justiciary and made other beneficial changes in the judicial system.

James was killed by the accidental bursting of a cannon during the siege of Roxburgh castle in 1460.

GOLD

Mints: *Aberdeen, Edinburgh, Linlithgow, Perth, Roxburgh, Stirling.*

First coinage, 1437-51

		F	VF
		£	£

5219

5217	**Demy**. IVa. As James I (5189), but quatrefoils on *rev.* with large central pellets, annulet stops	1250	3500
5218	— Similar, but annulet in centre of *rev.*	1500	4000
5219	IVb. As 5217, but saltire stops	1250	3500

Second coinage, 1451-60

5220

5220	**Lion** (10s, wt. 54 grs.) Fist issue. Crowned shield between two small crowns. ℞ St Andrew on cross between two lis, **SALVVM FAC** etc.	2000	6000

		F	VF
		£	£

5222   5223

5221 Lion. Second issue (10s). I. As 5220, but *mm.* crown on *obv.*, cross on *rev.*
R Crowned lis by saint, **XPC REGNAT** etc. 1850   5500
5222 — II. Crowned shield between two lis. R Crowned lis by saint,
mm. crown both sides.. 1750   5250
5223 Half lion (5s). II. Uncrowned shield. R Crown either side of saint. 2500   7500
5224 — Similar, but small crown over shield. 2750   8000

SILVER

First coinage, 1437-51

5225   5226

5225 Groat (= 6d) Third fleur-de-lis issue. *Edinburgh*. As 5200, but tall,
thinner crown, bushy hair, no extra ornaments 200   750
5226 — Similar, but king's name both sides 475   1500
5227 — As 5225, but sceptre to r. 225   850

5228   5230

5228 — *Linlithgow*. Similar to 5225 750   2500
5229 — *Stirling*. Similar to 5225 675   2000
5230 — Fourth fleur-de-lis issue. *Edinburgh*. As 5225, but bust in mantle and
hair more wavy. Spreading ornate crown with tall central lis 275   900

		F £	VF £

Second coinage, 1451-60

5231   5233

5231 Groat (= 12d, wt. 59 grs.) First issue. Edinburgh. Bust in mantle as last.
R Crowns and thee pellets in alternate angles of cross 425 1500
5232 Second issue. I. *Edinburgh*. Large crowned bust of English style, pellet
pointed spikes in crown, annulets by neck, *mm*. cross. R As last. 400 1350
5233 II. *Edinburgh*. Similar, but different lettering without annulets by
neck, *mm*. crown or cross (*rare*) 250 950
5234 — — — Similar, but saltires by neck 275 975

5236   5237

5235 III. *Edinburgh*. As 5233, but crown with trefoil pointed spikes . 275 975
5236 — — — Crosses or saltires by neck 225 900
5237 — — — Trefoils by neck 250 950
5238 — *Aberdeen*. Saltires or nothing by neck, VILLA ABIRDEN 950 3000
5239 — *Perth*. Saltires by neck 450 1500

5240   5241

5240 — *Roxburgh*. Saltires by neck, VILLA ROXBVRGh 1750 5250
5241 — *Stirling*. Lis or saltires by neck, VILLA STERLING 1000 3250
5242 IV. *Edinburgh*. New unjewelled crown without trefoils, beaded
circles, lettering partly similar to light groats and placks of James
III, *mm*. crown or cross 1100 3500

	F £	*VF* £

5243

5243 **Halfgroa**t (= 6d). *Edinburgh*. As 2nd issue groats, but crown with
small plain spikes and usually mm. cross on *obv.*, crown on *rev.* 625 1500
5244 — *Aberdeen* 900 2500
5245 — *Perth* 800 2250

BILLON
First coinage, 1437-51

5246

5250

5246 **Penny** (*c*.16 grs.) *Edinburgh*. Group D. Bust and lettering as 5225.
R Cross and pellets 425 1350
5247 — *Stirling*. Similar 575 1750

Second coinage, 1451-60
5248 **Penny** (10-12 grs.) *Edinburgh*. First issue. Clothed bust. R Cross
with pellets in two angles only.. 350 1000
5249 *Edinburgh*. Second issue, type Ai, Unclothed bust, initial mark
cross fourchée. R Crown in one quarter and trefoil of pellets
joined by a central annulet in three quarters 375 1250
5250 — Type Aii. Obverse as 5249. R Trefoil of pellets in
each angle.. 175 525
5251 — Type Bi. Obverse initial mark crown. With or without saltires
by neck and within trefoils of pellets on reverse. 200 575
5251A— Type Bii. No obverse initial mark. Plain both sides 200 575
5251B— Type Biii. Obverse initial mark lis. Obverse plain.
Reverse plain or with saltires between pellets. 200 575
5252 — Type Ci. No obverse initial mark. Lis to either side of neck
and on chest. Reverse plain or with saltires between pellets. 225 625
5252A— Type Cii. As Ci, but obverse initial mark lis......................... 200 575
5253 *Aberdeen*, type Bi 475 1500
5254 *Perth*, type Bi 325 900
5255 *Roxborough*, type Ci 750 2250

JAMES III 1460-1488

James III was crowned at Kelso in 1460 at the age of 9. During his minority Henry VI was received at the Scottish court, Berwick was acquired and the truce with England prolonged. The Boyds, in whose custody he had ben since 1456, arranged a marriage in 1469 with Margaret of Denmark, part of whose dowry was the Orkney and Shetland islands.

James' extravagance and partiality to favourites alienated him from the loyalty of his nobles who eventually placed his eldest son at their head. He was murdered following his defeat at Sauchieburn and buried at Cambuskenneth.

During his reign new denominations were introduced; in gold, the rider with its half and quarter, and the unicorn (issued at a baser standard of 21 cts.), although the half-unicorn may not have been issued until the next reign; and in billon, the plack and half plack. The thistle-head makes its first appearance as a Scottish emblem, and the numeral '3' occurs on some coins to denote the third king bearing the name of James.

An innovation during this reign was a coinage bearing the likeness of the monarch in the new renaissance style, thus pre-dating English coins of similar style by several years.

All the silver issues are of sterling silver (0.925 fineness) except for the base silver penny of *c*.1471 which is of 0.770 fineness only.

Mints: *Edinburgh. Berwick, Aberdeen.*

Mint-master's initials: A or L = Alexander Livingston. R = Thomas Tod.

GOLD

	F £	VF £

Issue of 1475-83

5256

		F £	VF £
5256	**Rider** (= 23s, wt. 78½ grs.) I. King in armour with sword, galloping r. R Crowned shield over long cross, **SALVVM** etc.	2500	7500
5257	— Similar, but A below king, small lis in front...........................	2750	8000
5258	II. King riding l., inscriptions reversed	3250	10000

5260   5261

		F £	VF £
5259	**Half-rider.** II. As last	2500	7500
5260	— Similar, but lis is below sword arm	2250	7000
5261	**Quarter-rider.** II. As 5260	3000	8500

	F £	VF £

Issue of 1484-88

5262

5262 Unicorn (= 18s, wt. 59 grs.) Unicorn l. with shield. ℞ Large
wavy star over cross fleury, **EXVRGAT** legend both sides. Roman
Ns, *mm.* cross fleury 3250 9500

SILVER

I. Light issue, *c.*1467

5263

5264

5263 Groat (= 12d, wt. 39¼ grs.) *Edinburgh.* Facing bust, saltires by neck,
mm. cross pattée. ℞ Trefoil of pellets and mullets of six points in
alternate angles 325 1000

5264 — Similar, but 'heavy' facing bust without saltires by neck 300 950

5265

5266

5265 — T and L by neck 375 1250

5266 *Berwick.* As above, T and L by neck 575 1750

5267

5269

5267 Halfgroat (= 6d). *Edinburgh.* As groat, crosses by neck, numeral
'3' after king's name 1350 3500

5268 — Similar, but no numeral 1100 2750

5269 *Berwick.* As 5267 .... 1250 3000

	F	VF
	£	£

II. Base silver issue of 1471 to *c.*1483 (0.770 fineness)

5270   5272

5270 **Groat** (= 6d, wt. c.33½ grs.) *Edinburgh.* Bust half-right in surcoat
and armour. ℞ Floriate cross, with thistleheads and mullets in
alternate angles 450   1500
5271 — Similar, but T to l. of king's head 525   1750
5272 **Halfgroat.** *Edinburgh.* As 5260 900   2750

III. Light issue of 1475

5273   5274

5273 **Groat** (12d). *Edinburgh.* Small facing bust with crown of five tall
fleurs, *mm.* cross pattée. ℞ Mullets of six points, and three pellets
in alternate angles, EDINBVRGh 275   950
5274 — Similar, but crown of three tall fleurs 250   900
5275 — Similar, but saltires by bust 300   1000

5276

5276 *Berwick.* As 5273, VILLA BERWICIh 625   2000
5277 — As 5274 675   2250

5278   5279

5278 **Halfgroat.** *Berwick.* As groat (5274) with crown of three tall fleurs 850   2500
5279 **Penny** (= current for 3d). *Edinburgh.* Neat round face with low crown.
℞ Mullet of six points and pellets as groat, no outer circles 375   1250

F	*VF*
£	£

IV. Light issue, *c*.1482

5280   5280A

5280	**Groat** (= 12d). *Edinburgh*. Small facing bust with low crown of five fleurs, *mm*. cross fleury. R Mullets of five points, and three pellets, in alternate angles. EDENBEOVRGE	225	675
5280A	— Similar, but pellets and mullets in opposite angles	225	675
5281	— Similar, but reverse as 5273	325	900

5282   5282A

5282	**Halfgroat.** *Edinburgh*. Crown of four fleurs, I above, A and T by neck. R I in centre of cross	575	1750
5282A	— No initials on obverse	625	1850
5283	**Penny.** *Edinburgh.* As 5279, but mullets of five points	225	750

5283

Heavy issue of 1484-1488 (Rough issue)

5284	**Groat** (1s 3d, wt. 47^{1}/$_8$ grs.) *Edinburgh*. Draped bust with crown of five fleurs (double punched to show ten fleurs), *mm*. cross fleury. R Pellets and crowns in alternate angles, EDINBRVG	1100	3500
	(This may be an irregular civil war issue, struck in 1488.)		

F	*VF*
£	£

VI. Main issue, 1484-1488

5287   5288

5285	**Groat** (1s 2d). *Edinburgh*. Bust half-left with arched crown. R Pellets with annulet, and crowns, in alternate angles, *mm*. cross fleury	350	1350
5286	— Similar, but crown and saltire before bust, lis behind	750	2500
5287	— As 5285, but annulet on inner circle before face	325	1250
5288	— As 5285, but annulet on inner circle before bust	325	1250
5289	— As 5285, but annulet on inner circle behind head	350	1350

5292

5290	*Aberdeen*. As 5285, but *mm*. mullet on obv.	625	2000
5291	— As 5287	575	1750
5292	**Halfgroat**. *Edinburgh*. As groat 5285, but *mm*. plain cross on *rev*.	950	2750

BILLON

5293   5296

5293	**Plack** (= 4d, wt. 31½ grs., 0.500 fineness). *Edinburgh*. Shield in tressure of three arcs, crown above, cross pattée either side. R Floreate cross fourchée, saltire in central panel, crowns in angles	175	525
5294	— Similar, but star in centre of *rev*.	185	550
5295	— As 5293, but I in place of saltire in centre of *rev*.	200	600
5296	**Half plack.** *Edinburgh*. As 5293	165	500
5297	— Similar, but no marks by shield	175	525
5298	— As 5295, with I in place of saltire on *rev*.	200	600

	F £	*VF* £

5300

5299 **Penny.** *Edinburgh.* A. Bust as on first issue light silver.
      R Long cross and pellets 175   525

The following varieties occur:
      Aa1. Reverse initial mark crown. Obverse and reverse normally plain,
      but is known with saltires beside bust.
      Aa2. As Aa1, but points within the trefoils of pellets on reverse.
      Ab1. Reverse initial mark cross fourchée. Reverse plain.
      Ab2. As Ab1, but points with the trefoils of pellets on reverse.
      Ab3. As Ab1, but saltires within the trefoils of pellets on reverse.
      Ab4. As Ab1, but annulets within the trefoils of pellets on reverse.

5300 — B. Facing bust, *mm.* cross fourchée. R Short cross as on base silver
      coins, slipped trefoils or quatrefoils in angles 200   550

5301 — C. Facing bust with five fleurs (as on light coins), *mm.* plain
      cross. R Cross and pellets 150   450

5302 — — Similar, but with three fleurs in crown 165   475

5303 — D. Bust nearly facing, with annulets by crown (sometimes
      above) and with pellets in angles of *rev., mm.* cinquefoil 325   950

5304 **Halfpenny.** As C, but three fleurs in crown 575   1500

COPPER (or BRASS)

Regal issues (known as 'Black Money')

5305 **Farthing.** I. (*c.*1465-6?). Edinburgh. Large crown, I REX SCOTORVM.
      R Saltire cross, small saltire either side 325   900

5306

5306 II. (c.1466-7?). Crown of five fleurs, IR below, IACOBVS etc. R Crown
      over saltire cross, small saltires in angles, VILLA EDINBVR 350   1000
      Mules are known with obverse of 5306 and reverse of 5305.
      5306 is known with royal titles both sides.

	F £	VF £

Other issues once regarded as Ecclesiastical

Crux Pellit copper ('Three-penny penny'), previously known as 'Crossraguel' of Bishop Kennedy pennies.

5307   5309

5307	I L(i). IACOBVS DEI GRA REX, orb tilted downwards to left. R CRVX PELLIT OIE CRIM etc. Latin cross in quatrefoil	100	325
5308	I L(ii). CRVX legend both sides	125	400
5308A	I R. Orb tilted downwards and to right		
5309	II L. Orb tilted upwards to left	110	350
5309A	II R. Orb tilted upwards to right		
5310	II R*. As above, a pellet/jewel in each section of orb	135	450

5311

5311	III L. Rosette in centre of orb, orb tilted upwards to left	90	300
5311A	III L*. As above, with annulet(s) on orb	90	300
5311B	III R. Rosette in centre of orb, orb tilted upwards to right	90	300

5314

5312	**Farthing.** I. IACOBVS D G R, crown over IR. R MONEPAVP, cross with crowns and mullets in alternate angles	275	800
5313	II. Large trefoils containing mullet and three lis, crowns in top angles, no legend. R As last	225	650
5314	— Similar, but MO PAVPER	250	70

JAMES IV 1488-1513

James IV was crowned at Scone in 1488 at the age of 15. In 1495 he received Perkin Warbeck at the Scottish court and arranged his marriage to Lady Katherine Gordon. For two years he carried out border raids in Warbeck's favour but later made a truce with Henry VII, whose daughter, Margaret Tudor, he married in 1503. Well educated and an able administrator, he instigated numerous legislative reforms. he patronised learning and was interested in astrology and surgery.

Despite rising national opposition to the treaty with England he preferred the alliance to continue while Henry VII was still alive, although closer ties with France were being formed. With the accession of Henry VIII relations between the two countries deteriorated, culminating in James assisting Louis XII of France against Henry. At the head of a large army he invaded Northumberland and was killed at the slaughter of Flodden Field in 1513.

The unicorn continued to be struck at a fineness of 21 carats or worse, while the crown (or lion) was apparently even baser. All the silver was struck at 11.1 deniers (0.925) but the billon plack was very base indeed, some having the appearance of pure copper.

All the coins were struck at Edinburgh.

GOLD

5315

5315	**Unicorn.** (= 18s, wt. 59 grs., 21 cts. or less). I. As James III, except royal title on *obv.*, Lombardic Π. Crown of three lis around neck of unicorn. Six-pointed star, 'V' or broken star stops, *mm.* lis		1500	4500
5317	II. Crown of five lis. Lis or pellet stops, *mm.* cross pattée		1750	5250
5319	III. Roman letters, 4 after king's name, no annulet or chain below unicorn, *mm.* crown.		3000	8500
5321	**Half unicorn.** I. Similar to unicorn 5315, Roman N, *mm.* lis		1350	4000

5322

5322	— Similar but lombardic Π, *mm.* lis, two stars or cross pommée		1250	3500
5323	II. Similar, QR at the of obv. legend. R I in centre of sun of 14 wavy rays, *mm.* cross potent		*Extremely rare*	
5324	III as 5319, Roman letters but no numeral, annulet below unicorn, *mm.* crown		2750	8500

	F £	*VF* £

5325 **Lion or crown** (= 13s 4d, wt. 52¼ grs.) I. St Andrew standing l.,
holding saltire cross. ℞ Lis either side of crowned shield .... *Extremely rare*

5326 II. Crowned shield, lis either side, IIII at end of legend, mm. crown.
℞ St Andrew on long saltire cross 3250   10000

5327 **Half lion.** I. Crowned shield between crowned lis. ℞ St Andrew
on cross between crowned lis 3500   11000

5328 II. As 5326 with IIII at end of legend, no *mm.* on rev. 3750   12000

5328A **Pattern Angel**, on heavy flan, wt. 491 grs. IACOBVS 4 etc., St. Michael
spearing dragon. ℞ Shield on ship, I 4 above, **SALVATOR**
IN HOC SIGNO VICISTI .... *Extremely rare*

		F	VF
		£	£

SILVER

Heavy coinage, 1489-c.1496

5330   5333

5329 Groat (= 1s 2d, wt. 47¹/₈ grs.) Ia. Neat unclothed bust with crown
of five fleurs, annulet stops. ℞ Crown and pellets in alternate angles
of cross, lis in centre 750   2500
This is a reverse of James III with a lis added.

5330 Ib. Taller bust. ℞ As above, but no lis on cross 575   2000

5331 Ic. Similar, but medieval 4 after king's name 900   3000

5332 IIa. (= 1s 2d, wt. 47½ grs.). *Edinburgh*. Facing bust with thin cheeks,
crown of five fleurs, annulet on breast, six-pointed star stops.
℞ Pellets and annulet in two angles, crown opposite lis in the other
two, ЄDIПBRVG 525   1850

5333 IIb. Larger bust with heavy eyelids, crown of three fleurs, short
spikes between, no annulet on breast.. 475   1750

5334 IIc. Similar, but tall spikes in crown 525   1850

5336

5335 Halfgroat. Ia. Facing bust with crown of five fleurs. Ω or 4 at end
of legend. ℞ As 5330 750   2250

5336 Ib. No numeral at end of legend. ℞ As 5330 .... *Extremely rare*

	F	*VF*
	£	£

Light coinage, *c*.1496-1513

5338

5337 **Groat** (= 12d, wt. 39¼ grs.) III. Neat facing bust, mm. crown.
R Pellets and mullets in alternate angles, **SALVVM** legend 525 1850
5338 — Similar, but medieval 4 at end of *obv.* legend 725 2500
5339 — — Also star by neck 800 2750

5340   5341

5340 — QRA or QT (quartus) at end of *obv.* legend 475 1750
5341 — — Also stars by neck 525 1850

5342   5343

5342 — As above but IIII at end of *obv.* legend 450 1600
5343 IV. (approx. 33 grs) Bearded bust, jewels in band of crown, 4 after
king's name. R As above, but with **EXVRGAT** legend 2000 6500
Struck as Maundy money from 11 lbs 1½ ozs. of silver ordered by the king
to be coined into twelvepenny groats for distribution in *Cena Domini* in 1512.

5345   5347

5344 **Halfgroat.** III. As groat, no numeral, **SALVV** legend 725 2250
5345 — — With stars by neck 750 2400
5346 — As 5344, but *obv.* legend ends IIII 800 2500
5347 **Penny** (= 3d). Facing bust, no numeral, mm. crown. R Cross
with mullets and pellets 950 3000

BILLON

5351   5354

		F £	VF £
5348	**Plack** (= 4d). I. Shield in tressure, crowns above and at sides, legend ends QRA. Lombardic lettering	100	350
5349	II. No QRA	40	125
5350	III. Similar, but Roman lettering on one side	50	150
5351	IV. Similar, but 4 after king's name, pellet and trefoil stops, Roman lettering both sides	45	135
5352	— Similar, star stops	60	200
5353	**Half plack.** I. Lombardic lettering, QR at end of obv. legend ...	175	525
5354	II. Similar, but without QR	135	450
5355	— Similar, but omitting crowns by shield	150	475
5356	— Similar, but lis by shield	150	475

5357   5359

		F £	VF £
5357	**Penny.** First issue. Tall bust with crown of five fleurs, annulets by neck. R Cross and pellets	125	375
5358	— Similar, but no annulets. Saltire stops	125	375
5359	Second issue. I. Small bust with fleurs and points in crown. R Crowns and lis in alternate angles of cross, **SALVVM** legend in place of mint name	175	600
5360	— II. Small neat bust. R As above, but with mint name	70	200
5361	— III. Larger bust	60	175

5362

		F £	VF £
5362	— IV. Rounder bust; usually a smaller, thicker flan	50	135

JAMES V 1513-1542

James V was a little over a year old at his father's death. Taken by his mother to Stirling, she was later forced to hand him over to the Regent Albany to be educated. He was declared competent to rule in 1524 although he did not rule absolutely until 1528 after his escape from Edinburgh and the clutches of Angus, who had held him in close confinement since 1526. He married Madeleine, daughter of Francis I of France in 1537 and on her early death married Mary of Guise (mother of Mary Queen of Scots) the following year.

He refused to support the English reformation and was given the title 'defender of the Faith' by Pope Paul III. His quarrel with the Douglases and other prominent nobles eventually led to the annexation to the Crown of all the Western Isles. He died at Falkland in 1542, being succeeded by his only legitimate daughter, Mary, then only one week old.

The unicorn continued to be struck in 21 ct. gold although now current for 20s, and was later to be raised to 22s. An 'eagle crown' current for 17s. and possibly struck from 22½ ct. gold may belong to this period, although no specimens are now known to exist.

A gold crown current at 20s. was struck to a 21½ ct. standard, and the introduction of the ducat or 'bonnet piece' of 40s. dated 1539 provides the first example of a dated Scottish coin.

Silver groats were not struck until late in the reign, all of which are scarce. The commonest coin in circulation continued to be the billon plack which was joined by a new coin in 1538, the bawbee, current for 6d.

The coinage continued to be struck in Edinburgh but gold crowns were struck at Holyrood and are often referred to in contemporary documents as 'Abbey crowns'. Those gold coins countermarked with a cinquefoil were probably struck for James, Earl of Arran, who supplied the gold, this being a family device.

GOLD

| | F | VF |
| | £ | £ |

First coinage, c.1518-26

5365

		F	VF
5364	**Unicorn** (20s, wt. 59 grs.) Roman lettering, similar to James IV, but no numeral, **X** or **XC** below unicorn. R With cinquefoil countermark, *mm*. crown	2250	6500
5365	— — Similar, but without countermark	2500	7000
5366	**Half unicorn.** Roman lettering, no numeral, **X** below unicorn ..	3000	9000
5367	**'Eagle crown'** (17s, wt. 53½ grs.) Crowned shield, saltires beside. R Dove with halo (Holy Spirit) facing, **IOHANNIS ALBANIE DVCIS GVBERNA**	*No extant specimen*	

	F	*VF*
	£	£

Second coinage, 1526-39

5370

5368	**Crown** (20s, wt. 52¼ grs.) I. Pointed shield with saltire each side, arched crown above. ℞ Cross fleury, thistles in angles, **PER LIGNV CRVCIS SALVI SVMVS**	2250	6500
5369	II. Shield with smaller open crown. ℞ As above but **CRVCIS ARMA SEQVAMVR**, annulet stops	1500	4500
5370	III. Similar, but shield with rounded base, trefoil stops	1250	3500
5371	IV. Similar, but pellet stops	1350	3750
5372	V. Similar, but very small crown above shield	*Extremely rare*	

Third coinage, 1539-42

5373

5373	**Ducat**, or 'Bonnet piece' (= 40s, wt. 88⅓ grs.) Bearded bust of king r., wearing bonnet. ℞ Crowned shield over cross fleury		
	1539	4500	13500
	1540	4250	12000

5374　　　　　　　　　　　　　　　　　　5375

5374	**Two-third ducat** (= 26s 8d). 1540. Similar. ℞ Crowned shield dividing I 5	3500	9500
5375	**One-third ducat** (= 13s). 1540. As above	4500	12500

SILVER

	F £	VF £

Second coinage, 1526-39

5376   5377

5376 Groat (1s 6d, wt. 42 grs., 0.833 fineness). I. Bust r., mantled, double-arched crown. ℞ Pointed shield over cross fourchée, VILLA EDINBRVGH .... | 450 | 1500

5377 II. Similar bust, but single-arched crown. ℞ As last, but OPPIDVM EDINBVRGI .... | 275 | 850

5378

5378 III. Similar, but with open mantle, sometimes trefoil of pellets in field. ℞ Rounded shield, OPPIDV, trefoil stops .... | 225 | 700

5379 IV. Similar, head with pointed nose, ℞ Similar to last, but mainly colon stops .... | 250 | 750

5380

5380 One-third groat (= 6d). IV. As groat .... | 200 | 700

BILLON

	F £	VF £

First coinage, 1513-26

5381

			F	VF
5381	**Plack** (= 4d, wt. 31½ grs.) As James IV, but no numeral. ℞ Crowns and saltires in alternate angles of cross, mullet in centre		25	125
5382	— (1532/3). Similar, but ornamental Roman letters, annulets in spandrils. Crowns in all four angles of cross, VILLA DE EDINBVRG		125	450

Third coinage, 1538-42

5384

		F	VF
5383	**Bawbee** (= 6d, wt. 29 grs., 0.250 fineness). Crowned thistle dividing I 5. ℞ Crown on saltire cross, lis each side	30	125
5384	— Similar, but annulet over I or on inner circle	30	125
5384A	— — Annulet over 5	40	150
5385	— — Annulet over I and 5	50	175

5388

		F	VF
5386	**Half bawbee.** As 5383, but without lis on rev.	100	400
5387	— Annulet over I	90	375
5388	— Annulet over 5	110	450
5389	**Quarter bawbee** (wt. 8.2 grs.) *Obverse* type doubtful. ℞ Crown on saltire cross, *mm.* crown	*Extremely rare*	

MARY 1542-1567

One of the most romantic, and tragic, figures in Scottish history, Mary became queen when only seven days old. Educated in France with the French royal children and brought up in the Catholic faith, she married the Dauphin, Francis, in 1558 and was prostrated on his death two years later. In 1565 she married Henry Stewart, Lord Darnley and the following year bore him a son, who later became James I of England. Suspicion implicated her and her favourite, the Earl of Bothwell, in Darnley's death by explosion in a house at Kirk o'Field, Edinburgh, in 1567. That same year she married Bothwell with Protestant rites and agreed to her abdication.

She escaped to England in 1568 after the battle of Langside and was imprisoned by Elizabeth. After numerous intrigues and plots she was beheaded at Fotheringhay Castle in 1587. Few historical periods are mirrored so closely in the coinage as that of Mary.

In the first period, before her marriage, the 1553 gold coinage, still being struck to a 22 ct. standard, bear the initials IG for Jacobus Gubenator (James, Earl of Arran, Regent and Governor of Scotland), while some of the testoons and half testoons have the letter A (Acheson, the mint master) by the shield.

The second period sees the transition in the royal titles and arms after the Dauphin became Francis I of France.

The first widowhood of 1560-5 is represented by a unique piece in gold, and in silver by a testoon and its half bearing a superb portrait of Mary said to have been inspired by the portrait by the French painter, François Clouet, also known as Janet.

No gold was struck after the first widowhood. Of the last two periods, her marriage to Darnley is noted with the change of titles to Henry and Mary etc., and on a unique ryal the couple are shown face to face, although the commonest coins of this and the final period after Darnley's death are the non-portrait ryals and their parts.

Among the billon coins, the bawbee continues to be prolific, and is joined by a 12d groat commonly called a 'nonsunt' and a 1½d piece known as a lion or 'hardhead' which at its worst was 23/24 alloy.

The mint of Stirling was used for an issue of bawbees and is the last occasion that coining took place outside Edinburgh.

NB. The testoons and ryals (and their parts) are often found countermarked with a crowned thistle (see p. 76) and the billon placks and hardheads with a heart and star (see p. 85).

GOLD

	F	VF
	£	£

First period, 1542-58. Before marriage

5390

5390	**Abbey crown** or écu (issued at 20s in 1542, raised to 22s 10d in 1543, wt. 52¼ grs.) Crowned shield, cinquefoil each side. ℞ Cross fleury with thistles in angles, CRVCIS ARMA SEQVAMVR	2750	8000

	F	*VF*
	£	£

5391   5394

5391 **Twenty shillings** (44¹/₆ grs.) 1543. Crowned shield. ℞ Crowned
MR monogram, cinquefoil below, ECCE ANCILLA DOMINI   3250   9500

5392 **Forty-four shillings** (78½ grs.) 1553. First issue. Crowned shield
dividing I G. ℞ Crowned monogram of MARIA REGINA dividing I G,
DILIGITE IVSTICAM   3000   8500

5393 — Similar, but cinquefoil in place of I G on both sides, 1553 ...   2500   7500

5394 — Similar, but I G on *obv.*, cinquefoils on *rev.*, 1553   2250   6500

5395 Second issue. Crowned arms dividing M R. ℞ Crowned monogram
of MARIA with crowned cross potent each side, 1557 ....   *Extremely rare*

5396

5396 **Twenty-two shillings.** As 5394, but crown on *obv.* divides legend.
℞ MR, cinquefoil each side, 1553   2000   5250

5397   5398

5397 **Three pound piece** or portrait ryal (117³/₄ grs.) Bust l. ℞ Crowned
arms, IVSTVS FIDE VIVIT

1555   7500   22500

1557 ....   *Extremely rare*

1558 ....   *Extremely rare*

5398 **Thirty shilling piece** or half ryal. Similar.

1555   8500   25000

1557 ....   *Extremely rare*

1558 ....   *Extremely rare*

	F	*VF*
	£	£

Second period, 1558-60. Francis and Mary

5399

5399   **Ducat** (= 60s, 117³/₄ grs.) 1558. Busts of Francis and Mary face
        to face, crown above. ℞ Cross of eight interlinked dolphins, Lorraine
        crosses in angles, **HORVM TVTA FIDES** 52500 150000

Third period. 1560-65. First widowhood

5400   **Crown** (50½ grs.) 1561. Crowned arms. ℞ Four crowned Ms crosswise,
        thistleheads in angles, **EXVRGAT** legend. Possibly a pattern .... *Extremely rare*

SILVER

First period, 1542-58. Before marriage

5401

5401   **Testoon.** Type I (= 4s, wt 78½ grs., 0.916 fineness) 1553. Crowned bust r.
        ℞ Crowned shield, cinquefoil each side, **DA PACEM DOMINE**   4750   15000

5402

5402   Type II (= 5s, wt. 117³/₄ grs., 0.725 fineness) 1555. Large **M**
        crowned, crowned thistle each side. ℞ Shield over cross potent,
        DILICIE DNI COR HVMILE   275   950
5403   — Similar, but annulet over left thistle   300   1000

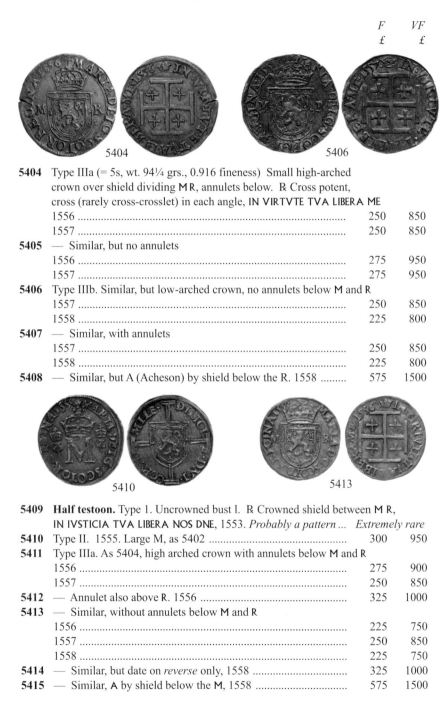

		F £	VF £

5404 Type IIIa (= 5s, wt. 94¼ grs., 0.916 fineness) Small high-arched crown over shield dividing M R, annulets below. ℞ Cross potent, cross (rarely cross-crosslet) in each angle, IN VIRTVTE TVA LIBERA ME

1556		250	850
1557		250	850

5405 — Similar, but no annulets

1556		275	950
1557		275	950

5406 Type IIIb. Similar, but low-arched crown, no annulets below M and R

1557		250	850
1558		225	800

5407 — Similar, with annulets

1557		250	850
1558		225	800

5408 — Similar, but A (Acheson) by shield below the R. 1558 .... 575 1500

5409 **Half testoon.** Type 1. Uncrowned bust l. ℞ Crowned shield between M R, IN IVSTICIA TVA LIBERA NOS DNE, 1553. *Probably a pattern ... Extremely rare*

5410 Type II. 1555. Large M, as 5402 .... 300 950

5411 Type IIIa. As 5404, high arched crown with annulets below M and R

1556		275	900
1557		250	850

5412 — Annulet also above R. 1556 .... 325 1000

5413 — Similar, without annulets below M and R

1556		225	750
1557		250	850
1558		225	750

5414 — Similar, but date on *reverse* only, 1558 .... 325 1000

5415 — Similar, A by shield below the M, 1558 .... 575 1500

		F	*VF*
		£	£

Second period, 1558-60. Francis and Mary

5416

5416 **Testoon** (= 5s, wt. 94¼ grs., 0.916 fineness) I. Crowned arms of
Francis (as Dauphin) and Mary over cross potent. ℞ Large **FM** monogram
crowned, Lorraine cross each side, FECIT VTRAQVE VNVM

1558	....	275	950
1559	....	275	950

5417   5418

5417 II. 1560. Arms of Francis (as King of France) and Mary, Scottish crown
above, cross on l., saltire on r., VICIT LEO DE TRIBV IVDA 250   900

5417A— Similar, but no crowns on *reverse* 375   1250

5418 — Similar, but crown of five lis over arms

1560	....	275	950
1561	....	450	1350
1565, a die sinker's error for 1560	....	475	1500

5418A— Transitional issue (?), as 5418 but obverse legend as 5416,
ending D D VIEN. 1560 750   2000

5419 **Half testoon.** I. As 5416.

1558	....	300	900
1559	....	375	1100

5420 II. 1560. As 5417, with Scottish crown 325   1000

5421

5421 — — As 5418, with crown of five lis 325   1000

	F	VF
	£	£

Third period, 1560-65. First widowhood

5422   5423

5422   **Testoon** (= 5s, wt. 94¼ grs.) Bust l. in contemporary costume, date
below in tablet. ℞ Crowned arms of France and Scotland, crowned **M**
each side, **SALVVM** legend

1561	4250	12500
1562	4500	13500

5423   **Half testoon.** Similar.

1561	4500	12500
1562	5250	15000

Fourth period, 1565-57. Mary and Henry Darnley

5424

5424   **Ryal** (= 30s, wt. 471¼ grs.) I. Busts of Henry and Mary face to face,
date below, **HENRICVS & MARIA.** etc. ℞ Crowned shield. thistle each
side, **QVOD DEVS COIVNXIT HOMO NON SEPARET**, 1565   45000   135000

	F £	VF £

5425

5425 II. Crowned shield, thistle each side, **MARIA & HENRIC**, etc.
R Tortoise climbing a palm tree, **DAT GLORIA VIRES** on scroll,
EXVRGAT legend. Sometimes called a 'Crookeston' dollar.

1565	575	1750
1566	525	1600
1567	650	2000

5426

5426 **Two-thirds ryal.** As above.

Undated	1500	4500
1565	475	1350
1566	475	1450
1567	750	2250

5427

5427 **One-third ryal.** As above.

1565	475	1500
1566	650	1850

		F £	VF £

Fifth period, 1567. Second widowhood

5429

5429	**Ryal.** 1567. As 5425, but name of Mary only	675	2000
5430	**Two-thirds ryal.** 1567. As 5426, but name of Mary only	475	1500

5431

5431 **One-third ryal.** As 5427, but name of Mary only.

1566	750	2250
1567	650	1850

BILLON

First period, 1542-58. Before marriage.
Issue of 3/4 alloy

5432   5433

5432 **Bawbee** (= 6d, wt. 29½ grs.) *Edinburgh.* Crowned thistle dividing M R,
MARIA D G REGINA SCOTORV or MARIA D G R SCOTORVM
R Plain saltire cross through crown, cinquefoil each side, OPPIDVM
EDINBVRGI 40   135

5433 — Similar, but voided saltire cross 45   150

	F	*VF*
	£	£

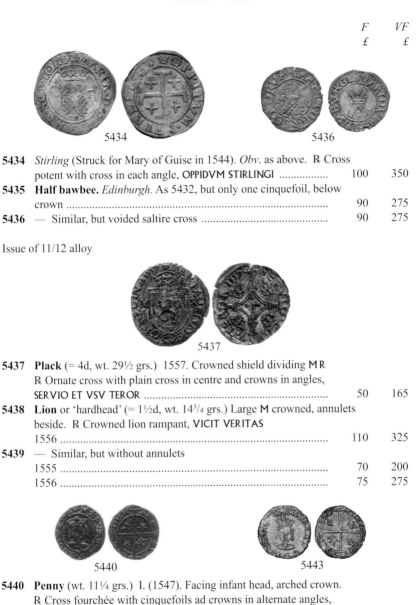

5434   5436

5434 *Stirling* (Struck for Mary of Guise in 1544). *Obv.* as above. ℞ Cross
potent with cross in each angle, OPPIDVM STIRLINGI 100 350
5435 **Half bawbee.** *Edinburgh.* As 5432, but only one cinquefoil, below
crown 90 275
5436 — Similar, but voided saltire cross 90 275

Issue of 11/12 alloy

5437

5437 **Plack** (= 4d, wt. 29½ grs.) 1557. Crowned shield dividing M R
℞ Ornate cross with plain cross in centre and crowns in angles,
SERVIO ET VSV TEROR 50 165
5438 **Lion** or 'hardhead' (= 1½d, wt. 14¾ grs.) Large M crowned, annulets
beside. ℞ Crowned lion rampant, VICIT VERITAS
1556 .... 110 325
5439 — Similar, but without annulets
1555 .... 70 200
1556 .... 75 275

5440   5443

5440 **Penny** (wt. 11¼ grs.) I. (1547). Facing infant head, arched crown.
℞ Cross fourchée with cinquefoils ad crowns in alternate angles,
OPIDVM EDNBVR 275 950
5441 — Similar, but open crown 325 1050
5442 II. Similar, but older face. ℞ OPIDV EDINBVRGI 375 1250
5443 III. (1554). Crowned facing bust with no inner circle. ℞ Cross
fourchée with lis and crowns in angles, OPPIDVM EDINBVRG...... 450 1500

	F	*VF*
	£	£

Issue of 45/48 alloy

5444

5444 Penny. Cross potent with four small crosses potent in angles.
℞ Crown over **VICIT / VERITAS / 1556** 250 850

Issue of 23/24 alloy

5445

5445 Lion (= 1½d). As 5439, but dated 1558 .... 40 125

Second period, 1558-60. Francis and Mary

Issue of half alloy

5447    5448

5447 Twelvepenny groat or 'nonsunt' (wt. 26¼ grs.) Crowned **FM** monogram,
on l. a crowned heraldic dolphin looking r., crowned thistle on r.
℞ **IAM NON / SVNT DVO / SED VNA / CARO** in panel, date below.
1558 .... 110 375
1559 .... 100 350
5448 — Similar, but dolphin looking left, 1559 .... 100 350

Issue of 23/24 alloy

5449

5449 Lion, or 'hardhead' (= 1½d). 1559. Crowned FM monogram, dolphin
each side, looking r. ℞ Crowned lion rampant 50 150
5450 — Similar, but dolphins looking left, date 1558 .... 40 125
(date '58' only are probably all contemporary forgeries)
1559 (genuine) 40 125
1560 (genuine) 70 225

JAMES VI 1567-1625

James VI acceded to the throne of Scotland on his mother's abdication in 1567, aged one year. A council of regency was established and his excellent education was largely due to George Buchanan. He married Anne of Denmark in 1589. The death of Elizabeth I left James as her nearest heir and he therefore ruled both kingdoms from 1603.

Following the gunpowder plot of 1605 he ordered severe sanctions against Romanist priests and during his reign the King James, or 'authorised' version of the Bible was published.

The frequent calling-in and changes of design has left us with a legacy of the most beautiful designs and varied legends, especially the gold coins, of any reign in the Scottish series. The half-length figure of the young king in armour and holding a sword must rank among the very finest of portraits on a British coin.

Billon and copper coins were issued in much reduced quantities, none at all being struck during the first sixteen years of the reign. Scottish documents of 1585 refer to the striking of coins at Dundee and Perth because of the pestilence in Edinburgh, but no coins are known with other than an Edinburgh mint-signature. Due to the number of forgeries in circulation hardheads and placks of Mary were called in in March 1575 and the genuine coins re-issued with a heart and star countermark, the arms of the Earl of Morton, regent at that time.

By 1578 the value of silver had risen so much that the silver coins of both Mary and James were called in and countermarked with a crowned thistle. The ryals were re-issued at 36s 9d and the testoons of Mary at 7s 4d. In 1611 the value of the gold unit and its fractions were raised by 10%.

After his accession to the English throne, James established a currency of similar weight and fineness in both realms although a 12:1 ratio between the Scottish and English denominations was still maintained.

GOLD
BEFORE ACCESSION TO ENGLISH THRONE

Note. There is no gold corresponding to the First coinage of silver.

Second coinage

	F £	VF £

5451

5451   Twenty pound piece (471¼ grs., 22 ct.) Half length bust of the
young king in armour. ℞ Crowned shield, PARCERE SVBIECTIS &
DEBELLARE SVPERBOS

	F	VF
1575	27500	80000
1576	25000	75000

Third coinage

5452

5452 Ducat (= 80s, wt. 94½ grs., 21 ct.) 1580. Bust in ruff l. ℞ Crowned
shield dividing date. **EXVRGAT** legend 8000   25000

Fourth coinage

5453

5453 Lion noble (= 75s, wt. 78½ grs., 21½ ct.) Crowned lion sejant with
sword and sceptre, **POST 5 & 100** etc. ℞ Four crowned **IR** cyphers
crosswise, **S** in centre, **DEVS IVDICIVM TVVM REGI DA**
1584 12000   35000
1585 .... *Extremely rare*
1586 .... *Extremely rare*
1588 .... *Extremely rare*

5454

5455

5454 Two-thirds noble (= 50s). Similar.
1584 10000   30000
1585 .... *Extremely rare*
1587 .... *Extremely rare*
5455 One-third noble (= 25s). Similar, 1584 8000   25000

	F	VF
	£	£

Fifth coinage (1588)

5456

5456 **Thistle noble** (= 146s 8d or 11 merks, wt. 117³/₄ grs., 23½ ct.)
Crowned shield on ship, thistle below. ℞ Thistle plant with crossed
sceptres and lions rampant in panel surrounded by eight thistles, undated.
FLORENT SCEPT PIIS REGNA HIS IOVA DAT NVMERATO 3500   10000

Sixth coinage

5457

5457 **Hat piece** (= 80s, wt. 69³/₄ grs., 22 ct.) Bust in tall hat r., thistle
behind. ℞ Crowned lion std. l. holding sceptre, cloud and 'Jehovah'
in Hebrew above, TE SOLVM VEREOR

	F	VF
1591	6750	20000
1592	6250	18500
1593	6250	18500

		F £	VF £

Seventh coinage

5458   5459

5458 Rider (= 100s, wt. 78½ grs.) King in armour with sword, on horse galloping r. R Crowned shield, SPERO MELIORA

	F	VF
1593	1350	4000
1594	1250	3750
1595	1350	4000
1598	1500	4500
1599	1250	3750
1601	1650	5000

5459 Half-rider. Similar

	F	VF
1593	1350	4000
1594	1250	3500
1595	1500	4500
1598	1500	4500
1599	1350	3750
1601	1350	3750

Eighth coinage

5460   5462

5460 Sword and sceptre piece (= 120s, wt. 78z grs., 22 ct.) Crowned arms. R Crossed sword and sceptre, crown above, thistles at sides, SALVS POPVLI SVPREMA LEX

	F	VF
1601	750	2000
1602	750	2000
1603	800	2250
1604	850	2250

5462 Half sword and sceptre piece. Similar

	F	VF
1601	575	1500
1602	625	1350
1603	*Extremely rare*	
1604	675	1750

AFTER ACCESSION TO ENGLISH THRONE

I. Ninth coinage, 1604-9, and II. Tenth coinage, 1609-25

5463   5464

5463 **Unit or sceptre piece** (= £12 Scots or £1 sterling, wt. 154^{5}/$_{6}$ grs., 22 ct.)
I. King half-length r. wearing Scottish crown and holding orb and sceptre.
℞ Crowned shield dividing I R. English arms in 1st and 4th quarters.
FACIAM EOS etc. 950   2750
5464 II. Similar, but Scottish arms in 1st and 4th quarters 850   2500

5466

5465 **Double crown** (= £6 Scots, wt. 77^{2}/$_{5}$ grs.) I. As 5463 but without
sword and orb; king's name abbreviated and rev. legend HENRICVS
ROSAS REGNA IACOBVS 2250   6500
5466 II. Similar, but Scottish arms in 1st and 4th quarters 1750   5000

5468

5467 **Britain crown** (= £3 Scots, wt. 38^{3}/$_{5}$ grs.) I. As 5465 1500   4500
5468 II. Similar, but Scottish arms in 1st and 4th quarters 525   1500

		F	VF
		£	£

5469    5470

5469 **Halfcrown** (= £30s Scots, wt. 23²/₃ grs.) I. As 5465 but I D G
ROSA SINE SPINA ℞ TVEATVR etc. 575   1750

5470 II. Similar, but Scottish arms in 1st and 4th quarters 475   1350

5471

5471 **Thistle crown** (= 48s Scots). I. Crowned rose. ℞ Crowned thistle,
TVEATVR legend 425   1250

SILVER

BEFORE ACCESSION TO ENGLISH THRONE

First coinage. See p. 76 for countermarked coins

5472

5472 **Ryal,** or 'Sword dollar' (= 30s). Crowned shield dividing I R.
℞ Crowned sword, pointing hand on l., XXX on r. PRO ME SI MEREOR IN ME

1567	....	450	1300
1568	....	500	1500
1569	....	475	1350
1570	....	450	1300
1571	....	450	1300

	F £	VF £

5474

5474 Two-thirds ryal. Similar, but **XX** on *rev*.

1567	275	850
1568	300	900
1569	325	950
1570	325	950
1571	275	850

[Varieties are known dated 1561 in error, also 1571 exists without the crowns above I R]

5476

5476 One-third ryal. Similar, but **X** on *rev*.

1567	325	900
1568	375	1050
1569	525	1500
1570	325	900
1571	350	1000

Second coinage

	F	VF
	£	£

5478    5479

5478 Half merk, or 'noble' (= 6s 8d, wt. 104³/₄ grs., ²/₃ fine). Crowned
shield between 6 and 8. ℞ Ornate cross with crowns and thistles
in alternate angles, SALVVM FAC etc.

1572	100	300
1573	110	325
1574	100	325
1575	125	350
1576	135	375
1577	100	325
1580	100	325

5479 Quarter merk, or 'half-noble' (= 3s 4d). As above, but 3 and 4 by shield.

1572	90	300
1573	90	300
1574	90	300
1576	135	375
1577	110	325
1580	135	375

5480

5480 Two merks, or 'thistle dollar' (= 26s 8d, wt. 342²/₃ grs., 0.916 fine).
Crowned shield. ℞ Leaved thistle between I and R, NEMO ME
IMPVNE LACESSET

1578	3250	8000
1579	2500	6500
1580	3000	7500

	F	VF
	£	£

5481

5481 **Merk** (= 13s 4d). As above

| 1579 | .... | 3750 | 9000 |
| 1580 | .... | 3500 | 8500 |

Revaluation of 1578. Countermark crowned thistle

	F £	VF £

As 5405

	F £	VF £
Testoon of Mary. As 5402-3. (Value 7s 4d)	275	1000
— — As 5404-8. (Value 7s 4d)	250	850
— of Francis and Mary. As 5416. (Value 7s 4d)	275	950
— — As 5417-18. (Value 7s 4d)	250	900
— of Mary alone. As 5422. (Value 7s 4d)	3750	10500

As 5425   As 5426

	F	VF
Half-testoons, similar. (Value 3s 8d)	4250	12000
Ryal of Mary and Darnley. As 5425. (Value 36s 9d)	500	1500
Two-thirds ryal. As 5426 (Value 24s 6d)	425	1250
One-third ryal. As 5427. (Value 12s 3d)	450	1350
Ryal of Mary alone. As 5429. (Value 36s 9d)	625	1750
Two-thirds ryal. As 5430 (Value 24s 6d)	475	1500
One-third ryal. As 5431. (Value 12s 3d)	575	1650
Ryal or 'Sword dollar' of James VI. As 5472. (Value 36s 9d) .	400	1200
Two-thirds ryal. As 5474. (Value 24s 6d)	250	750
One-third ryal. As 5476. (Value 12s 3d)	300	850

Third coinage

F   VF
£   £

5482

5482   Sixteen shillings (wt. 171⅓ grs, 0.916 fine). 1581. Crowned shield.
℞ Crowned thistle dividing I R, NEMO legend 3250   7500

5483

5483   Eight shillings. 1581. Similar 2500   6000

5484   5485

5484   Four shillings. 1581. Similar 3000   6500
5485   Two shillings. 1581, Similar .... *Extremely rare*

	F	VF
	£	£

Fourth coinage

5486

5486 **Forty shillings** (471¹/₆ grs., 0.916 fine). 1582. Half-length figure l.
     in armour, holding sword. ℞ Crowned shield between I R and XL S,
     HONOR REGIS IVDICIVM DILIGIT 6250   18500

5487

5487 **Thirty shillings.** Similar, but X^XXS

1581	900	2750
1582	475	1500
1583	500	1600
1584	575	1750
1585	650	2000
1586	750	2250
5488 — XXX on one line, 1582	650	2000

		F	VF
		£	£

5489

5489 **Twenty shillings.** Similar, but **XX S**

1582	....	375	1350
1583	....	400	1400
1584	....	650	2250
1585	....	750	2500

5490

5490 **Ten shillings.** Similar, but **X S**

1582	....	325	1100
1583	....	475	1500
1584	....	375	1350

Sixth coinage

5491

5492

5491 **Balance half merk** (= 6d 8d, wt. 71⅓ grs., 0.875 fine). Crowned shield
between two thistles. ℞ Balance with sword behind, **HIS DIFFERT
REGE TYRANNVS**

1591	....	275	900
1592	....	325	1100
1593	....	325	1100
5492	**Balance quarter-merk.** 1591. Similar	575	1750

Seventh coinage

	F £	VF £

5493   5494

5493 **Ten shillings** (wt. 92¼ grs., 0.916 fine). Bare-headed bust in armour r.
R Crowned, triple-headed thistle, **NEMO** legend

	F	VF
1593	125	450
1594	110	425
1595	125	450
1598	125	450
1599	125	450
1600	350	950
1601	475	1250

5495   5496

5494 **Five shillings.** Similar

	F	VF
1593	300	850
1594	125	400
1595	150	450
1598/6	175	500
1599	150	450
1600	475	1100
1601	525	1250

5495 **Thirty pence.** Similar

	F	VF
1594	125	375
1595	135	400
1596	175	525
1598/6	175	525
1599	150	450
1601	225	675

5496 **Twelve pence.** Similar, but single pellet behind head

	F	VF
1594	200	650
1595	135	400
1596	225	675

Eighth coinage

<table>
<tr><td></td><td></td><td>F
£</td><td>VF
£</td></tr>
</table>

5497

5497 **Thistle merk** (= 13s 4d, wt. 104³/₄ grs., 0.916 fine). Crowned shield
R Crowned thistle, REGEM IOVA PROTEGIT

	F	VF
1601	110	450
1602	100	400
1603	110	450
1604	125	525

5498

5498 **Half thistle merk.** Similar

	F	VF
1601	75	275
1602	65	250
1603	85	300
1604	150	525

5499   5500

5499 **Quarter thistle merk.** Similar

	F	VF
1601	65	275
1602	60	250
1603	135	475
1604	125	450

5500 **Eighth thistle merk.** Similar

	F	VF
1601	70	200
1602	45	135
1603	100	300

	F £	VF £

AFTER ACCESSION TO ENGLISH THRONE

5501

5501 **Sixty shillings** (= 5s English). I. King on horseback r. wearing
Scottish crown, thistle on housings. ℞ Shield with arms of England
in 1st and 4th quarters, QVAE DEVS legend 475   1600
5502 II. Similar, but Scottish arms in 1st and 4th quarters 525   1750

5504

5503 **Thirty shillings.** I. Similar to 5501 150   475
5504 II. Similar to 5502 175   525

5506   5507

5505 **Twelve shillings.** I. Bust r., XII behind. ℞ Similar to 5501 150   525
5506 II. As last. ℞ Similar to 5502 135   475
5507 **Six shillings.** I. As 5505 but VI behind bust. ℞ Date over shield
1605 750   2500
1606 750   2500
1609/7 850   2750

		F £	VF £
5508	II. As last, but shield as 5502		
	1610	525	1600
	1611	525	1600
	1612	525	1600
	1613	575	1750
	1614	575	1750
	1615	525	1600
	1616	575	1750
	1617	525	1600
	1618	525	1600
	1619	500	1500
	1622	500	1500

5509   5510

5509 **Two shillings.** I. Crowned rose, I D G ROSA SINE SPINA ℞ Crowned
thistle with angular scales, TVEATVR legend, *mm.* thistle 25 110

5510 **One shilling.** I. Similar, but uncrowned rose and thistle, *mm.* thistle 60 175

BILLON and COPPER

BEFORE ACCESSION TO ENGLISH THRONE

5511   5512

5511 **Eightpenny groat** (wt. 28 grs., 0.250 fine). Crowned shield. ℞ Crowned
thistle, no inner circles, OPPIDVM EDINBVRGI (1583-90) 30 110

5512 — OPPID EDINB, hairline or no inner circles 30 110

5513 — — Similar, but beaded inner circles 35 120

		F £	VF £

5515

5517

5514	**Twopenny plack**. As 5511	150	475
5515	As 5512	125	400
5516	As 5513	150	425
5517	**Hardhead** (= 2d, wt. 23½ grs., ²³/₂₄ alloy). I. (issued August 1588). IR crowned. ℞ Crowned shield, VINCIT VERITAS (1588)	125	375

5518

5519

| 5518 | II. (issued November 1588). Similar, but lion rampant on *rev.*, two pellets behind .... | 50 | 175 |
| 5519 | **One penny plack.** Simlar to last, but no pellets .... | 225 | 650 |

5520

5521

| 5520 | **Fourpenny plack.** (wt. 23½ grs., ²³/₂₄ alloy). Thistle over two sceptres in saltire. ℞ Lozenge with thistle-head at each point (1594) .... | 200 | 575 |
| 5521 | Æ **Twopence** or 'Turner'. Bare-headed bust r., IACOBVS 6 etc. ℞ Three thistle heads, OPPIDVM EDINBVRGI (1597) .... | 110 | 375 |

5522

| 5522 | Æ **Penny.** As 5521, but single pellet added behind head (1597) | 425 | 1250 |

	F	VF
	£	£

Countermarking of 1575. (Genuine coins countermarked with a heart and star)

As 5437

Plack of Mary. As 5437	75	225
Lion, or hardhead of Mary. As 5438, 5439	70	200
Lion, or hardhead of Mary and Francis. As 5445, 5449, 5450 .	60	150

AFTER ACCESSION TO ENGLISH THRONE

5524

5525

5523	**Æ Twopence** or 'Turner'. I. Issue of 1614, Triple thistle. ℞ Lion rampant, two pellets behind. FRANCIE ET HIBERNIE REX	30	135
5524	II. Issue of 1623. Similar, but FRAN & HIB REX	25	125
5525	**Æ Penny.** I. As 5523, but single pellet	125	375
5526	II. As 5524, but single pellet	150	450

CHARLES I 1625-1649

Charles I, second son of James VI and Anne of Denmark, became heir apparent to the throne in 1612 and king in March 1625 at the age of 25. He was married by proxy to the Princess Henrietta Maria of France in June the same year. His Scottish coronation did not take place until 1633.

The history of this unfortunate king's reign culminating in civil war and his execution is well known, but numismatically it is of the highest interest, and the English and Scottish issues together represent the largest number of coins and types of any British monarch.

Although coining ceased on the death of James VI, a directive was made authorising the use of the old dies until new irons could be prepared by Charles Dickieson. Apart from the change in title and a slight difference in the style of the beard the first issues of Charles I bearing his name are similar in type to James's last issue.

Nicholas Briot, a Frenchman, previously employed at the French and English mints, received an appointment as master of the Scottish mint in August 1634 and was later joined by his son-in-law John Falconer, who eventually succeeded him in 1646.

Briot's work is of the highest calibre, and his introduction of the use of the mill and screw press (albeit no more popular with fellow mint workers in Scotland than in England) has given both the English and the Scottish series coins of a technical excellence previously unknown.

It should be noted that on some coins Charles is shown wearing the English crown, with central cross, rather than the Scottish crown, with central lis. The only coins made in Scotland during the Civil War years, 1642-1660, were copper *turners*, which were struck in 1642, 1644, 1648 and 1650.

GOLD
First coinage, 1625-35

	F	VF
	£	£

5527

5527   Unit. As James I last coinage, but for king's name and CR at shield. 1350   4000

	F £	VF £

5528

5528	**Double crown.** Similar	2750	8500
5529	**Britain crown.** Similar	3500	9500
5530	**Milled angel** (= 10s, wt. 64²/₃ grs., 23 ct. 3½ grs. fine). 1633. Coronation issue. St Michael spearing dragon, **X** to r. ℞ Ship with English arms on sail, **B** before bowsprit, AMOR POPVLI PRÆSIDIVM REGIS	12500	35000

Third coinage, 1637-42

5531

5531	**Unit**. I. (Briot's coinage). Similar to 5527, thistle and **B** after *obv.* legend. ℞ Crowned **C R** at shield, HIS PRÆSVM VT PROSIM	1750	5000
5532	— Similar, but *obv.* legend begins with **B** and ends with thistle .	2000	6500
5533	II. (Falconer's coinage). Similar, but thistle and **F** after *obv.* and *rev.* legend	8500	25000

5534

5534	**Half unit.** I. Bust l., **B** below. ℞ VNITA TVEMVR	1350	4250
5535	II. Similar, but **F** after *obv.* legend	6000	17500

		F	*VF*
		£	£

5536   5538

5536 Britain crown. Crowned bust l. breaking legend which ends with B.
        R Crowned C R at shield 1500   4500
5537 — Similar, but B before *obv*. legend 1750   5250
5538 Britain halfcrown. As crown, B below bust, C R uncrowned 750   2000
5539 — Similar, B over crown on rev. 850   2250

SILVER

First coinage, 1625-34

5540

5540 Sixty shillings. As last coinage of James I 950   2750

5541

5541 Thirty shillings. Similar 175   650

	F	*VF*
	£	£

5542

5542 **Twelve shillings**. Similar 200 725

5543

5543 **Six shillings.** Similar, date over shield on rev.

1625	450	1350
1626	500	1500
1627	525	1650
1628	450	1350
1630	500	1500
1631	500	1500
1632	450	1350
1633	425	1250
1634	525	1650

5544

5545

5544 **Two shillings.** As James I last coinage 50 150
5545 **Shilling.** Similar, C struck over I 135 475

Second coinage (Briot's hammered issue, 1636)

F   VF
£   £

5546

5547

5546 Half merk. Crowned bust l. to edge of coin, **VI/8** behind. ℞ Crowned
arms, CHRISTO AVSPICE REGNO 110   350
5547 — Milled pattern. Similar, but crowned CR added to *rev.*, dated
1636 above crown .... *Extremely rare*

5548

5551

5548 Forty pence. Similar, but **XL** behind head. ℞ SALVS REIP SVPR(EM)
LEX around large crowned and leaved thistle 125   425
5549 — Milled pattern. Similar, but crowned CR added to *rev.,* undated *Extremely rare*
5550 Twenty pence. Similar, but **XX** behind head. ℞ IVST THRONVM
FIRMAT 90   275
5551 — Milled pattern. Similar, but crowned CR added to *rev.,* undated 375   1250

Third coinage, 1637-42

1.   Briot's issue
II.   Intermediate issue
III. Falconer's first issue with F
IV. Falconer's second issue with F
V.   Falconer's anonymous issue

5552

5552 Sixty shillings. I. King riding l. ℞ Crowned arms, QVAE DEVS
legend, mm. B over thistle and B after *rev.* legend 525   1750

	F £	VF £

5555

5553	**Thirty shillings.** I. Similar to last, B and flower on obv., B and thistle on *rev*. (i.e. a London *obv*. die)	200	725
5554	II. As last, but without B	175	675
5555	IV. As last, but F by horse's hoof, smooth ground below horse. Ɍ Lozenges, stars, or nothing over crown	135	500
5556	— Similar, but rough ground below horse	135	500
5556A	— F over crown on *rev*.	150	575
5557	V. Similar, but no F	135	500

5559

5558	**Twelve shillings.** I. Bust to edge of coin, B at ends of legends...	125	550
5559	II. As last, but thistle at end of obv. legend and above the crown on *rev*.	135	475

5560

5560	III. As last, but F over crown on *rev*.	125	450

	F	*VF*
	£	£

5561

5561	IV. Bust of new style, only slightly breaking inner circle, F after *obv.* legend		110	400
5562	— R Thistle before legend and F over crown		110	400
5563	— Bust wholly within inner circle. R As last		120	425
5564	V. As 5561, but without F. MAG.BRIT		110	400

5569   5571

5565	**Six shillings.** I. Bust to edge of coin, B at end of *obv.* legend	100	325
5566	— Similar, but B and lis at end of *obv.* legend	100	325
5567	— As last, but B over crown on *rev.*	135	450
5568	— As last, but B after *rev.* legend	125	400
5569	III. Bust to edge of coin, F over crown on *rev.*	90	300
5570	— Mule. Briot *obv.* of class I. R As last	135	450
5771	IV. Bust within legend as 5563, *mm.* thistle	90	300
5771A	— Bust slightly breaking inner circle. R Thistle before legend, F over crown.	90	300
5772	V. Bust of new style within inner circle, but without F	100	325

5573

5773	**Half merk.** I. Crowned bust l. to edge of coin. R Crowned CR by shield, B under bust and above crown	100	325
5574	— Similar, but B after legend on *rev.*	125	425

	F £	VF £

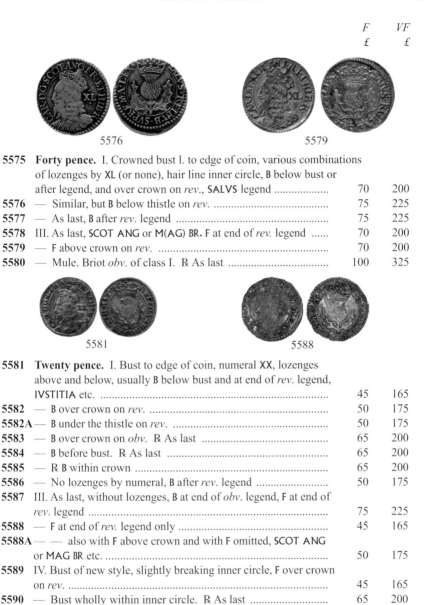

5576   5579

5575 **Forty pence.** I. Crowned bust l. to edge of coin, various combinations
of lozenges by **XL** (or none), hair line inner circle, **B** below bust or
after legend, and over crown on *rev.*, **SALVS** legend .... | 70 | 200

5576 — Similar, but **B** below thistle on *rev.* .... | 75 | 225

5577 — As last, **B** after *rev.* legend .... | 75 | 225

5578 III. As last, **SCOT ANG** or **M(AG) BR**. **F** at end of *rev.* legend ...... | 70 | 200

5579 — **F** above crown on *rev.* .... | 70 | 200

5580 — Mule. Briot *obv.* of class I. ℞ As last .... | 100 | 325

5581   5588

5581 **Twenty pence.** I. Bust to edge of coin, numeral **XX**, lozenges
above and below, usually **B** below bust and at end of *rev.* legend,
IVSTITIA etc. .... | 45 | 165

5582 — **B** over crown on *rev.* .... | 50 | 175

5582A — **B** under the thistle on *rev.* .... | 50 | 175

5583 — **B** over crown on *obv.* ℞ As last .... | 65 | 200

5584 — **B** before bust. ℞ As last .... | 65 | 200

5585 — ℞ **B** within crown .... | 65 | 200

5586 — No lozenges by numeral, **B** after *rev.* legend .... | 50 | 175

5587 III. As last, without lozenges, **B** at end of *obv.* legend, **F** at end of
rev. legend .... | 75 | 225

5588 — **F** at end of *rev.* legend only .... | 45 | 165

5588A — — also with **F** above crown and with **F** omitted, **SCOT ANG**
or **MAG BR** etc. .... | 50 | 175

5589 IV. Bust of new style, slightly breaking inner circle, **F** over crown
on *rev.* .... | 45 | 165

5590 — Bust wholly within inner circle. ℞ As last .... | 65 | 200

5591 V. As 5589, but no **F** .... | 45 | 150

5591A — Similar, but **MAG BRIT** .... | 70 | 200

Fourth coinage, 1642

	F	VF
	£	£

5592   5593   5595

5592 Three shillings. Crowned bust l., thistle behind. R Crowned arms,
        SALVS legend 100   375
5593 Two shillings. Similar, but large II behind bust, IVST THRONVM
        FIRMAT legend 60   175
5594 — Small II behind bust 75   225
5595 — Without numerals, B below bust which extends to edge of coin   90   350

COPPER

Coinage of 1629

5596   5597

5596 Twopence, or Turner. As james VI, but CAROLVS etc.   30   125
5597 Penny. Similar 150   525

Earl of Stirling coinage, 1632-39

5598   5599

Twopence, or Turner (wt. 13 grs.)
5598 1. 'English' crown, *mm.* lozenge (*obv.*), flower (*rev.*)   18   75
        a — *mm.* lozenge (both sides)   18   75
        b — *mm.* lozenge – rosette   15   70
        c — *mm.* flower (over lozenge) – flower   18   75
5599 2. 'Scottish' crown with jewelled band and arches, *mm.* lozenge   15   70
        a — *mm.* lozenge (*obv.*), star (*rev.*)   18   75
        b — *mm.* lozenge – rosette   15   70
        c — *mm.* lozenge – flower   15   70
        d — *mm.* lozenge – stop and saltire   15   70
        e — *mm.* stop and saltire (both sides)   15   70
        f — *mm.* trefoil – lozenge. With trefoil stops, instead of lozenges,
            below C II R   25   100

	F £	VF £

5600   5601

5600   3. 'Scottish' crown with plain band and arches, *mm*. flower   15   70
    a — *mm*. lozenge (*obv.*), flower (*rev.*)   18   75
    b — *mm*. flower – rosette   18   75
    c — *mm*. flower – lozenge   18   75
    d — *mm*. flower – star   18   75
5601   4. Crown with five crosses
    a — *mm*. saltire (both sides)   20   80
    b — *mm*. lozenge (*obv.*), flower (*rev.*)   20   80
    c — *mm*. lozenge – rosette   20   80
    NB There are many variations in the legends of these Turners and also
    many contemporary forgeries (including those with mintmarks lis and
    lion).

Penny
Known to have been struck, but none extant.

Coinages of 1642, 1644, 1648 and 1650

5602   5603

5602   **Twopence**, Turner or Bodle. Crowned CR. ℞ Thistle, no mark of
    value, mm. lozenge. LACESSET   20   85
5602A— LACESSIT   25   100
5602C **Pattern** (?) As 5602. With small neat letters ....   *Extremely rare*
5603   **Pattern threepence.** Striking in silver for a copper threepence (26 grs).
    Two interlinked Cs, large thistle on rev., NEMO etc. ....   *Extremely rare*
5603A— — Similar, but bust of Charles I on obv. ....   *Extremely rare*

CHARLES II 1649-1685

Charles II the eldest surviving son of Charles I and Henrietta Maria, was proclaimed King of Scotland in Edinburgh less than a month after his father's execution.

After being virtually a prisoner at the hands of Argyll he was crowned at Scone on 1 January 1561 following his acceptance of the Scottish Covenant.

Nearly ten years of exile passed before his return to London and coronation in April 1661 after the collapse of the Commonwealth, during which period no Scottish coins were struck, the mint being closed from about 1650 until 1663.

For the first silver coinage the punches were made in London by Thomas Simon and for the second coinage by John, Joseph and Philip Roettiers. The actual dies were made at the Scottish mint under the direction of Sir John Falconer, the Master of the Mint. Both coinages were machine made, the second coinage with new machinery obtained from London in 1675.

No gold coins were struck for Scotland and the fineness of the silver at 11 deniers (0.916 fine) is the same as those of Charles I.

In 1682 the Scottish mint was closed on account of the illegal activities of certain mint officials and remained inactive until 1687.

SILVER

First coinage. The die axis of the first coinage is usually with inverted *reverse* though there does not seem to have been a strict quality control in this matter, and coins with *en medaille* (upright) die axis and with other angles are known. Examples of these 'unusual' die axes may be worth a 10-20% premium above the prices quoted.

| | F | VF | EF |
| | £ | £ | £ |

5604 **Four merks** (53s 4d). I. 1664. Bust r., thistle above. ℞ Cruciform shields, crowned interlinked Cs in angles, value LII/4
in centre 850 2500 10000

5605 II. Similar, but thistle below bust

1664 .... 900 2750 10500

1665 .... 4000 — —

1670 .... 900 2950 —

1673 .... 1200 3500 —

1673 4 of value over horizontal I .... 1250 3750 —

	F	VF	EF
	£	£	£

5606

5606 III. Similar, but F below bust

1670	*? Exists*		
1674	850	2750	9500
1674/3	900	3000	—
1674 BR instead of BRI on rev.	950	3250	—
1675	900	3000	—

5607

5607 **Two merks** (= 26s 8d). I. 1664. As 5604, with thistle above head,
value XXVI/8 in centre of *rev.* 450 1750 5000

5608 II. As 5605, with thistle below bust

1664	475	1850	5250
1670	575	2250	—
1673	425	1500	4500
1674	475	1850	5250

5609 III. As 5606, F below bust

1673	*Extremely rare*		
1674	600	2250	—
1675	425	1500	4500
1675 BR instead of BRI on rev.	450	1650	4750

	F	*VF*	*EF*
	£	£	£

5611

5611 **Merk** (= 13s 4d). II. As 5605, thistle below bust and value XIII/4 in centre of *rev.*

1664 small thistle below bust	135	400	1350
1664 large thistle below bust	150	450	1450
1665	200	525	1600
1666	250	675	1750
1668	275	750	2000
1669 legend stops vary, some with colons	85	300	1200
1669 error with no stops on *obv.*	175	475	1500
1669 Scottish arms in 2nd and 4th quarters	250	675	1750
1670 legend stops vary, some with colons	100	350	1350
1671 legend stops vary, some with colons	90	325	1250
1672 legend stops vary, some with colons	90	325	1250
1672 — reversed 2 in date	175	475	1500
1673	90	325	1250
1673 error BRA for BRI	250	675	1750
1674	200	550	1650

5612

5612 III. As 5606, F below bust

1674	175	475	1500
1675	150	450	1450
1675 reverse error XII instead of XIII	175	475	1500

5613 IV. No thistle or F.

1675	275	750	2000

	F	VF	EF
	£	£	£

5614

5614 **Half merk** (= 6s 8d). II. As 5605 but VI/8 in centre of *rev.*

	F	VF	EF
1664	200	575	1500
1664 *cmk.* 1665 behind head (dated 1664 on *rev.*)	375	750	—
1665	200	575	1500
1666	225	700	1650
1667	250	750	1750
1668	225	650	1650
1669 stops both sides vary	85	300	950
1669 error no stops on *obverse*	135	450	1200
1669 error Scottish arms in 2nd and 4th quarter	175	525	1350
1670 stops on both sides vary	90	325	975
1670 error no stops on *obverse*	135	450	1200
1671 straight ribbon behind head	85	300	950
1671 curly ribbon behind head	85	300	950
1672	90	325	975
1673	110	375	1050

5615   5617

5615 — Error shields, England, France and Ireland transposed

	F	VF	EF
1665	225	650	1650
1666	250	750	1750
5616 III. As 5606, F below bust. 1675	150	475	1250
5617 IV. No thistle or F below bust. 1675	175	525	1350

Second coinage. This coinage has die axis with *reverse* inverted.

	F £	VF £	EF £

5618

5618 Dollar. Bust left, F before. R Cruciform shields, interlinked Cs
in centre, thistles in angles

1676 legend stops vary both side	525	1500	4750
1679	575	1650	5250
1680	750	2000	6000
1681	575	1650	5250
1682	475	1400	4500

5619

5619 Half dollar. Similar

1675	525	1200	3750
1676	675	1500	4750
1681	550	1250	4000

5620

5620 Quarter dollar. Similar

1675	175	475	1900
1676	125	375	1750
1676 error DR1 for DEI	150	425	1850
1677	135	400	1700
1677/6	150	425	1850

	F	VF	EF
	£	£	£

5620 Quarter dollar. Continued

1678	175	475	1900
1679	175	475	1900
1680 error CAROVLS for CAROLVS	135	400	1700
1681	135	400	1700
1682	150	425	1750
1682 error CAROVLS for CAROLVS	375	900	2750

5621 Quarter dollar. Error shields, 1682. Irish arms in first shield .. 300 750 2500

1682 — with CAROVLS error 425 1000 3000

5622

5622 Eighth dollar. Similar

1676	80	325	900
1676 struck with *reverse* at 90° die axis	100	375	1000
1677	85	350	950
1678/7	*Extremely rare*		
1679	200	525	1350
1680	85	350	950
1682	175	475	1250
1682 error, reversed 2 in date	350	750	1750

5623 Eighth dollar. Error shields, 1680, French arms in first shield.. 225 575 1500

5624

5624 Sixteenth dollar. Similar, but St Andrew's cross on rev., emblems in angles.

1677	60	200	475
1678	100	300	725
1678/7	90	295	700
1679/7	100	300	725
1680	75	275	600
1680/79	110	300	725
1681	60	200	495

COPPER

Coinage of 1663

	F £	VF £	EF £

5625

5625 Twopence, Turner or Bodle. Crowned CR with small II to r.
R Thistle, NEMO etc., *mm.* usually rosette or cross of pellets,
occasionally lion rampant or cinquefoil ....*from*   20   65   250

Coinage of 1677

5628   5630

			F	VF	EF
5626	**Bawbee**, or sixpence Scots, 1677. Bust l., ANG FR ET HIB REX R Crowned thistle		65	185	525
	— with AN G instead of ANG		75	200	575
5627	Similar, A NG FR ET HIB R 1677		65	185	525
5628	Similar, AN FR ET HIB R				
	1677		60	175	500
	1678		60	175	500
	1679		65	185	525
	1679 error, CAR H instead of CAR II		75	200	600
	1679 error, SOC instead of SCO		125	375	900
5629	Cruder head and irregular letters, 1679 (? forgery)			*fair*	25
5630	**Turner**, or Bodle. Crown over crossed sword and sceptre. R Thistle, NEMO etc.				
	1677		45	135	400
	1677 error FBA for FRA		65	150	425
	1677 error IIB for HIB		65	150	425
	1677 error REXI for REX		75	175	475
	1678		65	150	475
	1678 FRAN instead of FRA		70	160	450
	1679		*Extremely rare*		
5631	Similar, but error NMEO, 1677		85	200	550
5632	Similar, but error LAESSET, 1677		85	200	550
5633	Similar, but error LACSSET, 1677		85	200	550

JAMES VII (II of England) 1685-1689

James II, younger brother of Charles II, was created Duke of York in 1634 and Lord High Admiral in 1638. With the support of Samuel Pepys (the diarist) and Matthew Wren he greatly improved the organisation and efficiency of the Navy. In 1660 he married Annye Hyde, daughter of the Earl of Clarendon, His conversion to Catholicism and the possibility of a Catholic succession eventually led to William of Orange being assured of the support of the Army should he land in England. The defection of the Army, and also that of his daughter Anne, caused James to order his Queen and infant son to France. James landed in Ireland in March 1689 to rally support, but was completely defeated by William of Orange at the battle of the Boyne on 1 July 1690. James died at St Germain on 5 September 1701.

Only silver coins were issued during his reign, the largest of which, the forty shilling piece, is the first Scottish coin to bear a lettered edge.

The so-called '60 shilling' pieces were never issued and only late strikings of 1828 by Matthew Young are known.

A reduction in weight of the coins made the proportions to English a little over 13 to 1 as against 12 to 1 from the accession of James VI.

5634

5634 **Sixty shillings.** 1688. Laureate bust r. ℞ Crowned arms in the collar of the Order of the Thistle, edge plain. (Matthew Young restrike). Struck in silver .... *FDC* £3000

5635 Similar, struck in gold ....3 known *FDC* £75000

5636

		F £	VF £	EF £

5636 **Forty shillings.** 1687. Laurate bust r., IACOBVS etc., 40 below.
Ɽ Crowned arms. *Edge:* NEMO ME IMPVNE LACESSET ANNO
REGNI TERTIO 275 900 2500

5637 Similar, but IACOBUS, 1687. *Edge:* TERTIO 275 900 2500

— — Error edge: LACESSIET 325 975 2750

5638 Similar, but IACOBUS, 1687. *Edge:* QVARTO 325 975 2750

5639 Similar, but IACOBVS, 1688. *Edge:* QVARTO 300 950 2650

5640 Similar, but IACOBUS, 1688. *Edge:* QVARTO 300 950 2650

5641

5641 **Ten shillings.** Similar to 5637, but 10 below bust. Ɽ St Andrew's
cross and national emblems, stops vary both sides
1687 .... 150 525 1750
1688 .... 175 575 1850
1688 error, unbarred A in FRA on rev. 200 750 2000

WILLIAM AND MARY 1689-1694

William III was the son of William II Prince of Orange, and Mary, daughter of Charles I. Appointed Captain General of the Dutch forces in 1672 and later proclaimed Stadholder, he married Mary, daughter of James II of England in 1677.

On account of James II's Catholic leanings William became the chief hope of the Protestant cause and eventually accepted an invitation to lead an armed expedition to England and landed at Torbay in 1688. James II fled to Ireland and was defeated by William at the battle of the Boyne.

William formed the Grand Alliance with the United Provinces and was responsible for the vigorous treatment of Scottish rebels culminating in the massacre of Glenluce in 1692.

Mary died in 1694 and the Act of Settlement secured the ultimate succession of the House of Hanover.

SILVER

	F £	VF £	EF £

5642

5642	**Sixty shillings.** Conjoined busts, 60 below. ℞ Crowned arms.			
	Edge: PROTEGIT ET ORNAT ANNO REGNI TERTIO			
	1691	700	1850	5000
	1692	650	1650	4850
5643	*Trial striking in copper.* 1691. *Edge:* NEMO ME IMPVNE LACESS			
	O REGNI QVARTO	*Extremely rare*		
	Forty shillings. Similar, but 40 below busts, edge as 5642			
	(it is now thought that the **SEXTO** edge does not exist)			
5644	1689. *Edge:* PRIMO	350	850	2500
5645	1689. *Edge:* SECVNDO	375	950	2750
5646	1690. *Edge:* PRIMO	275	800	2350
5647	1690. *Edge:* SECVNDO	250	700	2250
5648	1691. *Edge:* SECVNDO	200	600	2000
5649	1691. *Edge:* TERTIO	185	575	1950
	1691. — error with no lozenges in Dutch shield	250	700	2250
5650	1692. *Edge:* TERTIO	225	600	2000

	F £	VF £	EF £

5651

5651	1692. *Edge:* QVARTO	185	625	2100
5652	1693. *Edge:* QVARTO	200	600	2000
5653	1693. *Edge:* QUINTO	200	600	2000
5654	1693. *Edge:* SIXTO	250	700	2250
5655	1693. — error with no lozenges in Dutch shield	200	600	2000
5656	1694. *Edge:* SIXTO	250	700	2250
	1694. — error with no lozenges in Dutch shield	275	880	2500

5657

5657	**Twenty shillings**. Similar, but 20 below busts.			
	1693 *obverse* stops vary	525	1500	3500
	1694	650	1750	4250

5660

5658	**Ten shillings.** Similar, but 10 below busts, GRATIA, small shield,			
	1689, English crown, die axis can vary	*Extremely rare*		
5658A	— 1690	250	675	1850
	— 1690, with 0 over 9	375	850	2250
5659	Similar, large 10 below bust, large shield, Scottish crown			
	1691, J type 1 in date	200	575	1650
	1691, small 10 below busts, I type 1 in date	175	525	1500
5660	1691, GRA, small 10 below bust	200	575	1650
5661	1692, GRATIA, small 10 below bust, I type 1	175	525	1500
5662	1692, GRATIA, large 10 below bust, J type 1	200	575	1650
5663	1694, GRA, small 10 below bust, I type 1	275	750	2000
	1694, GRA, large 10 below bust, J type 1	350	825	2250

	F	*VF*	*EF*
	£	£	£

5665

5664 **Five shillings.** Similar, but **V** below crowned **WM** monogram on *rev.*

1691	175	425	1000
5665 1694. Similar, but **V** below busts	135	350	850
1694. Inverted **A** for 2nd **V** in GVLIELMVS	150	375	900

COPPER

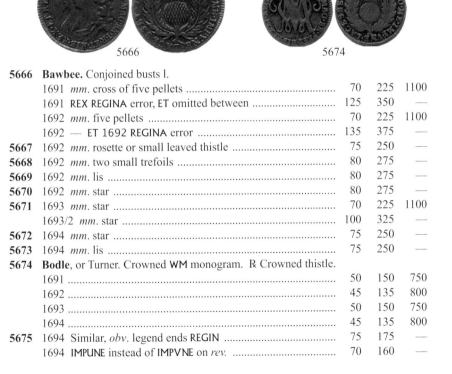

5666   5674

5666 **Bawbee.** Conjoined busts l.			
1691 *mm.* cross of five pellets	70	225	1100
1691 **REX REGINA** error, **ET** omitted between	125	350	—
1692 *mm.* five pellets	70	225	1100
1692 — **ET 1692 REGINA** error	135	375	—
5667 1692 *mm.* rosette or small leaved thistle	75	250	—
5668 1692 *mm.* two small trefoils	80	275	—
5669 1692 *mm.* lis	80	275	—
5670 1692 *mm.* star	80	275	—
5671 1693 *mm.* star	70	225	1100
1693/2 *mm.* star	100	325	—
5672 1694 *mm.* star	75	250	—
5673 1694 *mm.* lis	75	250	—
5674 **Bodle**, or Turner. Crowned **WM** monogram. ℞ Crowned thistle.			
1691	50	150	750
1692	45	135	800
1693	50	150	750
1694	45	135	800
5675 1694 Similar, *obv.* legend ends **REGIN**	75	175	—
1694 **IMPUNE** instead of **IMPVNE** on *rev.*	70	160	—

WILLIAM II (III of England) 1694-1702

GOLD

	F £	VF £	EF £

5676   5677

5676 **Pistole** (= £12 Scots, wt. 106 grs., 22 cts.) 1701. Bust l., sun rising from sea below. ℞ Crowned W R at sides of arms 5250 13500 25000

5677 **Half pistole.** 1701. Similar 3750 11000 18500
These coins were struck from gold dust imported by the Darien Company trading with Africa. The company badge, a sun rising from the sea, appears on the coins.

SILVER

5678 **Sixty shillings.** 1699. Bust l., 60 below. ℞ Crowned arms.
Recorded in the 19th century but no physical specimens ever seen in living memory and there are no records of it ever having been minted.

5679

Forty shillings. Similar, but 40 below bust, *edge* as William and Mary.

5679	1695. *Edge:* SEPTIMO	185	600	2000
	1695. — no stops on *obv.*	250	675	2350
	1695. — no lozenges in Dutch shield	225	650	2250
5680	1695. *Edge:* OCTAVO	185	575	2000
5681	1696. *Edge:* OCTAVO	200	625	2150
5682	1697. *Edge:* NONO	200	625	2150
5683	1698. *Edge:* DECIMO	250	675	2350
5684	1699. *Edge:* VNDECIMO	250	675	2350
5685	1700. *Edge:* VNDECIMO	*Extremely rare*		
	1700. *Edge:* DUODECIMO	1500	—	—

	F £	VF £	EF £

5686

5686 Twenty shillings. Similar, but 20 below bust.

	F	VF	EF
1695	200	700	2350
1696 with or without stop after date	200	700	2350
1697	375	1100	3250
1697 with inverted *reverse* die axis	400	1200	3500
1698	210	750	2500
1698/7	200	700	2350
1699	425	1250	3500

5687

5688

5687 Ten shillings. Similar, but 10 below bust.

	F	VF	EF
1695	150	475	1350
1696	150	475	1350
1697	175	525	1500
1697 with inverted *reverse* die axis	185	550	1600
1698	185	550	1600
1698/7	175	525	1500
1699	300	675	—

5688 Five shillings. Similar, but 5 below bust. ℞ Crowned thistle, GVL D G etc.

	F	VF	EF
1695	85	225	650
1696	85	225	650
1697	85	225	650
1697 with inverted *reverse* die axis	100	275	750
1699	140	325	850
1700	100	275	750
1701	300	600	1000
5689 1702 GVLIELMVS DEI GRATIA	250	450	900

COPPER

	F £	VF £	EF £

5690

		F	VF	EF
5690	**Bawbee.** 1695. Bust l., BR FR. ℞ Crowned thistle	90	375	950
5690A	— Similar, BRIT FRA	110	425	1050
5691	1696 Pellet stops both sides	95	400	1000
5692	— Pellet stops (*obv.*), annulets (*rev.*)	110	425	1050
5693	1697	125	475	1250

5697

		F	VF	EF
5694	**Bodle.** I. 1695. Flat sword and sceptre, crown above. ℞ Crowned thistle. GVLIELMVS and HIB R	65	200	575
5695	— GVLIELMVS and HIB REX	70	210	600
5696	— GVL and HIB REX	65	200	575
5696A	1696, GVL and HIB REX	70	210	600
5697	II. 1695. Sword and sceptres high, GVL, pellet stops on *rev.*	60	185	525
5698	1696. No stops on *rev.* (A variety known with stops)	70	210	600
5699	1697. No stops on *rev.*	75	225	625
	1697. — with *reverse* struck inverted	80	240	650

ANNE 1702-1714

Anne, second daughter of James II, was educated in the Protestant faith and married George, Prince of Denmark in 1683. Her reign is dominated by the wars of the Spanish succession and the ascendancy of the first Duke of Marlborough, culminating in the Treaty of Utrecht.

The Act of Union uniting the realms of England and Scotland is an important numismatic landmark as it provided for a coinage of the same standard and value in both countries.

The purpose or function of the 5 or 6 pointed star mark on some coins is not known.

The After Union coins, although technically now British rather than Scottish coins, are included as they were produced at the Edinburgh mint.

The coins of 1709 are the last native coins to be struck in Scotland.

SILVER

	F £	VF £	EF £

Before Union

5700

		F	VF	EF
5700	**Ten shillings.** Draped bust l., 10 below. ℞ Crowned arms, legend ends REG. 1705	125	375	1500
	1706	175	575	1650
5701	1706, legend ends REGINA	175	575	1650

5702

		F	VF	EF
5702	**Five shillings.** 1705. Similar, 5 below. ANNA DEI GRATIA	40	125	400
5703	1705 ANNA D G M BR FR ⁞ HIB REG	45	135	425
	1705/4	45	135	425
5704	1705 AN D G M BR FR ⁞ HIB REG	40	125	400
	1705 no stops on rev.	45	135	425
	1705/4	60	175	575
5705	1705 AN D G MAG BR FR ⁞ HIB R	50	150	450
5706	1706 AN D G MAG BR FR ⁞ HIB R	45	135	400

	F £	VF £	EF £

After Union

5707

5707 Crown. 1707. 'Second' bust l., E below. ℞ Four shields crowned,
Garter star in centre. *Edge:* SEXTO 185   525   2400
5707A 1707. *Edge:* SEPTIMO 1750   —   —
5708 1708. *Edge:* SEPTIMO 200   575   2750
5708A 1708/7. *Edge:* SEPTIMO 210   600   2850

5709

5709 Halfcrown. 'Second' bust, E below. 1707. *Edge:* SEXTO 100   325   1600
5710 1707. *Edge:* SEPTIMO 475   2250   7500
5710A 1708. *Edge:* SEPTIMO 100   325   1600
5711 1709. *Edge:* OCTAVO 275   950   —

5715

5712 Shilling. 'Second' bust. E below. 1707 110   400   1350
5712A— 1707 E no stops on *rev.* 250   750   —
5713 — 1707 E* 150   475   1750
5714 — 1708 E 175   625   2000
5714A— 1708 E no rays to garter star 475   —   —
5715 — 1708 E* 150   475   1750
5715A— 1708/7 E* 325   —   —

		F £	VF £	EF £
5712	**Shilling.** 'Second' bust. E below. 1707	125	475	1750
5712A—	1707 E no stops on *rev.*	250	850	—
5713	— 1707 E*	175	525	2000
5714	— 1708 E	175	625	2250
5714A—	1708 E no rays to garter star	525	—	—
5715	— 1708 E*	175	550	2000
5715A—	1708/7 E*	350	—	—
5716	'Third' bust. 1707 E	90	275	1100
5717	— 1708 E	100	300	1200
5717A—	1708/7 E	125	350	1250
5718	'Edinburgh' bust. 1707 E	525	—	—
5718A—	1708 E*	225	750	2500
5718B	'Edinburgh' bust struck from cruder local dies with two very large top curls to hair. 1708 E*	375	1250	—
5719	— 1709 E	325	1000	—
5720	— 1709 E*	225	750	2500

5723

5721	**Sixpence.** 'Second' bust. 1707 E	45	135	500
5722	— 1708 E	55	165	550
5722A—	1708/7 E	70	200	700
5723	— 1708 E*	60	175	600
5723A—	1708/7 E*	70	200	700
5724	'Edinburgh' bust 1708 E*	65	185	675

Proof strikings of the 1707 E shilling and sixpence with plain edges are known, all are very rare. Late strikings only of fourpence and twopence are known from original dies, dated 1711, which were never used.

JAMES VIII 1688-1766
(The Old Pretender)

In 1708 James, Prince of Wales (son of James II of England) made a vain attempt to invade Scotland.

Dies were prepared by Nortbert Roettiers for what was itended to be a British crown piece dated 1709, styling James as IACOBVS III MAG BRIT FRAN ET HIB REX. He was also responsible for the 'Restoration of the Kingdom' medal which was struck in silver and copper.

During a second invasion in 1715 James actually landed in Scotland and his coronation was planned at Scone for 23 January 1716. This never took place and he was forced to return to France in February 1716.

Dies were again prepared by Roettiers, this time for a Scottish coinage, styling James as IACOBVS VIII SCOT ANGL FRAN ET HIB REX and bearing the arms of Scotland instead of those of Great Britain as on the crown of 1709. No contemporary strikings are known from the 1716 dies but a number of pieces were struck from the original dies in 1828 by Matthew Young, after which the dies were defaced; however, there are modern reproductions of this restrike.

5725

5725	**Guinea.** 1716. Bust r. ℞ Cruciform shields, with sceptres in angles. *Struck in silver*	*FDC*	£1750
5726	Similar. *Struck in gold*	*FDC*	£17500
5727	Similar. *Struck in bronze*	*FDC*	£1500

5728

5728	Bust l. IACOBVS TERTIVS. Struck in silver	*FDC*	£1750
5729	Similar. *Struck in bronze*	*FDC*	£1500

5730

5730 **Crown.** 1709. Bust r. IACOBVS III etc. ℞ Crowned oval shield.
Edge plain .... *Unique*

5731

5731 1716. Bust r. IACOBVS VIII etc. ℞ Crowned square shield .... *FDC* £3500
5732 Similar. *Struck in gold* .... *Extremely rare*
5733 Similar. *Struck in white metal* .... *FDC* £1500
5734 Similar. *Struck in bronze* .... *Extremely rare*

CHARLES III 1720-1788
('Bonnie Prince Charlie', the Young Pretender)

Charles Edward Stewart, titular heir to the Scottish throne, was the son of James VIII and grandson of James II of England.

His French expedition to invade England in 1744 was foiled by the English fleet at Dunkirk, and he finally landed in Scotland at Glenfinnan in 1745, After several minor victories he was crushingly defeated at Culloden Moor in 1746 by forces under the command of the Duke of Cumberland, nicknamed the 'Butcher'. His months as a fugitive in the Highlands and his escape to France are the source of much Scottish lore. He died in Rome at the age of 68.

Charles is said to have carried on the age-old superstition of 'touching' for the King's evil. The 'touch-piece' used was in silver with the *obv.* legend **CAR III D G M B F ET R H**. The *rev.* legend **SOLI DEO GLORIA** is the same as on the touch-pieces of earlier British monarchs

HENRY IX 1725-1807

The younger brother of Prince Charles, Henry Benedict Maria Clement, Cardinal York attempted to come to England to support the rising of 1745. On his brother's death in 1788 he styled himself as Henry IX. He also touched for the King's evil and contemporary touch pieces in silver and pewter (or tin) are known, pierced for suspension. It is possible that unpierced specimens in gold, silver and bronze may be of somewhat later origin. On his death, in 1807, the Stewart jewels (carried off by James II) were left to George IV.

UNITED KINGDOM COINS BEARING SCOTTISH EMBLEMS

Shillings of George VI were struck bearing a Scottish lion seated on a Scottish crown, with a shield bearing the cross of St Andrew on the left and a thistle on the right. Shillings of Elizabeth II were struck bearing the Scottish shield with lion rampant.

These coins were struck as a compliment to the Scottish ancestry of Queen Elizabeth Queen Consort of George VI (died 30 March 2002), but it should be emphasised that these were part of the United Kingdom coinage and were not issued exclusively for use in Scotland

For a detailed listing of these coins, see nos 4083, 4101, 4109, 4140 and 4148 in the *Spink Standard Catalogue of British Coins*, vol. 1, *Coins of England and the United Kingdom*.

IRELAND

INTRODUCTION TO IRISH COINS

In dealing with the coinage of Ireland there are three main groups to consider: the Hiberno-Scandinavian issues of the Scandinavian kings of Dublin, the Anglo-Irish coinages of Ireland under the English monarchy, and the republican coins of the Irish Free State and Éire. If it is objected that the latter should not be included in a catalogue of 'British' coins the editor can only reply that they have been included for convenience and that it is not part of a plot to take over the South! Northern Ireland, of course, uses United Kingdom coinage (see Volume 1).

Currency is not necessarily *coin*, as coins by definition are objects (normally of metal) of definite weight and value, stamped with an officially authorised device. In ancient Ireland gold ornaments are likely to have circulated as a form of currency and some types of ornaments are known as 'ring money', but cattle or possibly horses were probably used as the standard unit of wealth. Without large urban settlements the Irish did not require the complications of a coinage system until very late in their history and then it was imposed by foreigners.

Coinage began in Asia Minor in the seventh century BC, reached Western Europe at the end of the third century BC and coins of Gaulish type were circulating in South East Britain by the end of the second century BC. Roman coins have been found on the east coast of Ireland, brought from Britain by raiders or traders, but it was not until almost 1000 AD that coins are known to have been struck in Ireland and then they were issued by the Norsemen of Dublin, not by the Irish.

Many of the medieval coins are quite rare, especially the later Hiberno-Norse types, the earliest Anglo-Irish coinage of John and some of the issues of Henry VI and Edward IV, and unpublished varieties may well come to light with the discovery of new hoards. The early Tudor coins tend to be from poorly engraved dies, many being carelessly struck. The coinages of the Civil War period and of James II's abortive attempt to hold Ireland after his flight from England are particularly interesting. The coins of the Irish Free State have been particularly admired for their fine animal designs.

LATIN AND IRISH LEGENDS ON IRISH COINS

ANO DOM (In the year of the Lord). James II gunmoney crown.

CAPUT IONIS REGIS, etc. (The head of King John). Halfpence of John.

CHRISTO AVSPICE REGNO (I reign under the auspices of Christ). Charles I halfcrowns of the Confederated Catholics.

CHRISTO VICTORE TRIVMPHO (I exalt in the victory of Christ). James II gunmoney crown.

ECCE GREX (Behold, the flock !). Charles II, St Patrick's halfpenny.

EXVRGAT DEVS DISSIPENTVR INIMICI (Let God arise and let his enemies be scattered: *Psalm* 68, 1). Shillings of James I.

FLOREAT REX (May the King flourish). St Patrick's halfpenny and farthing.

MELIORIS TESSERA FATI ANNO REGNI SEXTO (An improved token uttered in the sixth year of the reign). James II pewter crown.

POSVI DEVM ADIVTOREM MEVM (I have made the Lord my helper: *comp. Psalm* 54, 4). Groats and halfgroats, Edward I - Henry VII, and on some later Tudor coins.

POSVIMVS DEVM ADIVTOREM NOSTRVM (We have made the Lord our helper). Shillings and groats of Mary & Philip of Spain.

PROVIDEBO ADIVTORIVM (I will provide help). On some groats of Henry VII.

QVIESCAT PLEBS (He calms the common people). Charles II, St Patrick's farthing.

TIMOR DOMINI FONS VITÆ (The fear of the Lord is the fountain of life: *Prov.* 14, 27). Base shillings of Edward VI.

TVEATVR VNITA DEVS (May God guard the united, i.e., the kingdoms). Sixpences of James I.

VERITAS TEMPORIS FILIA (Truth, the daughter of Time). Mary Tudor.

Saorstát éireann (the Irish Free State)

éire (Ireland)

Deić scilling (Ten Shillings)

éirí amać na cásca (the Easter Rising)

Leat ćoróin (Half Crown)

Flóirín (Florin)

scilling (Shilling)

Reul (Sixpence)

Leat Reul (Half Sixpence)

pingin (Penny)

Leat pingin (Half Penny)

Feoirling (Farthing)

SELECT BIBLIOGRAPHY OF IRISH COINS

The earliest accounts of Irish coinage occur in Sir James Ware's *De Hibernia & anti-quitatibus eius disquisitiones*, London, 1654 (Chap. XXV), followed by Bishop William Nicolson's *The Irish Historical Library*, London, 1724 (Chap. VIII). James Simon's work is the first book devoted solely to the coinage of Ireland.

COFFEY, G. *A catalogue of the Anglo-Irish Coins in the Collection of the Royal Irish Academy.* 1911.

COLGAN, E. *For Want of Good Money: The Story of Ireland's Coinage.* 2003.

DOLLEY, M. *Medieval Anglo-Irish Coins*. 1972.

DOWLE, A & FINN, P. *A Guide Book to the Coinage of Ireland, from 995 A.D. to the present day.* 1969.

LINDSAY, J. *A View of the Coinage of Ireland, from the Invasion of the Danes to the Reign of George IV.* 1839.

NELSON, Dr. P. *The Coinage of Ireland in Copper, Tin and Pewter*. 1905 (reprinted from *BNJ*).

SIMON, J. *Essay towards an Historical Account of Irish Coins*. 1749.

— Ditto, together with *Supplement to Mr. Simon's Essay on Irish Coins* (first pub. 1776). 1810.

WITHERS, P. & B.R. *Irish Small Silver, John - Edward VI.* 2004.

YOUNG, D. *Coin Catalogue of Ireland 1722-1968.* 1969.

See also Herbert Grueber's *Handbook of the Coins of Great Britain and Ireland in the British Museum* (1899), and, for numerous statutes relating to Irish coinage, Rev. Rodgers Ruding, *Annals of the Coinage of Great Britain*, etc. (3rd ed. 1840). Various specialised papers on Irish numismatics have appeared in the following periodicals: *Transactions/Proceedings of the Royal Irish Academy (TRIA/PRIA), Proceedings of th Royal Society of Antiquaries of Ireland (PRSAI), Journal of the Royal Society of Antiquaries of Ireland (JRSAI), Numismatic Society of Ireland, Occasional Papers (NSI), Irish Numismatics (IN), Numismatic Chronicle (NC), British Numismatic Journal (BNJ), Seaby's Coin & Medal Bulletin (SCMB)*, and Spink's *Numismatic Circular (SNC)*. In addition to 'Notes on Irish Coins' by Dr. E.J. Harris (*SCMB* 1964-65), we note the following specialist works:

HIBERNO-SCANDINAVIAN COINAGE

BLACKBURN, M. 'Currency under the Vikings. Part 4. The Dublin Coinage, *c.*995-1050'. *BNJ* 78, 2008.

DOLLEY, R.H.M. *The Hiberno-Norse Coins in the British Museum.* (*SCBI* 8), 1966.

— 'Some New Light on the early Twelfth Century Coinage of Dublin'. *SCMB*, Oct. 1972.

HILDEBRAND, B.E. *Anglo-Saxon Coins in the Royal Swedish Cabinet of Medals at Stockholm, all found in Sweden.* 1881.

NAISMITH, R. and WOODS, A. 'Ireland to 1170', in *Medieval European Coinage with a Catalogue of the Coins in the Fitzwilliam Museum, Cambridge. VIII. Britain and Ireland c. 400-1066,* 2017.

O'SULLIVAN, W. 'The Earliest Irish Coinage'. *JRSAI* LXXIX, 1949.

ROTH, B. 'The Coins of the Danish Kings of Ireland'. *BNJ* VI, 1909.

SEABY, W.A. *Hiberno-Norse Coins in the Ulster Museum.* (*SCBI* 32), 1984.

WOODS, A. 'Monetary activity in Viking-Age Ireland: the evidence of single-finds', in R. Naismith, M. Allen and E. Screen (eds), *Early Medieval Monetary History: Studies in Memory of Mark Blackburn,* 2014.

— *Economy and authority: a study of the coinage of Hiberno-Scandinavian Dublin and Ireland.* 2014.

ANGLO-IRISH COINAGE: JOHN - EDWARD III

ALLEN, M. 'John de Courcy and the early Anglo-Irish coinage', *BNJ* 88, 2018.

BYRNE, G. 'The first Irish ('Henricus') coinage of Edward I', in R. Fitzpatrick (ed.), *The Numismatic Society of Ireland Occasional Papers 59– 66*. 2017.

CASSIDY, R. 'Documents of the Irish exchanges and mint, 1251–64', *BNJ* 87, 2017.

CASSIDY, R. 'The Irish exchanges and mints in the reign of Edward I', *BNJ* 87, 2017.

CLARKE, D.T.D., SEABY, W.A. & STEWART, I. 'The 1969 Colchester Hoard'. The Anglo-Irish Portion. *BNJ* XLIV, 1974.

DOLLEY, R.H.M. 'The Irish Mints of Edward I in the light of the coin-hoards from Ireland and Great Britain'. *PRIA* LXVI, 1968.

DOLLEY, M. & O'SULLIVAN, W. 'The Chronology of the First Anglo-Irish Coinage', in *North Munster Studies*, 1967.

DOLLEY, M. & SEABY, W. *Anglo-Irish Coins: John-Edward III in the Ulster Museum.* (*SCBI* 10), 1968.

DYKES, D.W. 'The Irish Coinage of Henry III'. *BNJ* XXXII, 1963.

— 'The Coinage of Richard Olof'. *BNJ* XXXIV, 1964.

— 'The Anglo-Irish Coinage of Edward III'. *BNJ* XLVI, 1976.

— 'King John's Irish *Rex* Coinage Revisited. Part 1: The dating of the coinage.' *BNJ* 83, 2013.

— 'Another Dublin penny of Richard Olof', *BNJ* 83, 2013.

— 'King John's Irish Rex coinage revisited. Part II: The symbolism of the coinage', *BNJ* 84, 2014.

NORTH, J.J. 'The Anglo-Irish Halfpence, Farthings and post-1290 Pence of Edward I and Edward III'. *BNJ* 67, 1997.

O'SULLIVAN, W. *The Earliest Anglo-Irish Coinage.* 1964.

SEABY, W.A. 'A St Patrick Halfpenny of John de Courci'. *BNJ* XXIX, 1958.

SLEVIN, G. *Henry III Dublin Mint Voided Long Cross 1251– 1254.* 2016.

SMITH, A. 'On the Type of the first Anglo-Irish Coinage'. *NC*, 1864.

— 'Inedited Silver Farthings coined in Ireland'. *NC*, 1863.

HENRY VI - HENRY VII

ALLEN, D. 'The supposed halfpence of King John', *NC*, 1938.

BURNS, J. *Irish Hammered Pennies of Edward IV, Edward V and Richard III.* 3rd ed. 2015.

— *Irish Hammered Pennies of Edward IV - Heny VII.* 5th ed. 2017.

CAYLYON-BRITTON, R. 'On the proposed attribution of certain Irish coins to Edward V', *NC*, 1941.

DOLLEY, M. 'A note on the Attribution of the Regally Anonymous "Three Crowns" Coinage'. *SNC*, April 1968.

— 'The sequence and chronology of the "portrait" Anglo-Irish groats of Henry VII'. *SNC*, Nov. 1969.

DYKES, D.W. 'The Anglo-Irish Coinage and the Ancient Arms of Ireland', *JRSAI* 96, 1966.

— 'The Anglo-Irish coinage of Henry VI', *BNJ* 84, 2014.

MAC CONAMHNA, O. 'The Irish portrait pennies of Edward IV, Edward V and Richard III, 1465-1483', *BNJ* 87, 2017.

— 'A Dublin penny of Edward V', *BNJ* 89, 2019.

SMITH, A. 'On the Irish coins of Edward the Fourth'. *TRIA* XIX, 1839.

— 'On the Irish coins of Henry the Seventh'. *TRIA* XIX, 1841

SYMONDS, H. 'The Irish silver coinages of Edward IV'. *NC*, 1921.

HENRY VIII & EDWARD VI

CARLYON-BRITTON, R. 'Henry VIII Harp Groats and Half-Harp Groats and Edward VI Harp Groats'. *NC*, 1955.

CHALLIS, C.E. 'The Tudor Coinage for Ireland'. *BNJ* XL, 1971.

DOLLEY, M. 'Was there an Anglo-Irish Coinage in the Name of Edward VI'. *SNC*, Sept. 1969.

— & HACKMANN, W.D. 'The Coinages for Ireland of Henry VIII'. *BNJ* XXXVIII, 1969.

ELLIS, S. G. 'The Struggle for control of the Irish Mint, 1450-c.1506', *PRIA*, 78, C, 1978.

LAKER, A.J. *The Portrait Groats of Henry VIII.* 1978.

MAC CONAMHNA, O. 'The Irish portrait pennies of Edward IV, Edward V and Richard III, 1465−1483', *BNJ* 87, 2017.

— 'A Dublin penny of Edward V', *BNJ* 89, 2019.

POTTER, W.J.W. 'The Coinage of Edward VI in his own Name', Part 1. *BNJ* XXXI, 1962.

SYMONDS, H. 'The Irish Coinages of Henry VIII and Edward VI'. *NC*, 1915.

MARY TUDOR & ELIZABETH

SMITH, A. 'On the Irish Coins of Mary'. *PRSAI*, 1855.

SYMONDS, H. 'The Coinage of Mary Tudor'. *BNJ* VIII, 1911.

— 'The Elizabethan Coinages for Ireland'. *NC*, 1917.

JAMES I & CHARLES I

DOLLEY, M. 'A note on the Weight and Fineness of the 1646 "Ormonde" Pistole'. *BNJ* XXXV, 1966.

EVERSON, T. *The Farthing Tokens of James I & Charles I.* 2007.

NELSON, P. 'The Obsidional Money of the Great Rebellion'. *BNJ* XVI, 1919-20.

O'SULLIVAN, W. 'The only Gold Coins issued in Ireland.' *BNJ* XXXIII, 1964.

SEABY, W. & BRADY, G. 'The Extant Ormonde Pistoles and Double Pistoles'. *BNJ* XLIII, 1973.

SMITH, A. 'Notes on the Irish Coins of James I'. *NC*, 1879.

— 'On the Ormonde Money'. *PRSAI*. 1854.

— 'Money of Necessity issued in Ireland in the reign of Charles I'. *JRSAI* 1860.

CHARLES II - GEORGE IV

BATEMAN, D. & DOLLEY, M. 'Some Remarks on the "Pewter" (Tin) Petty Coinage of March/April 1690'. *IN* 50, March-April 1976.

DAVIS, W.J. *The Nineteenth Century Token Coinage of Great Britain, Ireland* etc. 1904.

DOLLEY, M. 'Some reflections on the Volume of the "Brass Money" of James II'. *SCMB*, Dec. 1974.

— 'A Provisional Note on the 1804 Bank of Ireland Token for Six Shillings Irish'. *IN* 35, Sept.-Oct. 1973.

— 'Some Preliminary Observations on the Pennies Irish of 1822 and 1823'. *IN* 36, Nov.-Dec. 1973.

— 'The Armstrong and Legge (*recte* "Knox"?) Halfpence Irish with dates 1680-4'. *SCMB*, April 1979.

FRAZER, W. 'On the irish "St Patrick" or 'Floreat Rex" Coinage subsequently circulated in New Jersey by Mark Newbie'. *JRSAI* XXV, 1895.

MARTIN, S.F. *Saint Patrick Coinage [for Ireland and New Jersey].* 2018.

— *The Hibernia Coinage of William Wood (1722-1724).* 2007.

POWELL, J.S. 'The Irish Coinage of Armstrong and Legge'. *SCMB*, June 1978.

SMITH, A. 'Money of Necessity issued in Ireland in the reign of James II'. *NC*, 1870.

STEVENSON, D. 'The Irish Emergency Coinages of James II 1689-1691'. *BNJ* XXXVI, 1967.

TIMMINS, P. T*he Emergency Coinage of 1689-1691 for the Campaign of James II.* 2nd ed, 2020.

TURNER, R. 'The Gun Money Crowns of James II'. *SCMB*, July 1975.

WARHURST, Mrs. M. 'New Evidence for the Date of the so-called "St Patrick's" Halfpence and Farthings'. *IN* 59, Sept.-Oct. 1972.

IRISH FREE STATE & ÉIRE

REMICK, J.H. *The Coinage of the Republic of Ireland.* 1968.

YEATS, W.B. et al. *The Coinage of Saorstát Éireann.* 1928

IRISH MINTS

N

Carrickfergus ●

Downpatrick ●

Carlingford ●

Drogheda ●

Trim ●

Dublin ●

IRISH

SEA

Galway ●

ATLANTIC

OCEAN

● Limerick

✱ Kilkenny

● Wexford

Waterford ●

St. Georges Channel

Cork ✱   Youghal ✱

Bandon ✱   Kinsale ✱

Scale

0   50 Miles

Towns of Refuge. ✱

Map drawn by Alan Miles

HIBERNO-SCANDINAVIAN PERIOD
(late 10th century to early 12th century)

The Vikings began raiding the British Isles towards the end of the eighth century and in the first half of the ninth century large groups of Norsemen were settling in Ireland under leaders such as Turgeis, Olaf the White and Ivar the Boneless. The main centres of occupation were around Dublin, Dundalk, Wexford, Waterford, Cork, Limerick and other areas, and the newcomers were soon raiding along the waterways to the very centre of Ireland. Many of these Norsemen were driven out by the Irish in 901, but others returned a decade later and a succession of Norse kings held Dublin: Sihtric, Raghnall, Guthfrith, and the most famous of them all, Olaf Sihtricsson, known as Anlaf Cuaran, who was defeated at Tara by Maelsechnaill in 980 and then made a pilgrimage to Iona where he ended his life. Where the Norse (and Danes) did settle they intermarried and were converted to Christianity, and eventually they became the allies and naval auxiliaries of the Irish kings. The Norse fortresses, then, grew into commercial centres and it was the chief of them, Dublin (*O. Ir.* Dubh-linn, 'black pool'; *Old Norse*, Dyflinr), that the first Hiberno-Scandinavian coins were issued by the 'Ostmen', as the Scandinavians came to be called.

The first pennies known to have been minted in Ireland were produced at Dublin before the end of the tenth century, and at first directly in imitation of contemporary Anglo-Saxon coins. Many of these early coins have been found in Viking hoards buried in Scandinavia and the Baltic countries. Basically the earlier coins bear the name and stylised effigies of Æthelred II (987-1016), Cnut (1016-35) and of the contemporary king of the Ostmen Sihtric Anlafsson (Silkenbeard) who ruled over the Scandinavian settlers at Dublin and whose forces were defeated by the hosts of Brian Boru at the Battle of Clontarf in 1014. Some coins actually bear the names of English moneyers and English mints, e.g. LVND (London), LEIG (Chester), EFOR (York), PECED (Watchet), etc., but most of these seem to have been products of Norse imitators at Dublin.

As time went on the Hiberno-Scandinavian coins became more and more debased in style, the inscriptions meaningless, with the weight dropping considerably below that of contemporary Anglo-Saxon issues. After the Norman conquest of England in 1066, Hiberno-Scandinavian coins show in the many changes of design on the reverse the influence of the sterling pennies issued during the late 11th century, although the Irish coins being of such light weight did not circulate outside their country of origin. It is not known with certainty who were the authorities issuing these later coins, it is possible they were Hibernian as much as Hiberno-Scandinavians. Later still, in the early 12th century, the coins became so thin that they could not have been struck between hardened metal dies in the ordinary manner, but each design was impressed separately or else the coin was impressed on one side only. As such they are known as 'bracteates'.

Of this large coinage around 1,300 are contained in three major public collections. The largest and most important group is in the National Museum of Ireland at Dublin, and a summary of the types housed there has been published by Dr William O'Sullivan in *The Earliest Irish Coinage* (1949, revised 1961). A smaller but representative collection is in the British Museum, London, and this has been fully published by Mr Michael Dolley in a volume of the *Sylloge of Coins of the British Isles*, 'The Hiberno-Norse Coins in the British Museum' (1966). The third collection, also important, is that in the Ulster Museum made up chiefly from the Irish portion of the Carlyon-Britton collection.

A typical early coin reads SIHTRIC RE+ DYFLIN (Sihtric, King of Dublin), with the name of the moneyer and mint on the reverse, e.g. FÆREMIN MO[*netarius*] DYFLIN (Færemin, moneyer at Dublin).

All the coins of this period are silver pennies.

I. Sihtric Anlafsson and Related Issues, *c*.995-1020

Coins exist of some of the types in this group which have somewhat crude engraving or blundered legends, and these may be worth rather less than the prices indicated. Some close copies appear to have been minted in Scandinavia.

6100

6102

		F	VF
		£	£
6100	Group A. Imitation of Æthelred II of England, **CRVX** type, *c*.995-1000. With name 'Sihtric'. ℞ Voided cross, **CRVX** in angles. *Dublin. O'S* 1	1250	3250
6101	— — Similar, but with other mint name. *O'S* 2	1100	3000
6102	— With name 'Æthelred'. *Dublin. O'S* 3	1000	2750

6103

6104

6103	Group B. Imitation of Æthelred's *Long Cross* type, *c*.1000-1010. With name **SIHTRIC RE+DYFLIN**, etc. *Dublin. O'S* 6	375	1100
6104	— — Similar, but with other mint name. *O'S* 7	425	1250
6105	— — — With name **SIHTRIC CVNVNC**. *BM* 28	1500	4500

6106

6108

6106	— With name 'Æthelred'. *Dublin. O'S* 8	450	1350
6107	— — Similar, but with other mint name. *BM* 37-42	425	1250
6108	— With inscription **DYMN ROE+ MNEGNI**, etc., on obv. *Dublin. O'S* 9	575	1750
6109	— — Similar, but with other mint name. BM 30	625	1850
6110	— With name **OGSEN HEA MELNEM**. *O'S* 11	850	2500

F   VF
£   £

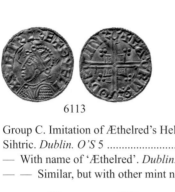

6113   6116

6113   Group C. Imitation of Æthelred's Helmet type, c.1004-1010. With name of
          Sihtric. *Dublin. O'S* 5   1750   5000
6115   — With name of 'Æthelred'. *Dublin. BM* 45-6   1650   4500
6116   — — Similar, but with other mint name. *BM* 46A & B   1500   4000

6117   6119

6117   Group D. Imitation of Æthelred's *Last Small Cross* type, *c.*1010-16. With
          name of Sihtric. *Dublin. O'S* 24   675   2000
6118   — — Similar, but with other mint name. *BM* 53-8   625   1850
6119   — With name of 'Æthelred', Dublin. *BM* 59   575   1750
6120   — — Similar, but with other mint name. *H.*3358   625   1850

6121   6121B

6121   Group E. Imitation of Cnut of England, *Quatrefoil* type, c.10156-20. With
          name of Sihtric. *Dublin. O'S* 25   1750   5750
6121A— With name of 'Cnut', *Dublin. H.*280-3   1350   4000
6121B— With blundered legends   750   2250

II. Later variants of Long Cross Coins, *c.*1020-35
Distinguished from earlier Long Cross pence by the addition of pellets in angles of cross.
Coins with unblundered legends (mostly 23-20 grs. weight, 1.5-1.3 gms.)

6122   6124

6122   Group F. With name of Sihtric, as 6103. *Dublin. O'S* 10   250   650
6123   — — Similar, but with other mint name. *S.*1   475   1350
6124   — With name of 'Æthelred'. *Dublin. S.*7   450   1250

Coins with blundered legends on one or both sides (mostly 20-12 grs., 1.3-0.78 gms.)

	F £	VF £

6125   6125A

6125 — As 6122, but generally cruder style 225   575
6125A— As 6122, inverted crozier behind head. *O'S* 12 250   750

Coins with blundered legends, and symbol in one or more quarters of reverse (mostly 12-9 grs., 0.78-0.58 gms.)

6126   6129

6126 As 6125, but ɯ on neck and in one angle of *rev. O'S* 14 275   800
6127 As 6125, but triquetra in one angle. *BM* 102 250   750
6128 As 6125, with spiral and millrind symbols. *BM* 110 .... 375 1000
6128B As 6125, but with hand behind neck... 450 1250
6129 *Obv.* as 6125. Hand of good style in one angle of cross, exhibiting
  stigma. BM 62 .... 575 1750
  See **Isle of Man** section for the Manx imitations of Hiberno-Norse *Long Cross* coins.

III. Long Cross and Hand Coinage, *c.*1035-60

Usually blundered legends (mostly 16-12 grs., 1.04-0.78 gms.)

6131   6132   6132A

6130 Bust with hand before face thumb to nose. ℞ One or two crude hands
  in angles of cross. *O'S* 18 .... 475 1350
6131 Bust with hand on neck. ℞ As above. *O'S* 19 250   750
6132 — Similar, but without hand on neck. ℞ Hands in two angles. *O'S* 16 200   500
6132A— Similar, but symbol on, before or behind bust, and one or two hands
  and other symbols on reverse). Many varieties. 210   525
6133 — — ℞ One crude hand, and sometimes **S** or other symbols. *O'S* 20. 225   550

IV. 'Scratched-Cross' Coins, *c*.1060-65

Reverse dies appear to have been part punched, part engraved.

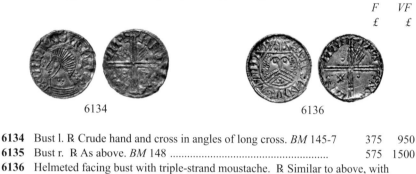

6134   6136

		F £	VF £
6134	Bust l. ℞ Crude hand and cross in angles of long cross. *BM* 145-7	375	950
6135	Bust r. ℞ As above. *BM* 148	575	1500
6136	Helmeted facing bust with triple-strand moustache. ℞ Similar to above, with various symbols in the angles. *O'S* 47	675	1750

V. Mainly Imitations of late Anglo-Saxon, Norman and North European Coins, *c*.1065-*c*.1100

Arranged in chronological order following the sequence of English types.

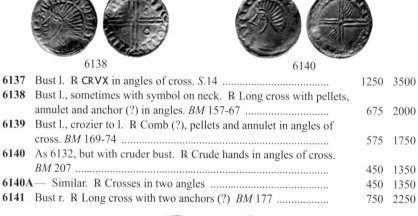

6138   6140

6137	Bust l. ℞ CRVX in angles of cross. *S*.14	1250	3500
6138	Bust l., sometimes with symbol on neck. ℞ Long cross with pellets, annulet and anchor (?) in angles. *BM* 157-67	675	2000
6139	Bust l., crozier to l. ℞ Comb (?), pellets and annulet in angles of cross. *BM* 169-74	575	1750
6140	As 6132, but with cruder bust. ℞ Crude hands in angles of cross. *BM* 207	450	1350
6140A—	Similar. ℞ Crosses in two angles	450	1350
6141	Bust r. ℞ Long cross with two anchors (?) *BM* 177	750	2250

6142A

6142	Bust l. ℞ As *rev.* of Cnut *Short Cross*. *O'S* 26	1000	3000
6142A	Bust l. ℞ As *rev.* of Cnut *Quatrefoil type*.	1200	3500
6143	Bust r. ℞ As last. *BM* 178-80	1100	3250
6144	Bust l. or r. ℞ As *rev.* of Harthacnut *Jewel Cross*. *S*.8	1350	4000
6145	Bust l. ℞ As *rev.* of Edward the Confessor *Expanding Cross* type. *BM* 176	1350	4000
6146	Bust l. ℞ As *rev.* of Edward the Confessor *Helmet* type. *BM* 218	1340	4000

F   VF
£   £

6147   6148A

6147 Bust l. ℞ As *rev.* of Edward the Confessor *Small Cross*. *O'S* 31. (6149) 750 2250
6148 As 6139. ℞ As 6147. *BM* 205. (6147).. 700 2000
6148A Bust l. ℞ Voided cross with trefoil ends, anchors in two angles . 750 2250
6149 Bust l. ℞ Cross pattée over cross with triple pellet ends. *BM* 219.
(6148).. 700 2000
6150 Bust r. ℞ Derived from Edward's *Pyramids* type. *BM* p.166...... 1000 3000
6150A Bust l., cross on neck. ℞ Short voided cross. small crosses at ends,
no inscription 850 2500

6151   6151A   6152

6151 Bust l. ℞ Derivative of rev. of Harold II **PAX** type. *O'S* 33 .... 1350 4250
6151A — — Similar, but bird above and below centre band of *rev. O'S* 35 1500 4500
6152 Bust r. of different style. ℞ Similar to 6151. *O'S* 34 .... 1350 4250
6153 Bust l. or r. ℞ As *rev.* of William I *Profile left* type. R.200, 202 1350 4250

6154   6154A   6154B

6154 Bust l. ℞ As *rev.* of William I *Bonnet* type. *BM* 222 .... 1500 4500
6154A Bust r. ℞ Similar to *rev.* of William I *Two sceptres* type. 1250 3750
6154B Bust l. ℞ 'Bow' cross, cross and pellets at centre. (6154A) 1300 4000
6155 Bust l. with various symbols on neck. ℞ Cross crosslet over celtic
cross. *O'S* 39 .... 1200 3500
6156 — Similar, but *rev.* as William I Two Stars type. *O'S* 40 .... 1350 4250

6156A   6157

6156A Bust l. ℞ Quadrilateral on cross fleury as William I *Sword* type. 1300 4000
6157 Bust l. ℞ As *rev.* of William I **PAX** type. O'S 27 .... 1750 5500

Hiberno-Scandinavian Issues, *c.*1065-1100

	F £	VF £

6158   6159

6158   Bust l. R As *rev.* of William II *Profile* type. *O'S* 43   1200   3500

6159   — Sometimes with pellets on neck or in field. R Three birds.
O'S 36-7   700   2000

6160   — R Small crosses and trefoils around central annulet or cross.
O'S 41-2   525   1500

6161   Bust r. R Cross and 'spectacles' in alternate angles of cross,
derived from Scandinavian prototype. *O'S* 30   650   1850

6162   6164

6162   Crude *Agnus Dei*, derived from Scandinavian prototype
(*Hauberg*, Magnus den Gode 15 and Svend Estridsen 60).
R Long cross, E and cross in alternate angles. *O'S* 63   1500   4750

6162A— Similar, but two hands above *Agnus Dei*. R Long cross,
'anchor' in one angle   1650   5000

6163   — R 'Bow' cross, annulet at centre. *O'S* 64   1500   4750

6164   Crude facing bust. R Long cross with symbols in angles. *O'S* 44   1750   5000

6165   6165A

6165   — R Type as Edward the Confessor *Facing Bust/Small Cross*, but
pellets in angles of cross. *BM* 189-92   1100   3250

6165A— R Long cross, hand and pellet in opposing angles   1200   3500

6165B   6166

6165B— R As Aethelred II *Long cross* type...   1100   3250

6166   — R Derived from Harold II **PAX** type. *BM* 184-5   1350   4000

6167   — R Short cross. *BM* 183   1000   3000

	F	VF
	£	£

6168    6169

6168 Bare-headed facing bust, with sword (?) in r. hand, l. hand upraised.
R As *rev.* of William I *Bonnet* type. *BM* 187 .... | 1750 | 5500
6169 Facing bust derived from William I *Canopy* type. R Three birds
around central point. *O'S* 57 .... | 1350 | 4000

6170    6172

6170 Facing bust, derived from William I *Two Sceptres* type. *O'S* 54. | 1350 | 4000
6171 — R As *rev.* of William II *Cross in Quatrefoil* type. *O'S* 55 ..... | 1500 | 4500
6172 — R Crude bird, cross above. *O'S* 56 .... | 1500 | 4500
6173 Facing bust derived from William I *Two Stars* type. R Long cross
with crude hand in one angle and/or other symbol. O'S 50........ | 1350 | 4000

6174

6174 — R Derived from rev. of William I PAX type. *O'S* 51-2 .... | 1500 | 4500
6175 Very crude facing head. R Crude hand and bird in alternate angles,
derived from Edward's *Sovereign* type. *O'S* 45 .... | 850 | 2500

6176    6178

6176 — R Similar, but hand and S (sometimes Ƨ) in angles. *O'S* 46 .. | 650 | 2000
6177 — R Similar, but Ƨ and other symbol in angles of cross potent.
O'S 48 .... | 750 | 2250
6178 — R Derived from rev. of William II *Cross in Quatrefoil* type.
O'S 49 .... | 850 | 2500

	F	VF
	£	£
6179 Crowned bust r., as William I Profile right type. *R*.207	1650	5000

6180

6180A

6180 Simple facing bust, two pellets either side, cross above. ℞ Two crosses and two scourges. *O'S* 53	750	2250
6180A— ℞ Similar, but pellet and scourges. *BM* 226	750	2250
6181 Cross with bar in two angles. ℞ Derived from Æthelred's **CRVX** type. *S. Supp.* 6	850	2500

6182   6184

6182 Annulet or cross at centre of four croziers in saltire, Ƨ to l., scourge (?) to r. ℞ Long cross with symbols. *O'S* 58-9	850	2500
6183 — ℞ As *rev.* of Cnut *Short Cross* type. *O'S* 60	900	2750
6184 — ℞ As *rev.* of Harthacnut *Jewel Cross* type. *BM* 199-201	1100	3500
6185 — ℞ As *rev.* of William I *Canopy* type. *O'S* 61-2	1100	3500
6186 Small flan coins. Types as 6153, 6161, 6168 etc.	575	1750

VI. Very Late and Degraded Imitations of Long Cross Coins, *c.*1100-*c.*1110

6187

6187 Very crude bust l., crozier to l. ℞ Long cross with sceptres and pellets, or annulets, in alternate angles. *O'S* 22	275	750
6188 — ℞ Sceptres and crosses in alternate angles. *O'S* 23	325	950
6189 As 6187, but bust to r. *R*.179	475	1350

	F	VF
	£	£

VII. Twelfth Century Semi-Bracteates and Bracteates, *c.*1110-*c.*1170

A. *Semi-bracteates – probably the obverse and reverse types struck in separate stages. c.1110-1115*

6192

6190	Crude bust l. ℞ Voided long cross, sceptres in angles. *O'S* 67 ..	1100	3500
6191	— ℞ Long cross and quatrefoil. *O'S* 65	1000	3250
6192	— ℞ Plain cross and cross botonnée. *O'S* 66	1100	3500

B. *Bracteates – coins struck with design on one side only (the same design appearing incuse on the reverse). c.1115-1170*

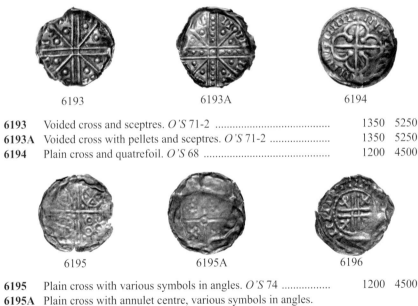

6193   6193A   6194

6193	Voided cross and sceptres. *O'S* 71-2	1350	5250
6193A	Voided cross with pellets and sceptres. *O'S* 71-2	1350	5250
6194	Plain cross and quatrefoil. *O'S* 68	1200	4500

6195   6195A   6196

6195	Plain cross with various symbols in angles. *O'S* 74	1200	4500
6195A	Plain cross with annulet centre, various symbols in angles. *O'S* 74	1200	4500
6196	Voided cross with various symbols in angles. *O'S* 79-80	1350	5250
6197	Cross pommée within quatrefoil. *O'S* 77	1200	4500

	F	*VF*
	£	£

6198

6199

6202G

		F	VF
6198	Cross with trefoils and quatrefoils in alternate in angles. *O'S* 78	1350	5250
6199	Cross with lis in each angle. *O'S* 73	1400	5500
6200	Cross potent with annulets in angles. *O'S* 82	1350	5250
6201	Hammer cross over quatrefoil. *O'S* 69	1350	5250
6202	Short cross pommée over long cross. *O'S* 70	1200	4500
6202A	Small cross pattée in inner circle, alternating sceptres and Is around.	1400	5500
6202B	Cross pattée, pellet in each angle	1200	4500
6202C	Small cross pommée in inner circle	1250	4750
6202D	Cross fleury in inner circle, annulets alternating with crescents and pellets in angles	1350	5250
6202E	Double cross pommée, fleury sceptres in angles	1350	5250
6202F	Double cross pommée over hammer cross	1350	5250
6202G	Cross over quatrefoil, pellet in each angle	1400	5500
6202H	Cross fleury over long cross	1350	5250
6202J	Long cross, formalized head in each angle	2000	6500
6202K	— Similar, but heads alternating with crosses	2000	6500

ANGLO-IRISH COINS

JOHN

Lord of Ireland, 1177 – Count of Mortain, 1189 – King, 1199-1216

The Anglo-Norman conquest of Ireland began in 1169, in the reign of Henry II of England, when a powerful group of Norman Lords from South Wales invaded Leinster with an army of Normans, Flemings and Welsh. Dermot MacMurrough, King of Leinster, had lost his kingdom in a feud with Tiernan O'Ruairc, Lord of Brefni; and he unwisely went for assistance in recovering his territory, first to Henry II, then to "Strongbow", Richard FitzGilbert, Earl of Pembroke, to whom he promised the hand of his daughter, Eva, and the succession to his kingdom. The Norman invaders soon carved out new estates for themselves and Henry had to act quickly to set a limit to their power. He visited Ireland to secure the homage of his powerful subjects and was able to obtain papal recognition of his *de facto* suzerainty of the island. In 1177 the king's son, young Prince John, was given lordship of the new dominion and he paid his first visit to the country in 1185. 'It is thought that this may have been the occasion when silver coins traditionally identified as halfpence, but that are probably pence on an Irish standard, bearing a profile bust with the name of John were struck by certain moneyers, probably in Dublin. Between no earlier than the mid-1180s and no later than 1208/9 another series of Irish pence ('halfpence') and halfpence ('farthings') bearing a round moon-like face in the name of John as 'Lord of Ireland' were minted at Dublin, Carrickfergus, Kilkenny, Limerick and Waterford. In the north also, John de Courcy, who had secured considerable territory for himself in Ulster, issued pence ('halfpence') and halfpence ('farthings') at his townships of Downpatrick and Carrickfergus.

From 1208 or 1209 King John had minted in Dublin silver pennies bearing his bust set in a triangle. He ordered the weight and fineness of these coins to be of the English sterling standard (0.925 fine silver) at about 22½ grains weight. This coinage was initially under the sole control of a mintmaster named Roberd, probably Robert de Bedford who later became Bishop of Lismore. The coins, also minted at Limerick and Waterford, were mainly for use overseas and were largely for war service. However, a number of circular halfpennies and farthings were struck for purposes of normal trading within the colony and at the other two principal Anglo-Irish ports.

First (Profile) coinage, c.1185
(has also been attributed to John De Courcy, Lord of Ulster)

F   VF

6203

£   £

6203 **Penny.** All *Dublin* ? IOHANNES, head r. ℞ Cross with lis and
pellet in each angle. *Elis de D[ ][e?]bne, Raul Blunt, Roger Tan,*
uncertain moneyers. 2500 7500

Second ('DOMinus') coinage, c.1185/1190 to no later than 1208/9

	F £	VF £

Group I, cross potent.

6204   6205

	F £	VF £
6204 **Penny.** *Dublin.* Ia. Facing diademed head, IOHANNES DOMIN YBER (or contraction). R Voided cross potent, annulets in angles. Large flans. *Norman, Rodberd*	175	525
6205 — Ib. Similar but smaller flan, *obv.* legend ends DOM, etc. *Adam, Nicolas, Norman, Rodberd, Tomas, Turgod*	110	350
6206 — Ic. As above, but *obv.* legend ends DEM. *Rodberd*	135	425
6207 *Carrickfergus* (CRAC). Ib. As 6205. *Roberd* (6216)	1250	3500

6208   6209   6211

	F £	VF £
6208 *Kilkenny* ('KIL', 'KEN'). Ib. As 6205. *Andreh, Simund, Waltex* (6213)	575	1750
6209 *Limerick.* Ib. As 6205, DOMI. *Siward* (6214)	675	2000
6210 *Waterford.* Ib. As 6205, DOM, etc. *Davi, Gefrei, Marcus, Walter, Wilmus, [Rob]ert* (6208)	125	400
6211 — Ic. As 6206, DE MO (of Mortain ?) *Gefrei* (6209)	150	475
6212 — Id. Similar, legend ends COMI. *Wilmus* (6210)	175	575

Group II, cross pommée.

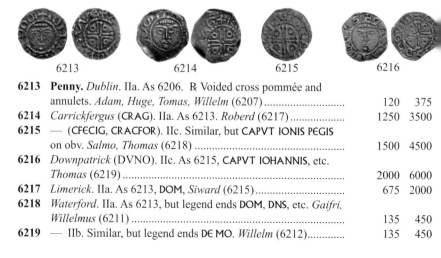

6213   6214   6215   6216

	F £	VF £
6213 **Penny.** *Dublin.* IIa. As 6206. R Voided cross pommée and annulets. *Adam, Huge, Tomas, Willelm* (6207)	120	375
6214 *Carrickfergus* (CRAG). IIa. As 6213. *Roberd* (6217)	1250	3500
6215 — (CFECIG, CRACFOR). IIc. Similar, but CAPVT IONIS PEGIS on obv. *Salmo, Thomas* (6218)	1500	4500
6216 *Downpatrick* (DVNO). IIc. As 6215, CAPVT IOHANNIS, etc. *Thomas* (6219)	2000	6000
6217 *Limerick.* IIa. As 6213, DOM, *Siward* (6215)	675	2000
6218 *Waterford.* IIa. As 6213, but legend ends DOM, DNS, etc. *Gaifri, Willelmus* (6211)	135	450
6219 — IIb. Similar, but legend ends DE MO. *Willelm* (6212)	135	450

	F £	VF £

6220

6220 Halfpenny (Without name of prince or mint). *Dublin*. Mascle with
trefoils at corners. ℞ Four letters of moneyer's name in angles of
cross. *Adam, Nico, Norm, Robd, Toma, Turg* 675 2000
6221 *Limerick*. Similar. *Siwa* (6222) 1500 4000
6222 *Waterford*. Similar. *Gefr, Marc, Walt* (6221).............................. 1200 3250

THE 'ST PATRICK' COINAGE OF JOHN DE COURCY,
LORD OF ULSTER, *c.*1185-*c.*1205

John de Courcy took a private army into Ulster in 1177, seizing Downpatrick. Within five
years he had subdued the whole kingdom of Uladh (Down and Antrim) which he ruled as an
independent prince, marrying the daughter of Godred, the Norse king of Man. Refusing to
pay homage to King John, he was outlawed and eventually taken prisoner by Hugh de Lacy
who was granted the earldom of Ulster.

I. Issues with de Courcy's name. No mint name, but probably Downpatrick

6223

6224

6223 Penny. As illustration. PATRICIVS ℞ IOh:S DЄ CVRCI .... *Extremely rare*
6224 Halfpenny. PATRICI, cross pattée. ℞ GOAN D CVRCI, voided
cross potent 2250 6500

II. Anonymous 'St. Patrick' issues.

6225

6226

6227

6225 Halfpenny. *Carrickfergus*. PATRICI, processional cross. ℞ Voided
cross pattée (6226).. 1100 3000
6226 — ℞ Voided cross pommée (6227).. 1200 3250
6227 *Downpatrick*. PATRICI, processional cross. ℞ Cross
with crescents in angles (6225)... 1100 3000

KING JOHN

Third ('Rex') coinage, 1208/9-*c.*1211/12.

6228   6229

	F	VF
	£	£
6228 **Penny.** *Dublin*. Crowned bust in triangle, hand holding sceptre.		
℞ Sun, moon and three stars in triangle. *Roberd*	85	225
6228A— Similar, but moneyers *Iohan, Willem, Wilelm P.*	125	350
6229 *Limerick*. Similar. *Willem, Wace*	175	475
6230 *Waterford*. Similar. *Willem*	475	1350

6231   6232   6234

	F	VF
6231 **Halfpenny.** *Dublin*. Similar bust but no sceptre. ℞ Cross, moon		
and stars in triangle. *Roberd, Willem*	100	275
6232 *Limerick*. Similar. *Willem, Wace*	175	475
6233 *Waterford*. Similar. *Willem*	325	950
6234 **Farthing.** *Dublin* (but without mint name). Head in triangle.		
℞ Whorled sun in triangle. *Roberd, Willem, Wace*	300	900
6234A *Limerick*. Similar. *Willem, Wace*	*Extremely rare*	

HENRY III, 1216-1272

In 1247 Richard, Earl of Cornwall, King Henry's younger brother, was granted the right to strike new money for a period of twelve years in England, Wales and Ireland, in consideration of a substantial loan which he had made to the king. The agreement gave Richard half the profits of the minting and the exchange. Coins of a new type, the *Long Cross* coinage, were struck in England the same year, but it was not until the autumn on 1251 that coining operations recommenced at Dublin. Roger de Haverhill was put in charge of the mint in Ireland, but the moneyers *Ricard* and *Davi* whose names appear on the coins may have been the London moneyers Richard Bonaventure and David of Enfield, operating *in absentia*. The dies form the coinage were sent from London.

The coinage was of fairly short duration as the Dublin mint was closed again in January 1254, probably after all the older money in the island had been re-coined and it was no longer profitable to incur the expenses of maintaining a mint. No halfpennies or farthings were coined, but pennies are sometimes found cut into halves or quarters along the line of the voided cross for use as small change. It seems that a large proportion of the pence produced were exported to England and the continent; there were, for instance, over 1600 of these pieces amongst the huge hoard of sterling pence found in Brussels in 1908, and the types were even copied in Saxony.

F   VF
£   £

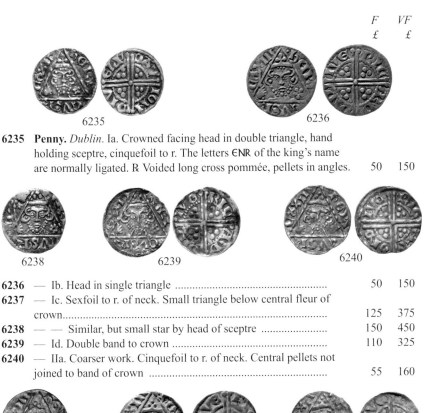

6235

6236

6235 **Penny.** *Dublin.* Ia. Crowned facing head in double triangle, hand
holding sceptre, cinquefoil to r. The letters ЄNR of the king's name
are normally ligated. ℞ Voided long cross pommée, pellets in angles.   50   150

6238   6239   6240

6236 — Ib. Head in single triangle   50   150
6237 — Ic. Sexfoil to r. of neck. Small triangle below central fleur of
crown...   125   375
6238 — — Similar, but small star by head of sceptre   150   450
6239 — Id. Double band to crown   110   325
6240 — IIa. Coarser work. Cinquefoil to r. of neck. Central pellets not
joined to band of crown   55   160

6241   6242A   6243

6241 — IIb. Similar, but band of crown jewelled with pellets   125   350
6242 — IIc. Three curls either side of head instead of two   100   300
6242A— IIc. Similar, but with beardless portrait   100   300

6243A

6243B

6243 — IId. Wide open shoulders   85   250
6243A Cut Halfpenny. As illustration   20   65
6243B Cut Farthing. As illustration   15   45

EDWARD I, 1272-1307

Lord of Ireland, 1254 – King, 1272-1307

It seems that no coins were minted in Ireland after 1254 until Richard Olof, a prominen
Dublin merchant, was placed in charge of the Dublin mint between 1278 and 1279. The coin:
of this issue are of the same basic type as Henry III's *Long Cross* (*Double Cross*) coins an
even continue the name hENRICVS; but, as on the English coins of the same period, ,
distinctive treatment of the king's hair distinguishes them from similar coins of the previou:
reign. Very few pieces of this issue have survived, which is not surprising as in 1280 ther
was a complete recoinage of earlier types.

Over the previous century there had been a gradual centralizing of control over the coinag
and it was now considered unnecessary for a coin to bear the name of the moneyer or min
master. The 1280 issue retains the king's head in a triangle, now inverted, and the revers
has a plain cross and pellets with the name of the mint. A branch mint was opened a
Waterford to help with the recoinage but it was closed by 1295, in which year a mint at Cor
was opened for a short period. Minting was intermittent and probably ceased in the openin
years of the 14th century. Coins with a rose on the king's breast seem to coincide with
similar feature on English sterlings in 1294. Round halfpence and farthings were again coine
for internal currency.

The normal obverse inscription is €DW'R / ANGL'D / NS hYB (*Edwardus, Rex Angliae
Dominus Hibernie* - Edward, King of England, Lord of Ireland) and on the reverse the nam
of the mint, CIVITAS DVBLIN, etc. Though many of the coins have three pellets on the king'
breast, the top pellet is sometimes stamped into the drapery and is not easily visible on
worn coin.

As in earlier reigns, a large proportion of pence coined were exported and imitations o
this type occur on the continental coins of Bar, Cologne and Lippe.

First ('hENRICVS') coinage, 1275-79

	F	VF
	£	£

6244

6244   Penny. *Dublin.* Facing crowned head in triangle, realistic hair.
Roman V or Lombardic U : hENRICVS or hENRICUS and DIV€
or DIU€. *Richard.*   1250   3750

Second ('€DW') coinage, 1279-1302.
The following classification has been retained in this edition on the grounds of simplicity.
The actual sequence of the series, based on close examination of the punches used, is mor
complex and is set out in J.J. North, 'The Anglo-Irish Halfpence, Farthings and post-1290
Pence of Edward I and Edward III', *BNJ* 67, 1997.

Second ('ЄDW') coinage, 1279-1302.

Early issues, 1279-1284. Open C and Є

6246   6246A   6247

6246	**Penny.** *Dublin.* I. No punctuation in legend. Crowned bust in triangle, trefoil of pellets on breast, no mark before ЄDW R	50	135
6246A—	Ia. As above but with punctuation in legend ЄDW.R.	50	135
6247	— Ib. Similar, but pellet before ЄDW.R	45	125
6248	— Ic. Similar, but small cross before EDW.R	65	200

6249

6249	*Waterford.* Ib. Trefoil of pellets on breast (6254)	45	125

6250   6251   6252

6250	**Halfpenny.** *Dublin.* Ia. Early lettering, no pellet before ЄDW R (6257)..	50	165
6251	— Ib. Pellet before ЄDW R (6258)	60	1785
6252	— Ic. Pellet before EDW R (6259)	100	275

6253   6254

6253	*Waterford.* Ia. Early lettering, no pellet before ЄDW R (6263)	80	240
6254	— Ib. Pellet before ЄDW R (6264)	75	225

6255   6256

6255	**Farthing.** *Dublin.* I. ЄRA / NG / LIЄ (6267)	90	275
6256	*Waterford.* I. Similar to 6255 (6268)...	100	325

	F £	VF £

6259   6262

Intermediate issues, 1294-1296? Closed ɑ and ɛ

6257	**Penny.** *Dublin.* II. Rose on breast, ᕮDW.R (6249)	300	900
6258	— III. Pellet in each angle of triangle (6250)	375	1250
6259	*Cork* (ɑORɑAɑIᕮ). III. Pellets in each angle of triangle (6256) .	450	1100
6260	*Waterford.* II. Rose on breast, regular dies	375	1250
6260A	— Rose on breast, local dies, irregular lettering (6255)	350	1000
6261	**Halfpenny.** *Dublin.* II. Rose on breast (6260)......................	325	900
6261A	— III. Pellet in each angle of triangle (6260A)	450	1100
6262	*Cork.* III. Wide crown, stringy hair (6266)	950	2750
6263	*Waterford.* III. Wide crown, stringy hair (as Cork) (6265)	175	525

Late issues, 1297-1302 Closed ɑ and ᕮ Single pellet below bust

6264   6265

6264	**Penny.** *Dublin.* IVa. small lettering on *obv.*, large letters on *rev.* (6251)	45	135
6265	— IVb. Similar, but pellet before ᕮDW.R (6252)	65	200
6266	— IVc. As 6264, but small lettering both sides (6253)	90	275

6267A   6268

6267	**Halfpenny.** *Dublin.* IVa. Tall narrow crown (6262)	110	375
6267A	— IVb. Similar, but no pellet on breast (6261)	100	325
6268	**Farthing.** *Dublin.* IVa. ᕮRA / NG / LIᕮ	100	325
6268A	— IVb. Similar, but no pellet on breast	110	350
6268B	*Counterfeits.* Contemporary copy of Edward I penny	75	225
6268C	— Contemporary copy penny with English type *obv.*	110	325

The sequence of the series, based on close examination of the punches used, is set out in J. North, 'The Anglo-Irish Halfpence, Farthings and post-1290 Pence of Edward I and Edward III', *BNJ* 67, 1997, and *Irish Small Silver*, P. and B.R. Withers, Galata 2004.

EDWARD II TO HENRY VI, 1307-1460

A great quantity of Irish silver had been drained out of the country by the export of 'sterlings' struck on the English standard by King John, Henry III and Edward I. To balance the shortage of native coinage some English money circulated, and Scottish coins also made their appearance, particularly in the North and West. Two extremely rare coins, Dublin halfpennies and farthings, are the only denominations to have survived of what must have been a very brief issue from the Dublin mint in 1339/30. Of similar types to the coins of Edward I, a star in the legends both sides link them to the base silver English coinage of 1334-43.

There was then a gap of many decades before another issue of coins was made in Ireland. Though the Norman conquest had been extensive, much of the country had been only thinly held. The descendants of the early settlers soon became largely assimilated in the South, West and North through intermarriage and the adoption by the conquerors of Irish customs and language. In the Eastern counties, in what became known as the 'Pale', closer links were maintained with England and the English crown, and the Anglo-Irish Parliament passed many restrictive ordinances which sought to keep the 'Irish enemy' under permanent subjection.

An ordinance of 1425 authorised a coinage at Dublin of the same weight and fineness as the English coinage and a moneyer was appointed the following year. Only four pennies are known of this issue, and the annulets in the inscriptions link the issue to the contemporary English 'Annulet Coinage' of 1422-26. Complaints about the state of the currency are borne out by finds which show that clipped and false English coins were in common use. The notorious 'Oraylly' money has been shown to refer to ingenious counterfeits of clipped groats manufactured from thin surface plates of silver soldered to a base metal core (See M. Dolley and W.A. Seaby, 'Le Money del Oraylly (O'Reilly's Money)', *BNJ* 36 (1967). English coins were free to circulate in Ireland, but a full weight *groat* (4 pence) might pass for as much as sixpence. Eventually, in 1460, an Irish Parliament called by Richard, duke of York, decided on a new coinage, but in order to prevent the coins being immediately exported it was planned to issue a groat containing only threepence worth of silver, and to prevent them getting into circulation in England the designs were to be quite distinctive. Before the coins could be issued the Yorkist Edward IV had ascended the throne.

EDWARD III, 1327-77

Coinage of 1339/40. 10 oz. fineness.

6269   6269A

		F £	VF £
6269	**Halfpenny.** *Dublin.* (Wt. *c.*10 grs.) As Edward I, but star before ЄDW / ARDV / SRЄX	2500	7500
6269A	**Farthing.** *Dublin.* (Wt. *c.*5 grs.) Similar. ЄDW / ARDV / SRЄX ...	2250	6500

HENRY VI, 1422-61

6270

Coinage of 1425-6. Wt. *c.*15 grs.

6270	**Penny.** *Dublin.* hЄNRICVS DNS hIBNIЄ, crowned bust in circle, star to. r. Annulet at end of obv. legend and after CIVI	3250	9500

EDWARD IV, 1461-1483
First reign, 1461-70

The coinage ordered in 1460 was issued in Dublin around the accession of Edward IV. Due to the prevailing uncertainties of the War of the Roses, it ommitted prudently any regnal name; and to make it distinguishable clearly from heavier English issues, it bore the distinctive device of a large crown on the obverse. To meet the needs of everyday commerce billon farthings and half-farthings, some in the apolitical name of Patrick, were issued in the early years of the reign.

Edward's name appears on the enigmatic and portraitless cross-on-rose issue, the dating of which is uncertain. On balance, it seems most likely that these coins were issued shortly after the battle of Towton, when the identity of the king could be assumed in safety. They bear Edward's heraldic device of a radiant sun, commemorating the sundogs that came with the dawn before his victory at Mortimer's Cross, prominently on the reverse.

Central to the numismatic diversity that developed from 1463 was the person of Thomas Fitzgerald, the seventh earl of Desmond (Deas Mumhan, South Munster), who was that year appointed Lieutenant Deputy of Ireland. Unusually for a holder of this office, he was of the most western, and gaelicised, of the Anglo-Irish earldoms, comprising parts of the modern counties of Limerick, Cork, and Kerry. Aligned enlightendly to his interests, he pursued a stimulatory policy of increasing the money supply to the Irish regions, authorising mint activity in Waterford, Limerick (where he was constable of the castle) and Trim (where he had been made lord of the manor by Edward) in 1463/4, with Galway following in 1465 Drogheda then or soon after, and Cork (which never received parliamentary approval for it activities) possibly in this period also. The 1463 coinage featured again an obverse crown this time with Edward's name and title as lord of Ireland. In 1465 the design was changed retaining Edward's Irish title but introducing a portrait to mimic the English coinage, at a lower weight standard (42 Troy grains to the groat versus the then-current English 48), so opening an obvious arbitrage opportunity for the spending of the coin in England. In addition to his monetary initiatives, Fitzgerald legalised and promoted trade between the Gaelic and Anglo-Irish communities in Munster.

He was replaced by John Tiptoft, the earl of Worcester, late in 1467. Tiptoft had Fitzgerald's head struck off immediately, and devalued the Irish currency by half. The former action would reverberate for generations in rebellion and strife, culminating in the fall of the House of Desmond and the Plantation of Munster under Elizabeth I, and the blood-lettin, that ensued in Munster during the War of the Three Kingdoms. The latter brought economi chaos and hardship, the Anglo-Irish parliament recording that the *"people are so greatl impoverished...that many of [them]...are like to perish from want"*. The devaluation wa implemented through the issue of "doubles" from the Pale mints of Dublin, Drogheda an Trim, at a standard of 45 Troy grains to a double groat of eight pence. The coins bore spectacular radiant sun on the reverse, to mark them clearly as Irish. The doubles act decree also the production of billon farthings, with some discretion to the mintmaster in their design and of which some with the distinctive radiant sun reverse survive. The doubles were demonetised, and the devaluation reversed, by the Irish parliament late in 1470, days afte Tiptoft – the *"fuigheall mallacht fear nereann"* (the wreck of the curses of the men of Ireland of the Annála Ríoghachta Éireann – lost his own head to the Lancastrians at the Tower. The recent discovery of a HENRIC' over EDWARDVS groat of Cork – and the existence of specimen from the die in the original name of Edward, coupled with a Cross and Pelle reverse, in the collection of the National Museum of Ireland – demonstrates that Cork wa issuing an autonomous, non-doubles coinage in 1470, prior to the doubles' demonetisation

Editor's note: since the 2015 edition of this catalogue was published there has been new research which we felt it was necessary to acknowledge; although we cannot state that these new findings are categorically correct, we believe that they will come to be seen as the standard. NB: the new numbers in this section have concordance to the 2015 edition (old numbers in parentheses), which in itself had a concordance to the original catalogue.

SILVER

I. Anonymous 'Crown' coinage, *c*.1460-63

		F	VF
		£	£

6280

6280	**Groat** (45 grs.) *Dublin*. Large crown in tressure of 9 arcs with pellets at points, no legend. ℞ Mint name, cross and pellets (6272)............................	750	2250

6280A

6280C

6280A—	Crosses in three top angles of tressure (6272A)	675	2000
6280B—	Similar, but 8 arcs to tressure, small sun in each angle (6273)	900	2750
6280C—	Similar, but arcs of tressure fleured, suns or rosettes in angles (6274)	1000	3000
6280D—	— Large rosette in each angle of tressure (6275)	1100	3250
6281	— Light issue (c. 35 grs.) As 6280 (6275A)..............................	675	2000

6282

6282D

6282	**Penny.** *Dublin*. As groat, 6280 (6276)...	1250	3500
6282A—	Crosses in top angles of tressure (6277)	1250	3500
6282B—	Saltire below crown (6278)...	1350	3750
6282C—	Crown in tressure of 8 arcs (6279)..	1250	3500
6282D—	No tressure (6280)..	1500	4000
6283	*Waterford*. Crown in tressure of fleured arcs (6281)	1750	4500
6284	**Halfpenny.** *Dublin*. Crown in tressure of 7 arcs, pellets in angles. (6281A)...	*Extremely rare*	

IMPORTANT: for full concordance with the previous edition of this catalogue please see Appendix 2 on page 299.

	F	VF
	£	£

II. Small Cross on Rose/Radiant Sun coinage, *c.*1462-3

6289

6290

6289 **Groat.** *Dublin.* Large rose, cross at centre, within tressure of five
arcs. ℞ POSVI etc., mint name, sun with face (6288)................... 3250 9000

6290 **Penny.** *Dublin.* Similar, but no tressure around rose. ℞ Mint name,
a sun with pellet in annulet at centre (6289) 1100 3250

III. Named and titled 'Crown' coinage, 1463

Mintmarks: rose *(Dublin),* cross *(Limerick, Waterford)*

6293

6294A

6293 **Groat.** *Dublin.* King's name and titles, large crown in tressure, small
annulets in spandrels. ℞ POSVI etc., cross and pellets. *Mm.* rose
(6282)... 3250 9000

6294 *Waterford.* Similar, but pellets in angles, *mm.* cross (6283) 3500 9500

6294A— Annulets in angles of tressure, saltires by crown (6284) 3750 10000

6295

6295 **Half groat.** *Dublin.* Pellets in angles of tressure, two saltires over
crown (6285).. 2250 6500

6296 *Waterford.* Pellets in angles of tresssure (6285A)........................ 2500 7000

6297 **Penny.** *Dublin.* Inscription around crown, no tressure (6286) 1850 5000

6298 *Limerick.* Similar. ℞ Mint name .... *Extremely rare*

6299 *Waterford.* Similar. ℞ Mint name (6287) 2000 5250

IMPORTANT: for full concordance with the previous edition of this catalogue please see Appendix
on page 299.

	F	*VF*
	£	£

IV. First 'Cross and Pellets' coinage, 1465

This coinage adopted the portrait design then current in England. At least initially, and for the Pale mints, die production was reserved to the Tower. Extra pellets, annulets, crosses or roses occur in one or more reverse quadrants on some coins. The pennies of this coinage may best be distinguished from those of the 1470s by their portraits, see Burns 2017.
Mintmarks: rose, pierced cross double fitchy

6301

6306	**Groat** (*c.*41 grs.) *Dublin.* Bust in tressure, no marks (6290)	150	450
6306A—	Pellets in one or three lower spandrels of tressure (6291)	165	500
6306B—	Pellet also to r. of crown (6292)...	175	500
6306C—	Stars by crown (6293)	275	750
6307	*Cork.* Irregular issue. Rosettes by neck (6295)...........................	2500	6000
6307A—	Crosses by neck (6296)	2250	5500
6308	*Drogheda.* Three pellets on some points of tressure, cross below bust (6297)	250	750
6308A—	Fleured tressure, cross below bust (6298)	250	750

6308B   6311

6308B—	Nothing below bust (6299)	240	725
6308C—	Pellet below bust (6299A)	225	700
6309	*Limerick.* Nothing on breast (6301)	575	1500
6309A—	L on breast, rosettes by neck, Irish title		
6310	*Trim.* Nothing on breast (6302)..	375	1000
6311	*Waterford.* Nothing on breast (6303)	210	650
6311A—	Crosses by neck (6304)...	225	700
6311B—	Annulets by neck. ℞ Crowned leopard's head at end of legend (wt. 45 grs.) (6305)...	575	1500
6311C—	V on breast (6306)...	225	700
6311D—	Ɛ on breast, crosses or saltires by neck (6307)......................	275	800

IMPORTANT: for full concordance with the previous edition of this catalogue please see Appendix 2 on page 299.

	F	VF
	£	£

6312 Half groat. *Dublin.* Pellets over crown and below bust (6308) .. | 675 | 1750
6312A— Similar, but pellets in each angle of tressure (6308A) .... | 675 | 1750
6312B— Annulets by neck, no pellets (6309) .... | 575 | 1500
6313 *Galway.* No marks by head. ℞ VILLA DE GALWEY .... | *Extremely rare* |
6314 *Trim.* Two small pellets over crown (6310) .... | 1350 | 3500

6315   6316A   6319

6315 Penny. *Dublin.* No marks by head (6311) .... | 70 | 200
6315A— Pellet either side of neck (6311A) .... | 75 | 225
6315B— Two pellets below head (6311B) .... | 80 | 250
6315C— Saltire either side of neck (6311C) .... | 90 | 275
6315D— Saltire either side of neck, cross either side of crown........... | 90 | 275
6316 *Drogheda.* No marks by head (6312)..................................... | 75 | 225
6316A— No marks by head. ℞ Rose in centre of cross (6370A)......... | 75 | 225
6316B— Saltire either side of crown .... | 75 | 225
6317 *Galway.* No marks by head (6313) .... | 1100 | 3000
6318 *Limerick.* No marks by head (6314) .... | 225 | 750
6318A— Cinquefoil either side of neck, Irish title .... | 225 | 750
6319 *Trim.* No marks by head. ℞ Mintmark after VIL-LA (6315)........ | 135 | 525
6319A— — ℞ Quatrefoil in centre of cross, mintmark after VIL-LA .. | 135 | 525
6320 *Waterford.* No marks by head (6316)..................................... | 150 | 475
6320A— Two crosses either side of neck, pellets by crown (6316A)... | 325 | 900
6320B— No marks by head. ℞ Quatrefoil in centre of cross .... | 150 | 475

6320C   6321

6320C— Annulets by neck. ℞ Plain cross (6383) .... | 125 | 500
6321 Halfpenny. *Dublin.* No marks by head (6317) .... | 475 | 1350

V. "Doubles" coinage. Bust/Rose on Sun, 1467

6328

6328 Double groat (45 grs.) *Dublin.* Crowned bust in fleured tressure.
     ℞ Rose at centre of large sun, suns and roses divide legend (6318) | 2500 | 7500
6328A— Similar, but unfleured tressure (6318A)................................. | 2750 | 8000

		F £	VF £

6329

| 6329 | *Drogheda.* As 6328 (6319).. | 3000 | 8500 |
| 6330 | *Trim.* Two pellets over crown and below bust(6230) .... | 3500 | 10000 |

6331   6333

6331	**Groat.** *Dublin.* As 6328A (6321)...	1750	5000
6332	*Drogheda.* Similar (6322)...	2000	5500
6333	*Trim.* Pellets over crown and below bust (6323)	2250	6250

6334A   6335

6334	**Half groat.** *Dublin.* As 6328 (6324)	1350	4000
6334A	— Similar, but crosses by neck (6324A)	1500	4250
6335	*Drogheda.* As 6329 (6325)...	2000	5500
6336	*Trim.* As 6334 (6326)	1750	5000
6336A	— Similar, but two pellets over crown (6326A)........................	1750	5000
6337	**Penny.** *Dublin.* No tressure (6327)...............................	1100	3500
6338	*Drogheda.* Similar (6328)...	1100	3500
6339	**Halfpenny.** *Dublin.* (Reported, not confirmed) (6382A)		

VI. Ungoverned coinage of Desmond, 1470

| 6341 | **Groat.** *Cork.* Rosettes at neck. Same obverse die as 6353, but
EDWARDVS. R POSVI, etc., mint name. .... | *Extremely rare* |

IMPORTANT: for full concordance with the previous edition of this catalogue please see Appendix 2 on page 299.

	F £	VF £

BILLON AND COPPER

Issues of *c.***1460-61**

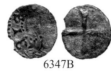

6347A   6347B   6348

6347   **Half farthing,** or 'Patrick' (Æ). PA branch TRIK branch, crown
       in centre. ℞ Quatrefoil tressure around large cross, no legend
       (6399)   1250   3000

6347A PA branch TRIK branch, crown in centre. ℞ Large cross, no legend
       (6400)   1000   2500

6347B — Similar, but retrograde inscription (6400A)   1100   2750

6347C — — ℞ P in one angle of cross (6400B)   1250   3000

Issue of 1462

6348   **Farthing** (billon). *Dublin.* Large crown, sun and roses in place of legend.
       ℞ Mint name, cross in centre (6401)..   1250   3000

Issue of 1463-65

6349   6351

6349   **Farthing** (Æ). PATRICIVS, mitred Saint's head facing, sun and
       rose. ℞ SALVATOR, cross with rose and sun in alternate angles.
       Several varieties, some with blundered legends (6402)..............   1500   3500

6350   **Half farthing** (Æ). Crown, no legend. ℞ Cross and pellets, no
       legend (6403)   1350   3250

Issue of 1467-70

6351   **Farthing** (Æ). Shield bearing three crowns. ℞ Cross with rose
       over sun at centre (6404)...   1500   3500

IMPORTANT: for full concordance with the previous edition of this catalogue please see Appendix
on page 299.

HENRY VI Restored, Oct. 1470 – Apr. 1471

Three Irish coins of the readeption of Henry VI, all groats of Cork, have been identified since the last edition of this catalogue appeared. The first of these chronologically is from a die originally in the name of Edward (from which a specimen in the original form exists in the National Museum of Ireland) which was overpunched with the name of Henry. The obverse die of the second readeption coin (and the first to be identified) is from new punches for the portrait and the letter I, the distinctive pre-readeption I perhaps being broken by the unusual stresses of the overpunching. The crown and the remaining letters are from the pre-readeption punches. The reverse die of the second specimen bears the pre-readeption I, and so predates the obverse. The third known readeption coin, in the collection of the National Museum of Ireland, is from the same obverse die as the second specimen, but from a different reverse die sunk with the new readeption I punch (and a new punch for the letter V). As was noted perceptively by the auction cataloguer of the second readeption coin when it was offered for sale in London, it shares its (pre-readeption) reverse die with another Cork groat in the name of Edward. This final Edward specimen, also with rosettes by neck, is from an obverse die sunk with the readeption portrait, I, and V punches, and a new crown punch. It thus post-dates the readeption, and therefore the three known readeption coins in the name of Henry are bracketed chronologically by punch- and die-linked coins in the name of Edward, all with rosettes by neck, thus securing the attribution of the coins of Henry beyond doubt.

	F	VF
	£	£

6353   6354

6353	**Groat.** *Cork.* HENRIC' over EDWARDVS Rosettes by neck. ℞ POSVI, etc., mint name.	*Extremely rare*
6354	— ENRIC' Rosettes by neck. ℞ POSVI, etc., mint name	*Extremely rare*

IMPORTANT: for full concordance with the previous edition of this catalogue please see Appendix 2 on page 299.

EDWARD IV, Second Reign, 1471-83

Following the demonetisation of the doubles in November 1470, the Irish parliament authorised a second cross and pellet issue in the English style, at a weight standard of 43.6 Troy grains to the groat, from Dublin, Drogheda and Trim. The coins are known to have been issued underweight, at least from Drogheda, and were often clipped, rendering them difficult to distinguish from the lighter third cross and pellets coinage of 1473, which was issued, initially from Dublin only, at a standard of 32 Troy grains to the groat. A systematic attempt to distinguish the pennies of these coinages has been made recently, but has not yet been attempted for the groats and halfgroats. The 1470 act, perhaps distracted by the fraught question of which regnal name to specify, mandated a title that was far too long for practical purposes, *"Edwardus dei gratia Rex Anglie & dominus hibernie, or the name of any other King for the time being."* As a result of this instruction, some Drogheda groats with Edward's English title may be attributed to the 1470 coinage with confidence, before the use of the Irish title became the standard (at the controlled mints) until the last years of the reign.

Activity at the controlled mints of Drogheda and Waterford was re-authorised by the parliament in July 1475, and Trim enjoyed a few months' resurgence during its occupation by Henry Grey from November 1478. In summer 1479, Edward, tiring of underweight but otherwise essentially indistinguisable Irish coin circulating in England, prohibited by personal decree all Irish mint activity outside of Dublin, and stipulated *"a notable difference of the* [device] *easy to be known to every body"*. From this came the Dublin Suns and Roses coinage, issued at 32 Troy grains to the groat. Intriguingly, some of these – those with larger obverse symbols, likely issued from 1480 under the mint mastership of James Keyting, the constable of Dublin castle and a leading figure in the rebellious rejection by the lords of the Pale of Grey's 1478 appointment by Edward as Lord Deputy of Ireland – bear Edward's English and French titles. In March 1483 Edward decreed the issue, from Dublin and Waterford, of what would become the Three Crowns coinage of Richard III and Henry VII (the design of which had been pre-figured by the obverse of the doubles farthing of 1467), but died before it could be implemented.

IMPORTANT: for full concordance with the previous edition of this catalogue please see Appendix 2 on page 299.

VII. Second Cross and Pellets Coinage (name of Edward), 1470

That only one groat and no halfgroats are assigned here to the second cross and pellets coinage of the governed mints of Dublin, Drogheda and Trim is not meant to imply that there were no others; but rather that it is not known how to distinguish the remainder from coins of the third cross and pellets coinage, under which all others are listed below.

	F £	VF £

6356

6356 Groat. *Drogheda.* English title (6329) .... *Extremely rare*

6357A

6358

			F	VF
6357	**Penny.** *Dublin.* No marks. ℞ Quatrefoil with pellet in centre of cross. Portrait as 6357A (6360)		45	225
6357A	— Two pellets above crown. ℞ Quatrefoil with pellet in centre of cross		35	200
6357B	— Two pellets above crown, pellet either side of neck. ℞ Quatrefoil with pellet in centre in centre of cross		35	200
6357C	— Suns either side of crown. ℞ Quatrefoil with pellet in centre of cross		35	200
6358	*Drogheda.* Pellets either side of crown. ℞ Quatrefoil with pellet in centre of cross.		135	525
6359	*Trim.* No marks. ℞ Quatrefoil with pellet in centre of cross (6380A)		135	525

IMPORTANT: for full concordance with the previous edition of this catalogue please see Appendix 2 on page 299.

VIII. Third, "Light", Cross and Pellets coinage, 1473

Many of the groats of this coinage have a G below bust, speculated to signify Germyn Lynche – and perhaps more as a control than a boast, given his indictment for striking underweight second coinage coin in 1472.

Mintmarks: pierced cross double fitchy, sun, rosette, plain cross, crown, trefoil

	F £	VF £

6366   6366D

		F £	VF £
6366	**Groat**. *Dublin*. G below bust (6330)..	125	400
6366A—	Similar, but annulets in two spandrels of tressure (6331)......	135	425
6366B—	As above, but with crosses by neck (6332).............................	175	525
6366C—	Annulets by neck (6333)	175	525
6366D—	Annulets by neck and in two spandrels of tressure (6334)	150	500

6366E

		F £	VF £
6366E—	Pellets in some spandrels of tressure (6335)...........................	175	525
6366F —	I on king's breast (6336)	325	900
6367	*Drogheda*. G below bust, annulets in two spandrels of tressure by crown (6339)..	175	525
6367A—	Similar, but annulets by neck and in two spandrels (6340) ...	225	650
6367B—	Trefoil on king's breast (6341)	225	650

6367C   6368A

		F £	VF £
6367C—	No marks other than G. ℞ Two extra pellets in one quarter (6341A)	175	525
6368	*Trim*. No letter on breast (6344)..	350	950
6368A—	Pellet in some spandrels of tressure and/or over crown (6345)..	325	900
6368B—	Pellets by neck (6346)	375	1000
6368C—	B on breast (6347)	475	1350

	F	VF
	£	£

6369 *Waterford*. No letter on breast, rosettes by neck (6348) .... | 240 | 700 |
6369A— Crosses or saltires by neck (6349) .... | 225 | 675 |

6369B

6369C

6369B— V on breast (6350) .... | 175 | 575 |
6369C— G on breast (6351) .... | 165 | 525 |

6369D

6370

6369D— No extra symbols on *obv*. ℞ Saltire in two quarters (6351A)
.... | 225 | 675 |

6370A

6371

6370 **Half groat.** *Dublin*. No marks by neck (6353) .... | 675 | 1750 |
6370A— Annulets by neck (6354) .... | 625 | 1600 |
6371 *Drogheda*. No marks by neck (6355).. | 1500 | 3750 |
6372 *Waterford*. No marks on breast or neck (6358) .... | 1500 | 3750 |
6373 **Penny.** *Dublin*. No marks by neck ℞ Rose in centre of cross ....
(6361A).. | 45 | 225 |
6373A— — ℞ D in centre of cross (6361B).. | 65 | 300 |
6373B— Crosses or saltires by neck. ℞ Plain cross (6362)................. | 45 | 225 |
6373C— — Similar, but with saltire to r. of crown ℞ Plain cross .....
(6363)... | 45 | 225 |
6373D— — ℞ Quatrefoil in centre of cross (6361) .... | 45 | 225 |
6373E— Similar, but with suns either side of crown .... | 45 | 225 |

IMPORTANT: for full concordance with the previous edition of this catalogue please see Appendix 2 on page 299.

	F	VF
	£	£

6373G

6373K

6374

6373F Penny. *Dublin.* Pellets by neck. ℞ Plain cross (6364) .... | 35 | 200
6373G— — ℞ Quatrefoil in centre of cross (6365) .... | 35 | 200
6373H— — ℞ Rose in centre of cross (6365A) .... | 45 | 225
6373 I — Pellets by crown and neck. ℞ Rose in centre of cross
(6365B) .... | 50 | 250
6373J — Mullets by neck. ℞ Quatrefoil in centre of cross (6366) ...... | 45 | 225
6373K— Mullets by crown ℞ Quatrefoil in centre of cross (6367)..... | 45 | 225
6374 *Drogheda.* No marks by neck. ℞ Plain cross (6369) .... | 50 | 250
6374A— — ℞ Quatrefoil in centre of cross (6370) .... | 45 | 225
6374B— Crosses by neck. ℞ Plain cross (6371) .... | 45 | 225
6374C— Pellets by neck. ℞ Plain cross (6372) .... | 45 | 225
6374D— — ℞ Small rose at centre of cross (6373) .... | 50 | 250
6374E — Pellets either side of crown. ℞ Plain cross........................... | 45 | 225
6374F — Pellets either side of crown and neck. ℞ Plain cross .... | 45 | 225
6374G— Pellets either side of neck. ℞ Quatrefoil in centre of cross... | 45 | 225
6374H— Pellets either side of crown and neck. ℞ Quatrefoil in centre
of cross .... | 45 | 225
6374 I — Pellets and rosettes by neck. ℞ Plain cross (6376) .... | 90 | 375
6374J — Pellet and rosette by neck, saltire by crown. ℞ Small rose at
centre of cross (6377).. | 110 | 475
6375 *Trim.* No marks. ℞ Plain cross (6380) .... | 135 | 525

6375A

6376

6375A— Similar, but crude bust of local style .... | 110 | 450
6376 *Waterford.* No marks. ℞ Quatrefoil in centre of cross (6382A) . | 125 | 500
6376A— Annulets by neck. ℞ Quatrefoil in centre of cross (6383A).. | 110 | 475
6376B— Pellets by neck. ℞ Quatrefoil in centre of cross (6384A) .... | 135 | 525
6376C— Crosses by neck and crown (6385) .... | 135 | 525
6376D— Crosses or saltires by neck. ℞ Quatrefoil in centre of cross
(6386).. | 110 | 425
6377 Halfpenny *Dublin.* Saltires by crown. ℞ Rose at centre of cross
(6387).. | 475 | 1250

IMPORTANT: for full concordance with the previous edition of this catalogue please see Appendix 2
on page 299.

IX. Issues of the Ungoverned Mints, c.1470-77.

Coins were issued outside of the governance of the Pale authorities by Limerick, Cork and Wexford during the 1470s, autonomously as a result of the Desmond rebellion by Limerick and Cork, and apparently opportunistically by Wexford. Most Limerick coins have rosettes or cinquefoils in opposite quadrants on the reverse.

		F £	VF £

6379   6379A

6379	**Groat.** *Cork.* Crude work. No marks by neck (6337)	2250	5500
6379A	— Pellets by neck (6338)...	2250	5500
6379B	— Rosettes either side of neck.	2250	5500

6380   6380A

6380	*Limerick.* L on breast, quatrefoils, crosses or saltires by neck, English and French titles (6342).................................	425	1100
6380A	— L on breast, rosettes or cinquefoils by neck, English and French titles (6343)	475	1250

6381   6383   6385

6381	*Wexford.* Very crude. R VILLA WEISFOR (6352)	3000	7500
6382	**Halfgroat.** *Limerick.* L on king's breast, rosettes or cinquefoils by neck (6356)	1350	3500
6382A	— Similar, no letter on breast (6357)	1250	3000
6383	*Wexford.* Crude work R VILLA WEISFOR (6359).........................	2750	7500
6384	**Penny.** *Cork.* Pellets by crown R Plain cross (6368)	375	1350
6384A	— Unusually large head R Plain cross (6368A)	425	1500
6384B	— Pellets by crown. R Quatrefoil in centre of cross (6368B) ...	375	1350
6385	*Limerick.* Rosettes or cinquefoils by neck, English and French titles (6378)	200	650
6385A	— Crosses or saltires by neck R Quatrefoil in centre of cross (6379)...	225	700

X. Bust with Suns and Roses/Rose on Cross coinage, 1479

6388   6388B

Mintmark: rose

	F	VF
	£	£

6388   Groat. *Dublin.* Sun and rose alternating at crown and neck.
R POSVI, etc., mint name. large rose at centre of cross................ 675   1850
6388A — Similar but rose and sun alternating at crown and neck
(6389)... 675   1850
6388B — Larger symbols by crown and neck, English and French titles
(6390)... 750   2000

6389   6389A   6398B

6389   Penny, small rose. *Dublin.* Sun and rose alternating at crown and neck.
R *Small* rose at centre of cross, rose and two suns and sun and two
roses alternating in angles (6395) 100   275
6389A — Similar, but rose and sun alternating at crown and neck
(6396)... 90   250
6389B — Similar, but larger symbols on *obv.*, English and French titles
(6397)... 110   300

6390B   6391

6390   Penny, large rose. *Dublin.* Sun and rose alternating at crown and neck.
R *Large* rose at centre of cross, no marks in angles (6393) 275   800
6390A — Rose and sun alternating at crown and neck (6393A)........... 250   750
6390B — Similar, but without symbols by crown (6393B) 350   950
6391   Halfpenny. *Dublin.* Saltires by crown. R Rose at centre of
cross, no marks in angles (6398).. 475   1250

IMPORTANT: for full concordance with the previous edition of this catalogue please see Appendix 2
on page 299.

EDWARD V, April – June 1483

It is thought, on the basis of recent research following earlier work by Carlyon-Britton, that coins were issued from Dublin and Drogheda during the reign of Edward V. The relevant punches were used continuously across the change of regnal name from Edward to Richard (one groat die of Drogheda was even overpunched from **EDW** to **RIC**), and both issues were, in different ways, in breach of Edward IV's commands of 1479 and 1483. For details of the portrait differences, see 'The Irish portrait pennies of Edward IV, Edward V and Richard III, 1465-1483', *BNJ* 87.

The best explanation appears to be that both mints seized the opportunity afforded them by Edward's death to either re-initiate, or revert to a type of, advantageous production which had been prohibited by Edward personally, but not by Irish statute. The Dublin pennies attributed to this short reign reverted to the standard English style, with the same portrait punch that was used for the pennies of Richard which followed them directly (and by which they may be identified), and were still underweight relative to their English counterparts; while the Drogheda mint, notwithstanding that its Suns and Roses output was compliant with the late king's 1479 command, was in breach of both this and his edict of 1483 by its very operation. An alternative explanation for these issues – that they were produced while Edward IV was still alive, but that mint activity everywhere in Ireland was ungovernably anarchic with respect to the Anglo-Norman legal framework and ignored the English king and feudal lord completely – is inconsistent with the historical evidence. In particular, it would be invalid to extrapolate from the conduct of the Desmond mints during the 1470s – which demonstrated these behaviours indeed, but in the context of outright sustained rebellion far beyond the Pale – to Dublin and Drogheda in 1483.

Note: The Edward V pennies, entirely by coincidence, have the same numbers after the current re-organisation and renumbering as they had under Edward IV in 2015.

6392

6393A

6392 Groat. *Drogheda.* Sun and rose alternating at crown and neck.
R **POSVI**, etc., mint name, large rose at centre of cross (6391)   600   1650
6392A— Similar but rose and sun alternating at crown and neck (6392)   675   1850
6393 Penny. *Dublin.* Portait as 6410. No obverse marks. R Quatrefoil in centre of cross
Extremely rare
6393A— — Pellets by neck. R Quatrefoil in centre of cross............... *Extremely rare*

6394

6394A

6394 *Drogheda.* Rose and sun alternating at crown and neck. R *Large*
rose at centre of cross, no marks in angles...................................   950   2750
6394A— Similar, but rose both sides at crown and neck   1000   3000

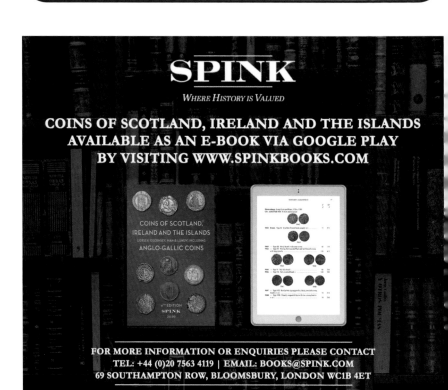

RICHARD III, 1483-1485 & HENRY VII, 1485-1509

The mints of Dublin and Drogheda continued issuing coins of the types of Edward V for a very brief period at the start of Richard's reign. On 18 July 1483, Richard issued a proclamation decrying the "*grete clamor, grugge, and complaints*" in England due to the spending of underwieght Irish coin there "*by subtill and crafty means of coveties persons*". He ordered the destruction of all punches and dies then existing in Ireland, and the production of a new coinage instead. That was to be the final end of the Drogheda mint, and of Irish portrait issues until the reign of Henry VII.

The new coins had the royal arms on the obverse and on the reverse the arms of Ireland, three crowns in pale, set over a cross with triple pellet ends, hence the coinage is known as the 'Three Crowns' issue. At one time it was thought that the coinage commenced in the reign of Edward IV, but it is now certain that it was first issued under Richard III and that rare coins with the name ЄDWARDVS were struck for Lambert Simnel, the Pretender 'Edward VI', who was crowned at Christchurch Cathedral, Dublin, on 24 May 1478.

The earliest Three Crowns coins struck in Henry's reign omit the sovereign's name, merely reading REX ANGLIE FRANCIE on one side and DOMINVS HYBERNIE or the Waterford mint name on the other. At Dublin, Gerald, Earl of Kildare, held what was virtually a royal court and it is noteworthy that the early coins bear no reference to King Henry. In contrast, at Waterford, which was a Butler (and anti-Yorkist) stronghold, the coins display the city's allegiance to Henry by having an initial 'H' below the lowest crown. After Simnel left Dublin on his abortive attempt to win the crown of England, the Three Crowns issue was continued but with the arms of the 'Great Earl' (the Fitzgerald saltire cross) inserted on small shields either side of the royal arms.

Simnel was defeated at the Battle of Stoke, and Henry then sent an envoy to Ireland to secure oaths of allegiance to the King and to grant a royal pardon to Kildare. It must be from this time that the later Three Crowns coins omit the Geraldine arms. The issue continued until about 1490 with Dublin as the sole mint. The half-groat normally had the DOMINVS VBERNIE legend or the mint name on the reverse, but there is an interesting variant which reads DOMINE KERIE and it has been postulated that this was a rendering of Domine Kyrie 'O Lord, O Lord' - a Latin-Greek mule.

There exist Irish portrait coins of Henry VII which may have been issued early in his reign, but the first regular portrait coinage was probably not issued before Kildare was allowed to return to Ireland in 1496 after his imprisonment at London for complicity in the Perkin Warbeck affair. The earliest groats of this issue are of English type and have an open crown, some are made from double-punched obverse dies and on some the normal POSVI DEVM legend is transformed to PROVIDEBO ADIVTORIVM, IVTOREVM, etc. These are superceded by arched-crown groats which become progressively cruder and on the latest coins the king's head appears in a plain circle without a tressure, often with grossly blundered inscriptions. The portrait halfgroats and most of the pennies are of comparatively good style and must come early in the series. A rare, but interesting penny has a large crowned H instead of a portrait, perhaps derived from the lower part of the Three Crowns type.

RICHARD III

Bust with Suns and Roses/Rose on Cross coinage

| | | F £ | VF £ |

6407

6408

6406	**Groat**. *Drogheda*. Sun and rose alternating at crown and neck. R Rose at centre of cross	2000	4750
6407	— — Similar, but RIC altered from ЄDW	2250	5000
6408	**Penny**. *Drogheda*. As 6406. R Large rose at centre of cross	2500	6000

Cross and Pellets coinage

6410

| **6410** | **Penny**. *Dublin*. Annulets by neck. R Quatrefoil in centre of cross. | 1350 | 3500 |
| **6411** | *Waterford*. Annulets by neck. R Quatrefoil in centre of cross ... | 1500 | 4000 |

The cross-and-pellets half-groat listed by Coffey is probably a coin of Edward IV's fifth coinage.

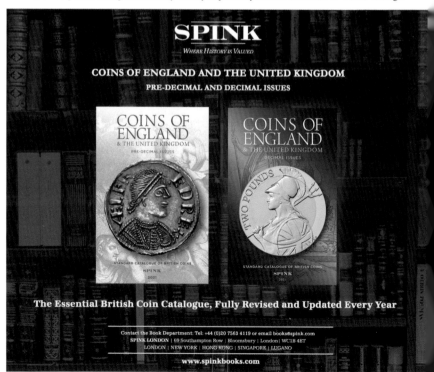

'THREE CROWNS' COINAGE, 1483-c.1490

Issued by Richard III, Henry VII, Lambert Simnel ('Edward VI') and Gerald, Earl of Kildare
Note: The earlier coins have the cross-ends terminating in triple pellets (pellet crosses); the later coins have triple annulets at the ends of the cross arms (annulet crosses). The change takes place at Waterford appreciably earlier than at Dublin and there are a number of pellet-annulet and annulet-pellet mules.

I. Richard III, 1483-85

	F	VF
	£	£

6412

6413

			F	VF
6412	**Groat**. No mint name (*Dublin*). RICARD, etc., arms over cross with pellet ends. ℞ DOMINVS hYBERNIE, three crowns in pale over cross		750	2250
6413	*Waterford*. Arms within tressure of four arcs. ℞ CIVITAS WATERFOORD, three flat crowns in tressure of eight arcs		2000	5250

Henry VII, early 'Three Crowns' issues, 1485-97

6414

6415

		F	VF
6414	**Groat**. No mint name (*Dublin*). As Richard III but REX ANGLIE FRANCIE. ℞ DOMINVS hYBERNIE. Pellet crosses	160	475
6415	— Similar, but DOMINVS hYBERNIE legend both sides. Pellet crosses	150	500

6416

		F	VF
6416	— As 6414 but ET REX hYBERNIE on *rev.*	175	650

	F £	VF £
6417 *Waterford.* hENRICVS etc., arms in quatrefoil. R Mint name, three crowns with h below, two lis by central crown, trefoils on points and angles of tressure. Pellet crosses	225	750
6418 — — No lis by centre crown, trefoils on points of *rev.* tressure but not in angles	225	750
6419 — Arms with no quatrefoil. R Three crowns with no tressure. Annulet crosses	300	1000

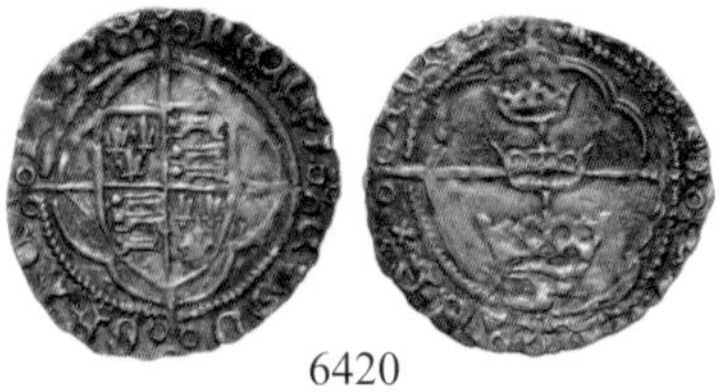

6420

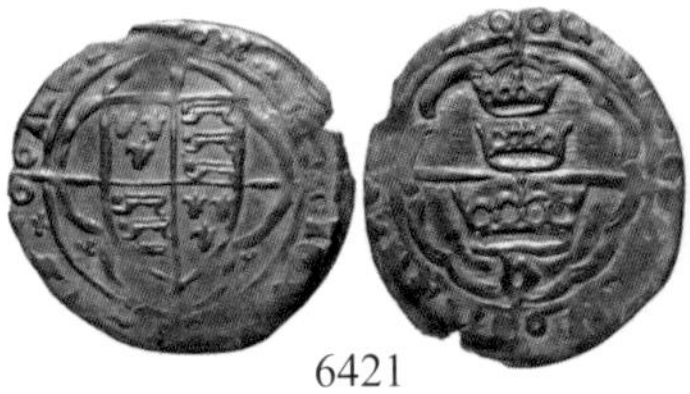

6421

	F	VF
6420 — Arms in quatrefoil. R Three crowns in tressure, h below. Annulet crosses	150	550
6421 — — Similar, but crosses or mullets in lower angles of quatrefoil.	165	600

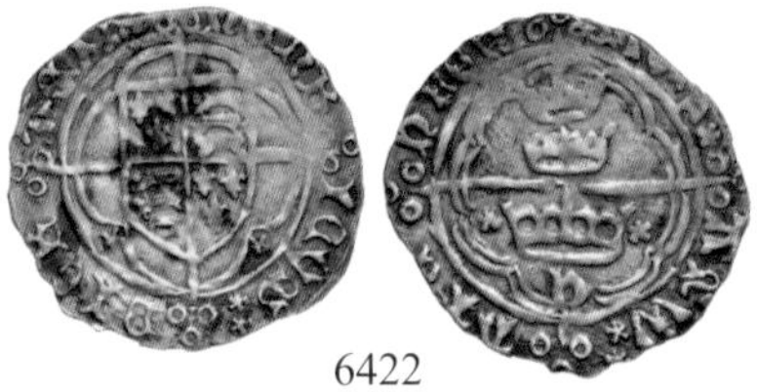

6422

| **6422** — — — Similar. R Stars by lower crown .... | 250 | 850 |

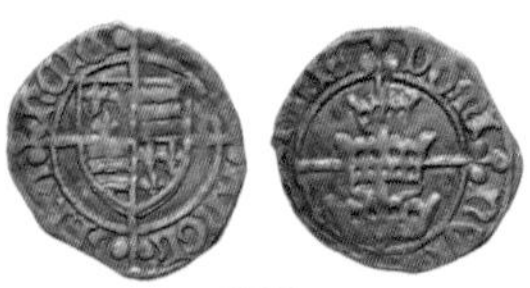

6423

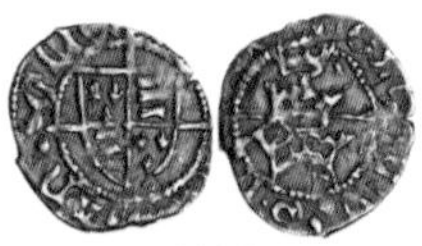

6424

	F	VF
6423 **Half groat.** No mint name (*Dublin*). As 6415, pellet crosses, REX ANGLIE FRANCIE R DOMINVS hIBERNIE	225	725
6423A — Similar, but lis below lower crown	275	850
6424 **Penny.** No mint name (*Dublin*). Similar	850	2500
6425 **Halfpenny.** No mint name (*Dublin*). Similar	1350	3500

III. Lambert Simnel, as 'Edward VI', May?-July? 1487

		F £	VF £

6426

6427

6426	**Groat.** No mint name (*Dublin*). As 6416, but €DWARDVS R€X ANL, etc. ℞ €T R€X hYB€RNI€. Pellet crosses	1750	5250
6427	— — €DWARDVS R€X ANGL FR etc. ℞ D€MINVS hYB€RNI€ ...	2000	5500
6428	*Waterford.* €DWARDVS etc., arms in quatrefoil, crosses in lower spandrels. ℞ CIVITAS WAT€RFORD, three crowns in tressure with reversed € below. Annulet crosses......................	2500	6500
6429	— — Similar *obv.* muled with Henry VII rev. die with h below crown	2500	6500
6430	— Henry VII *obv.* die muled with rev. similar to 6428	1750	4500
6430A	— Henry VII *obv.* die muled with a D€MINVS hYB€RNI€ die *rev.* having a reversed € over an h	1750	4500

IV. Geraldine issues, August?-October? 1487

6431

6432

6431	**Groat.** No mint name. R€X ANGLI€ Z FRAN etc., arms (not in quatrefoil) over cross with annulet ends, small shield with Fitzgerald arms either side. ℞ DOMINOS VR€RNI€ etc., three crowns above h within tressure	225	650
6432	— — Similar, but without h below crowns	200	600
6433	— As 6431, but muled with *Waterford* reverse	300	900

6434

6434	**Half groat**. No mint name. As 6432	525	1500
6434A	— DOMINOS legend both sides	600	1750

The Geraldine shields on the half groats are sometimes hardly visible.

Henry VII, late 'Three Crowns' issues, 1488-*c*.1490

	F £	VF £

6435   6436

6435 Groat. No mint name (*Dublin*). hƐNRICVS, etc. ℞ DOMINOS
VBERNIƐ, etc., h below crowns. Crosses with annulet ends .... | 200 | 600
6436 — — Similar, but obv. legend RƐX ANGLIƐ Z FRANC, etc......... | 175 | 525
6437 — — Similar, but DOMINOS VBERNIƐ both sides, h below crowns. | 225 | 700
6438 *Dublin.* hƐNRICVS, etc. ℞ Mint name, upper crown arched and
surmounted by cross, h below lower crown. Annulet crosses .... | 275 | 850

6440

6439 Half groat. No mint name (*Dublin*). RƐX ANGLIƐ Z FRANCIƐ,
cross with pellet ends. ℞ DOMINOS VBERNIƐ, h below crowns,
cross with annulet ends .... | 240 | 750
6440 — — Similar, but no h below crowns .... | 225 | 700
6441 — Annulet crosses both sides, no h .... | 225 | 700
6442 — DOMINOS legend both sides, h below crowns, annulet crosses. | 250 | 800
6442A— — Similar, but variant *obv.* reading DOMINƐ KƐRIƐ .... | 275 | 900
6443 — — As 6442, but no h .... | 250 | 800

6444   6446

6444 *Dublin.* As 6441, RƐX ANGLIƐ. ℞ Mint name, no h. Annulet crosses. | 240 | 750
6445 — hƐNRIC, etc. ℞ As above, but h below crowns .... | 350 | 1050
6446 Penny. No mint name (*Dublin*). RƐX ANG, etc., arms over cross
fourchée. ℞ DOMINOS VRƐRNIƐ, etc., h below crowns, no cross. | 750 | 2000
6447 — DOMINOS legend both sides, h below crowns .... | 850 | 2250
6448 *Dublin.* hƐNRICVS, etc. ℞ Mint name, no h below crowns .... | 750 | 2000

Portrait coinage

Early portrait issue?
It is not apparent at present exactly where this issue fits into the series.

F   VF
£   £

6450 **Penny.** *Dublin* ? Facing bust with open crown. R Large rose on
cross 1500 4000
The Waterford groat listed by Coffey as a Henry VII portrait issue coin is a piece of rather
poor style, the name is indistinct and it is possibly a coin of Edward IV's fifth coinage.

Late portrait issues, c.1496-1505
The standard weight of the groats of Groups I and IA is about 32 grains, but later groups
seem to have been struck to a standard of 28 grains.

6451   6452

6451 **Groat.** *Dublin*. I (at one time given to Henry VI). Broad facing head
(often from double-punched dies), open crown with straight band,
fleured tressure. R POSVI DEVM, etc., long cross pattée 200 525
6452 — — Similar, but *rev.* reads PROVIDEBO, etc. 300 750

6453   6455

6453 — — Smaller head, usually plain tressure. R POSVI, etc. 175 475
6454 — — — *rev.* reads PROVIDEBO, etc. 225 625
6455 — IA. Arched crown, bust breaks plain tressure. R As 6451 .... 200 525
6456 — — Similar, but *rev.* begins PROVIDEBO 225 625
6457 — IIA. Arched crown, trefoils on some points of tressure.
R Sideways h in centre of cross fourchée 350 950
6458 — — Similar, but annulets by crown and neck 450 1200

		F	VF
		£	£

6459 — IIB. Open crown with curved bands, plain tressure, saltires by neck. ℞ Cross fourchée 300 800

6460 — IIC. Similar, but saltires on points of tressure 275 725

6461   6464

6461 — IID. Open curved crown, no tressure, crosses by crown. ℞ Legends usually blundered 300 800

6462 — — Rosettes by crown 400 1050

6463 — — No marks by crown. ℞ Rosette in centre of cross........... 475 1250

6464 — III. Open flat crown, no tressure. ℞ Cross fourchée 225 625

6464A — — Similar, but reads SIVITAS 250 650

6465   6466   6467

6465 **Half groat.** *Dublin.* II. Arched crown, bust breaking tressure 1100 3000

6466 — — Arched crown, bust within fleured tressure, V (?) below bust. 1200 3250

6467 — — Similar, but V below bust inverted 1100 3000

Note: A half groat similar to 6460 (groats of group IIC) but with very blundered legends is in Ulster Museum. It may be a contemporary forgery.

6468   6470   6471

6468 **Penny.** *Dublin.* II. Large crown with jewelled arches over large h. ℞ Cross and pellets 1750 4500

6469 — — Facing bust with arched crown. ℞ Mint name, cross fourchée. 1250 3000

6470 — — Similar, but pellets by crown 1300 3000

6471 — — III. Bust with flat open crown. ℞ Mint name, cross and pellets.1100 2750

6471A — — Bust with open crown with curved band. ℞ Cross fourchée, rosette before DVBL 1350 3250

HENRY VIII, 1509-1547

No coinage was produced specifically for Ireland during the first twenty-six years of the reign of Henry VIII. A Tudor who believed in the central control of all the organs of state, particularly with regard to its fund-raising aspects, it was in keeping with Henry's policies that when a decision was taken to mint Irish money again, it was to be coined at London rather than in Ireland.

The new coins, known as 'Harp' groats, together with half groats, were made of silver debased slightly below the sterling standard and, after a second debasement in 1540, were forbidden to be re-imported into England. As on the Three Crowns coinage of the previous reign, the obverse type was the royal arms of England, though now the shield was crowned, and on the reverse a large crowned Irish harp appears for the first time in the Irish coinage. The earlier issues are of particular interest for, as on Henry's gold crowns, the initials of the royal consorts are inserted on the reverse: H A for Henry and Anne Boleyn, H I for Jane Seymour and H K for Katherine Howard. As queen succeeded queen perhaps it was to discourage ribald gibes that the consort's initials were eventually replaced with R for *Rex*.

Following the king's clash with Rome an Anglo-Irish parliament was prevailed upon to recognise Henry as the supreme head of the Church in Ireland and in June 1541, in order to dispose of the belief widely held amongst the Irish that the kings of England only held the temporal lordship of Ireland from the Pope, an Act was passed declaring Henry to be 'King of Ireland'. It is from 1541 that the title *Hiberniae Rex* replaces *Dominus Hiberniae* on the Harp coins.

Early in 1544 the silver content of the coins was reduced to two-thirds with one-third alloy and, at the same time, the current value of the groat was 'called up' to sixpence. Later the same year the fineness was decreased again to 50% silver. The Harp coins issued during the last year of the reign were minted at Bristol mint and these bear the WS monogram of William Sharrington, the Bristol mintmaster. They rival in baseness the most debased of henry's English coins, being struck in silver of only 0.250 fineness. Late Harp groats are the first Irish coins to be dated, having the regnal year '37' or '38' at the end of the reverse inscription. Harp groats are sometimes found with a small countermark of four pellets, possibly a mark of value which stamped on them in a later reign to indicate a reduction in value from 6d to 4d.

The Dublin coins which bear Henry's portrait were, in fact, minted after his death and are listed under the coins of Edward VI.

HARP COINAGE

1st Harp issue, 1534-40. Silver of 10 oz. 2 dwt. fineness (0.842). *Mm.* crown.

	F £	VF £

6472   6473

6472	**Groat.** With title *Dominus.* Crowned arms. ℞ Crowned harp dividing crowned h A (Henry and Anne Boleyn, 1534-5)	100	275
6473	— Similar, but with initials h I (Henry and Jane Seymour, 1536-7)	100	275

6474   6475

6474	— Similar, but with initials h K (Henry and Katherine Howard, 1540)	125	350
6475	— Similar, but with initials h R (*Henricus Rex*, 1540)	150	425

6476   6478

6476	**Half groat.** As 6462, h A (Anne Boleyn)	1000	2500
6477	— As 6373, h I (Jane Seymour)	1500	3750
6478	— As 6474, h K (Katherine Howard)	1250	3250

2nd Harp issue, 1540-42. Silver of 9 oz. 2 dwts. fineness (0.758). *Mm.* trefoil.

6479A

6479	**Groat.** With title *Dominus.* As 6475, except for mintmark	90	250
6479A	— — Similar, but omits VIII after king's name	125	350
6480	— With new title hIBERNIE REX on *rev.*	100	250

3rd Harp issue, 1543. Silver of 10 oz. fineness (0.833). *Mm.* rose.

	F £	VF £

6481   6482

6481	**Groat.** As 6480, except for *mm.*	110	275

4th Harp issue, 1544. Silver of 8 oz. fineness (0.666). *Mm.* lis.

6482	**Sixpenny groat.** As 6480, except for *mm.*	100	250

5th Harp issue, 1544-46. Silver of 6 oz. fineness (0.500). *Mm.* lis.

6483A

6483	**Sixpenny groat.** As above, but *rev.* legend ends 'REX S'	200	575
6483A	— — Similar, but regnal year '37' after REX	200	525

6th Harp issue, 1546-47. Silver of 3 oz. fineness (0.250). Made at Bristol under William Sharrington. *Mm.* lis.

6484   6484A

6484	**Sixpenny groat.** Different style, hENRIC 8. ℞ Legend commences with WS monogram and ends with regnal year '38'	175	450
6484A	— — Similar, but omits regnal year (issued posthumously)	275	750

6484B

6484B	**Harp groat** countermarked with quatrefoil or four pellets	475	1250

EDWARD VI, 1547-1553

The first coins issued in this reign were Harp groats which differ from the last issue of the previous reign only by the omission of the regnal year. Edward's ministers in England planned to finance the restoration of sound currency there by a continued but temporary issue of debased money. To conceal the means of reform from the general public the coins were minted with the name and portrait of Henry VIII, and when the Dublin mint was reopened in 1547 base groats, half groats, pence and halfpence of English type, and of marginally better alloy than the worst of Henry's Harp coins, were made current for 6 pence, 3 pence, 3 halfpence and 3 farthings. However in 1552 there was a reversion to the baser 0.250 fineness. Some of the dies are of English workmanship, though others of cruder style are obviously of local manufacture.

It sees likely that base English shillings, with a portrait of the young King Edward and with the harp mintmark, may have been struck expressly for Ireland in 1552 though there is no surviving documentary evidence for the issue. It is known that in Elizabeth's reign base Edward VI shillings were shipped to Ireland to pass first at sixpence and later at twopence and brass imitations known as 'bungals' continued to circulate in Connacht at a penny each. English base 'Rose' pennies of the York mint may also have been exported to Ireland. England's coinage was virtually restored to its old standards in 1551, but it was to be another ten years before an issue of 'fine' silver was made for Ireland.

For the first coins of the reign see no. 6484A of the Harp coinage, listed above.

Posthumous Old Head coinage, Henry VIII, 1547-c.1550

These have the name and portrait of Henry VIII, as do the English coins of the same period, the *sixpence* being the same size as the English *groat*. The earliest coins appear to be from dies made in England, others being from locally made dies.
Mintmarks: boar's head, harp, **P**.

	F £	VF £
6485 **Sixpence.** I. Bust of early London 'Tower' style. ℞ Arms over cross	125	575
6486 — II. Large facing bust of local style. Several varieties	200	850

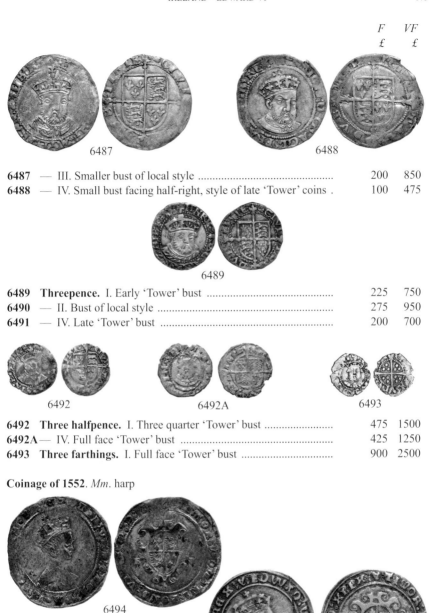

	F £	VF £

6487

6488

6487 — III. Smaller bust of local style 200 850
6488 — IV. Small bust facing half-right, style of late 'Tower' coins . 100 475

6489

6489 **Threepence.** I. Early 'Tower' bust 225 750
6490 — II. Bust of local style 275 950
6491 — IV. Late 'Tower' bust 200 700

6492   6492A   6493

6492 **Three halfpence.** I. Three quarter 'Tower' bust 475 1500
6492A— IV. Full face 'Tower' bust 425 1250
6493 **Three farthings.** I. Full face 'Tower' bust 900 2500

Coinage of 1552. *Mm*. harp

6494

6494A

6494 **Shilling.** Young crowned bust r. ℞ Arms in oval garnished shield,
      legend ends **MDLII** 750 3250
6494A— Contemporary brass imitation of the above, dated **MDXLIX** or **MDLII** 175 450

MARY TUDOR, 1553-1558

It was in this reign that the Pale and the power of the English crown was extended by the shiring and plantation of English settlers in Leix and Offaly and other areas. The quality of the silver used for the earliest of Mary's coins was an improvement on that of the previous reigns, but after Mary's marriage to Philip of Spain shillings and groats were issued with the heads of the two monarchs face to face and these were of only 0.250 fineness. To provide small change base 'rose' pennies from London mint were alse sent to Ireland.

Pre-marriage coinage, 1553-54. Base silver, 0.583 fineness, with a groat of about 32 grains *Mintmark:* fleur-de-lis.

Note: Counterfeits exist of most of these coins.

F   VF
£   £

6495

		F £	VF £
6495	**Shilling.** Crowned bust l. ℞ Crowned harp, legend ends MDLIII (1553)	1350	4500
6496	— Similar, but rev. legend ends MDLIIII (1554)	2500	7500

6497   6498

		F £	VF £
6497	**Groat**, undated. Similar type.	3750	10000
6497A	— Similar, but local dies, dated MDLIII......................................	*Extremely rare*	
6497B	— Similar, but local dies, dated MDLIV	*Extremely rare*	
	Doubt has been expressed about the authenticity of the above two coins.		
6498	**Half groat.** Undated. Similar. ℞ Harp, uncrowned	3250	9000
6499	**Penny.** Undated. As 6497, crowned harp	2750	8000

MARY AND PHILIP OF SPAIN, 1554-1558

Base silver, 0.250 fineness, with groat of about 48 grains. *Mintmarks*: portcullis, rose.

	F	VF
	£	£

6500

6500 Shilling. 1555. Busts face to face, date below. (ANGL to AN).
R Crowned harp. *Mm.* portcullis 275 1500

6501A   6501B

6501 Groat. 1555. Similar, but date by crown. *Mm.* portcullis, rose .. 85 300
6501A— 1556. *Mm.* portcullis, rose 85 300
6501B— 1557*. *Mm.* rose 80 275
  * The figure 7 on some of these coins looks like a 3.
6501C— — Similar, but 'Z' for 'ET' 75 275

6501D

6502

6501D— 1558. *Mm.* rose 100 350
6502 Penny of English type (made for currency in Ireland). (*London*).
  P. Z. M. D. G. etc., rose. R Royal arms, CIVITAS LONDON 60 225

ELIZABETH I, 1558-1603

The initial Irish coinage of Elizabeth was a continuation of the base issue of the previous reign, but in 1561 an issue of 'fine' silver shillings and groats restored the sterling standard to Ireland; the old base money was devalued and later called in. For the better part of the reign English money circulated in Ireland, as is evident from coin hoards and many single finds.

The shiring of Irish land and the extension of English law and land tenure proceeded apace; in the closing years of the century the final reduction of the independent and warlike Irish of the North who were led by O'Neill was conducted at first unsuccessfully by the Earl of Essex, until he was recalled to London to his execution, and later by Mountjoy. Large numbers of troops were involved in the campaign, and it was doubtless to help finance the war and pay the troops that an emergency Irish coinage of base silver money was ordered in 1601, with regal copper pence and halfpence also being coined.

Base coinage of 1558. Silver 3 oz. fine (0.250). *Mintmark*: rose.

	F £	VF £

6503    6504

		F	VF
6503	**Shilling.** Wt. 144 grs. Crowned bust l. R Crowned harp. (REGINA to RE)	275	1500
6504	**Groat.** Similar. (REGINA to REG)	110	525

'Fine' coinage of 1561. Silver 11 oz. fine (0.916). *Mintmark*: harp.

6505    6506

		F	VF
6505	**Shilling.** Wt. 72 grs. Crowned bust l. R Crowned shield. (REGI to REG, RGI)	250	1250
6506	**Groat.** Similar. (REGI to RE)	300	1500

Third (base) coinage, 1601-02. Silver 3 oz. fine. *Mintmarks*: trefoil, star. martlet.

	F £	VF £

6507

6507 Shilling. Wt. 88 grs. Arms. ℞ Crowned harp. *Mm.* trefoil, star, martlet. 150   650

6508

6509

6508 Sixpence. Similar. *Mm.* trefoil, star, martlet 150   525
6509 Threepence. Similar. *Mm.* trefoil, star, martlet 225   850

COPPER

6510

6510A

6510 Penny, 1601. E R at sides of shield. ℞ Date at sides of crowned
harp. *Mm.* trefoil, star 35   135
6510A— 1602. *Mm.* martlet 40   145
6510B— Undated. *Mm.* star 325   950

6511

6511 Halfpenny, 1601. Similar. *Mm.* trefoil, star 75   250
6511A— 1602. *Mm.* martlet 135   475

JAMES I, 1603-1625

The war in the North had ended in defeat and famine for the native Irish, and though with the accession of a Scottish monarch a general amnesty was declared, once the power of the Northern chiefs had been drastically curtailed it was only a matter of time before the confiscation of great tracts of land and the establishment of new plantations of Scot and English led to the final subjection of Ulster. In order to replace Elizabeth's war-time base money James issued a new coinage in 'fine' silver between 1603 and 1607 which was minted in London; but his objective was a uniform currency throughout his realm of 'Great Britain and Ireland' and thenceforward only the standard silver coins of the Tower mint were made for use in Ireland. The smaller Irish shilling was then tariffed at ninepence sterling, the groat at threepence.

In 1613 the farthing tokens manufactured under royal licence by Lord Harrington were authorized as legal tender for use in Ireland as well as England (though this was not confirmed by the Irish Parliament until 1622). Though these coins were made for circulation in both islands they are included in this catalogue owing to the prominence given to the Irish harp used as the reverse type, and because it has been suggested that the coins struck on oval flans were originally intended for use in Ireland only. These farthings were stamped in strips before being punched out, and sometimes can still be foun d in strips of various lengths.

Mintmarks: Bell 1603-4
                Martlet 1604-5
                Rose (large and small) 1605-6
                Escallop 1606-7

Latin legends: EXVRGAT DEVS DISSIPENTVR INIMICI
                  HENRICVS ROSAS REGNA IACOBVS
                  TVEATVR VNITA DEVS

SILVER

First coinage, 1603-4. With title 'ANG · SCO · FRA · ET HIB · REX'

	F	VF
	£	£

6512   6513

		F	VF
6512	**Shilling.** First bust r., short square-cut beard. ℞ EXVRGAT etc., crowned harp. *Mm.* bell	90	400
6513	— Second bust r., pointed beard. *Mm.* bell, martlet	100	425

	F	VF
	£	£

6514

6514 **Sixpence.** First bust. ℞ TVEATVR, etc. crowned harp. *Mm.* bell, martlet 70 300

Second coinage, 1604-7. With title 'MAG · BRIT · FRA · ET HIB · REX'

6515   6516

6515 **Shilling.** Third bust r., longer square-cut beard. ℞ HENRICVS etc. *Mm.* Martlet, rose, escallop 70 300
6516 — Fourth bust, long beard, less ornate cuirass. *Mm.* rose, escallop. 100 425

6517

6517 **Sixpence.** First bust, as 6514, but MAG BRIT. ℞ TVEATVR, etc. *Mm.* Martlet, escallop 65 300

COPPER, ETC.

Farthing tokens, issued under royal licence, from 1613

6520

6520 Farthing. I. Small size 'Harington' issued with tinned surface.
Crown over crossed sceptres. ℞ Crowned harp. *Mintmarks*
(sometimes between sceptres or on band of crown): A, B, C, D, F,
S, ermine, millrind, pellet, :L, trefoil, crescent, mullet or none ...   45   125
6520A— As last, but with untinned surface   40   100
6521   — II. Normal size, untinned 'Harington' issue. Similar. *Obv.*
inscription starts at 11 o'clock. *Mintmarks*: cinquefoil, saltire, lis,
martlet, mullet, trefoil   20   40

From 1616

6522   6523

6522 Farthing. III. 'Lennox' issue. Similar type, but slightly larger flan
and *obv.* inscription starts at 1 o'clock. *Mintmarks*: annulet, ball, bell,
coronet, crescent, cross fleury, cross fourchée, dagger, eagle's head,
flower, fusil, grapes, key, lion passant or rampant, 3 lis, mascle,
quatrefoil, rose, star, stirrup, thistle, trefoil, triangle, tun, woolpack.   10   30
6523   — IV. Similar, but oval flan, *obv.* legend starts at 7 o'clock.
Mintmark: cross pattée   60   120

The farthing tokens of James I and Charles I were minted on metal strips and
afterwards cut out. The above strip consists of tokens of Charles I, no. 6524.

CHARLES I AND THE GREAT REBELLION

English silver and the 'royal farthings' made privately under licence circulated in Ireland during the first fifteen years of the reign of King Charles, supplemented by some foreign coin, principally silver and a little gold from Scotland, the Low Countries, Spain or Spanish-America and from Portugal and even copper *tournois* from France and *turners* form Scotland.

Racial and religious discrimination and the dispossession of large numbers of the native Irish population earlier in the century had assured a permanently discontented majority of the population, and tension exploded into open rebellion in October 1641. Two protestant Lord Justices had prevented the Irish parliament passing a Royal bill to alleviate Catholic grievances. This precipitated an attempt to seize Dublin Castle which failed, but the irish rose in Ulster under Sir Felim O'Neill and slaughtered many thousands of the new 'planters'. The insurrection spread throughout Leinster and Munster and English troops and Protestant settlers fell back on fortified towns such as Londonderry and Drogheda in the North and Bandon, Kinsale and Cork in the South. An army raised in Scotland under General Munro landed in Ulster to suppress the insurrection, and when in 1642 civil war broke out in England between King Charles and the English parliament, Lord Inchiquin was appointed to command the Protestant forces in Munster.

Additional coin was urgently needed and the Lords Justices in Dublin issued an emergency currency consisting of pieces of silver plate cut to specified weights which were to circulate at their bullion value. The first issue of 1642 showed only the weights in pennyweights and grains, though later the lower denominations had the number of pence indicated by annulets.

The Irish Catholics set up their own Council, the Catholic Confederacy, at Kilkenny in 1642, where they proclaimed their loyalty to the king. They, too, issued their own coinage of silver halfcrowns, the so-called 'Blacksmith's Money', copying the type of the king's English coins; and they also struck large copper halfpence and farthings of the type of the small and unpopular 'royal' farthing. The following year the Confederacy issued crowns and halfcrowns with a large cross on one side.

In the meantime, the Lords Justices at Dublin followed their first 'weight money' issues with a new coinage, the first type of which had the sterling denomination stamped on both sides though later coins acknowledged allegiance to King Charles with a crowned 'CR' on the obverse. This latter coinage is usually known as 'Ormonde Money' after the Earl of ormonde who was appointed Lieutenant of Ireland in 1643. In 1646 another issue of 'weight money' was struck, this time in gold to the equivalent weights of the French pistole (*Louis d'or*) and double pistole which were legal tender in Ireland. These gold coins are now extremely rare.

Dissension amongst the Catholics prevented the capture of Dublin and in 1646 the arrival of the Papal Nuncio, Rinuccini, with financial aid from France, put an end to secret negotiations for a peace settlement between the Confederates and the king. After the battle of Naseby the king's cause seemed to be lost in England and Ormonde, a Protestant royalist, preferred to surrender the capital to a Cromwellian expedition rather than to risk a Catholic victory.

Counterstamped or crudely struck copper money, sometimes even stamped on foreign coins, had been issued by the parliamentary forces besieged at Bandon, Cork, Kinsale and Youghal; and the Cork garrison had also made crude silver shillings and sixpences from cut plate. The final coinage of the Rebellion period was issued by Ormonde after he returned to Ireland in 1648 to lead a more united royalist alliance. After the execution of Charles I he struck crowns and halfcrowns in the name of Charles II, 'Defender of the Faith'.

CHARLES I, 1625-1649

Farthing tokens, issued under royal license, 1625-44

COPPER

	F	VF
	£	£

6524   6525   6526

6524   Farthing. I. 'Richmond' issue. As 'Lennox' coins. Single arched
        crown, no inner circles. *Mintmarks*: A, annulet, bell, book, cinquefoil,
        crescent, cross with pellets, cross pattée, cross fitchy, cross patonce,
        cross saltire, dagger, ermine, estoile, eye, fish-hook, fleece, fusil, two
        fusils, gauntlet, halberd, harp, heart, horseshoe, leaf, lion passant,
        lion rampant, lis, demi-lis, three lis, martlet, mascle, nautilus, rose,
        shield, spearhead, tower, trefoil, woolpack   10   30

P6524 — Proof, *mm.* cross pattée .... *Silver*   EF £1250

6525   — II. Transitional issue. Similar, but double-arched crown.
        Mintmarks: harp, quatrefoil   20   50

6526   — III. 'Maltravers' issue. Similar, but inner circles. *Mintmarks*: bell,
        billet, cross pattée, cross fitchy, harl, lis, martlet, portcullis, rose,
        woolpack   15   35

6527   6529

6527   — IV. As 6524, but on oval flan and legend commences at bottom
        left. *Mintmarks*: crescent, cross pattée, demi-lis, martlet, millrind,
        rose, scroll, 9   75   150

6528   — V. Similar, but double-arched crown. *Mintmark*: lis   45   90

6529   — VI. 'Rose' farthing. Smaller thicker flan, usually with a brass
        wedge inserted. Crown over sceptre. ℞ Crowned single rose.
        Mintmarks: crescent, cross pattée, lis, martlet   15   35

P6529 — Proof, *mm.* lis .... *Silver*   EF £1250

6530   6531

6530   — VII. Similar, with single-arched crown. ℞ Crowned single rose.
        Mintmarks: crescent, mullet   10   25

P6530 — Proof, *mm.* crescent .... *Silver*   EF £1250

6531   — VIII. Similar, but sceptres below crown. *Mintmark*: mullet .   35   75

THE GREAT REBELLION

Coinages of the Lords Justices

Issue of 1642. Sometimes referred to as 'Inchiquin Money', stamped from cut pieces of flattened plate

	F £	VF £

6532   6533

		F	VF
6532	**Crown.** Irregular polygon stamped with the weight '19 dwt. 8 gr.' in circle both sides	3500	8500
6533	**Halfcrown.** Similar, but '9 dwt. 16 gr.'	1750	4250

6534   6536

6534	**Shilling.** Similar, but '3 dwt. 21 gr.'	2750	7500
6535	**Ninepence.** Similar, but '2 dwt. 20 gr.'	5500	13500
6536	**Sixpence.** Similar, but '1 dwt. 22 gr.'	6250	15000
6537	**Groat.** Similar, but '1 dwt. 6 gr.'	5000	12500

Note: Modern counterfeits exist of most of these coins, but there are also a number of genuine varieties.

Annulets issue of 1642

6538	**Ninepence.** *Obv.* as 6535. ℞ Nine annulets	8500	17500

6539

6539	**Sixpence.** *Obv.* as 6536. ℞ Six annulets	7500	15000
6540	**Groat.** *Obv.* as 6537. ℞ Four annulets	6000	12500
6541	**Threepence.** '23 gr' in circle. ℞ Three annulets	6500	13500

Issue of 1643. Sometimes called 'Dublin Money'

	F £	VF £

6542    6543

		F	VF
6542 Crown. V^s both sides		2250	7000
6542A— Similar, but from smaller dies		2500	7500
6543 Halfcrown. II^{s}VI^p both sides		3000	9000

Issue of 1643-44. Usually called 'Ormonde Money'

6544    6550

6549

6545    6546    6547    6548

		F	VF
6544 Crown. Crowned CR. ℞ V^s within double circle		400	1050
6545 Halfcrown. Similar. ℞ II^{s}VI^p		350	950
6546 Shilling. Similar. ℞ XII^p		250	800
6547 Sixpence. Similar. ℞ VI^p		150	475
6548 Groat. Similar. ℞ IIII^p		100	350
6549 Threepence. Similar. ℞ III^p		150	525
6550 Twopence. Similar. ℞ II^p		375	1100

For varieties, see Aquilla Smith, 'On the Ormonde Money', *PRSAI* (1854)

Ormonde's gold coinage of 1646

	F	VF
	£	£

6551   6552

6551 **Double pistole.** Irregular polygon stamped with '8 dwtt. 14 gr.' on
both sides 75000 175000

6552 **Pistole.** Similar, but stamped '4 dwtt. 7 gr.' both sides 40000 100000

Ormonde's silver coinage of 1649. Issued after the death of Charles I
Mintmark: lis

6553

6553 **Crown.** CAR · II · D · G · MAG · BRIT around large crown.
R FRA · ET · HIB · REX · FID · D. & around V^s 5000 12500

6554

6554 **Halfcrown.** Similar, but II^{s}VI^p on *rev.* 3500 9000

ISSUES OF THE CONFEDERATE CATHOLICS

Kilkenny issues of 1642-3

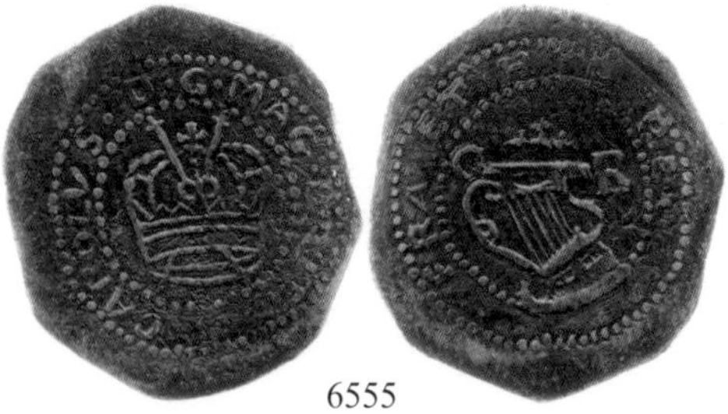

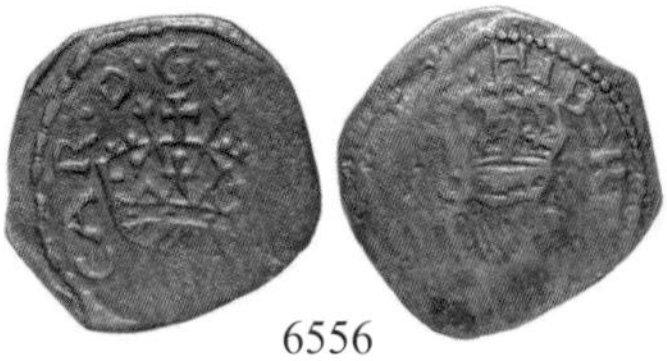

	F	*VF*
	£	£

6555

6556

6555 **Halfpenny.** Æ. Crown and two sceptres. ℞ Crowned harp. *Mint-mark.* harp 250   900

6556 **Farthing.** Æ. Similar 350   1250

Contemporary forgeries of the last two are common.

6557

6557 **'Blacksmith's Halfcrown** (date uncertain). Crude copy of London issue. King on horseback left, cross on housings. ℞ Oval shield between C R. *Mm.* cross (*obv.*), harp (*rev.*) 750   2250

6557A

6557A— Similar, but without cross on horse's housings 800   2500

Issues of 1643-4. Sometimes called 'Rebel Money'

F VF
£ £

6558

6558   **Crown.** Large cross, pellet or star in margin. ℞ Vˢ 4500 12500

6559

6559   **Halfcrown.** Similar, small star in margin. ℞ IIˢVIᴰ 5000 13500

LOCAL ISSUES OF THE SOUTHERN 'CITIES OF REFUGE'

6560   **Bandon (Bridge). Æ Farthing.** BB ℞ Three castles 800 2250

6561

6561A

6561   **Cork. Æ Shilling.** Octagonal. CORK / 1647. ℞ X.II 2750 9000
6561A— **Æ Sixpence.** Similar. ℞ VI 1350 4250

   Modern forgeries of the last two are not uncommon.

Modern forgery

F   VF
£   £

6562A

6562 — Æ **Halfpenny.** CORK in double circle. ℞ Castle 1250 4500
6562A— Æ **Farthing.** CORK or CORKE in circle of pellets. ℞ Castle   475 1750
6562B— — CORK countermarked on copper coin 325 1250

> The brass pieces countermarked with CORKE and a
> lion's head are struck on the 1677 tokens of William
> Ballard and may be of the period of the civil war, 1689-
> 91. This countermark also appears on worn English
> shillings of Elizabeth.

6563 **Kinsale. Æ Farthing.** K · S in circle of pellets. ℞ Chequered
      shield 350 1350
6563A **Kilkenny. Æ Halfpenny.** Castle with K below countermarked on
      copper coin 525 1750
6563B— — Five small castles (in form of a rosette) countermarked on
      copper coin (possibly New Ross ?) 575 1850
6564 **Youghal. Æ Farthing.** YT ℞ Ship (yawl) 650 2000

6565

6565 — Bird above YT, 1646 below. ℞ As above 375 1500
6565A— **Circular farthing.** YT ℞ Fish or whale ? 675 2250

THE COMMONWEALTH

The conquest of Ireland by Cromwell and his Puritan army continued until Galway finally
surrendered in 1652. Over 30,000 Irish Catholic soldiers were allowed to leave Ireland for
France and Spain, Catholic landowners were transported to the West of Ireland and nine
counties were confiscated to grant land to Cromwell's army or sold to pay his troops.

No coinage was minted especially for Ireland, but from 1649 the Commonwealth gold
and silver coins had a shield bearing the Irish harp set alongside the republican arms of
England, the cross of St George. However, a large number of copper tokens, mostly pennies
were issued by the merchants of the old cities and the new towns. Ireland was formally
declared part of the Protectorate in 1653, and the granting of free trade with England and
Scotland helped to raise the prosperity of the new merchant classes.

CHARLES II, 1645-1685

In 1660 Charles II granted a patent to Sir Thomas Armstrong for a term of twenty-one years for coining farthings and at the same time prohibited the use of all other tokens. The Irish authorities were, however, opposed to the circulation of these farthings in Ireland, though they were considerably heavier than the 'royal' farthings of the previous reign and, as a result, comparatively few were issued. In consequence, during the ten years 1663 to 1673, further large numbers of private merchants' tokens were put into circulation. It was probably about 1674 that the curious coins known as 'St Patrick's money' were made, though little is known of the circumstances of the issue. These have a figure of the saint on one side and a kneeling figure of King David playing the harp on the other, and most have a milled edge and a plug of brass impressed into the flan to discourage counterfeiting. As the obverse of the farthing closely copies the type of the Dublin farthing token of Richard Greenwood this coinage should, perhaps, be more properly treated as a token issue. After they were called in about 1680/1 a large quantity were taken by an emigrant named Mark Newby to the State of New Jersey, where they were allowed to circulate officially as currency. They also circulated in the Isle of Man.

More traders' tokens were issued between 1676 and 1679, and the City of Dublin issued its own halfpenny in that year, but the following year Irish regal halfpennies were minted under a new patent granted to Sir Thomas Armstrong and Col. George Legge for a term of twenty-one years. These coins were considerably larger and heavier than most of the traders' tokens and successfully drove them out of circulation.

	F	VF	EF
	£	£	£

Armstrong's coinage of 1660-1

6566

6566 Farthing. Crown and two sceptres. ℞ Crowned harp. *Mm.* plumes
or no mintmark. Undated. Inverted die axis 40 125 375
— Struck with upright die axis, *en medaille* 65 195 425
— — proof struck in silver .... *Extremely rare*

'St Patrick's' coinage. Usually with milled edge and brass spot on the rev.

6567

6567 Large size. King David playing harp, crown above, FLOREAT REX.
℞ St Patrick holding cross and crozier preaching to multitude, arms
of Dublin to r., ECCE GREX .... 1700 3000 —
— — Proof struck in silver .... *Extremely rare*
— Similar, with FLORE AT T REX instead .... 1950 3500 —

		F	VF	EF
		£	£	£

6568 Large size. Similar, but star in *obv*. legend 800   1750   —

— Similar, with plain edge 900   1950   —

— — proof struck in silver .... *Extremely rare*

6569

6569 Small size. As above. ℞ St Patrick with patriarchal cross driving
away reptiles, cathedral to r., QVIESCAT PLEBS 300   800   2500

6570 — Stars in *rev*. legend 400   950   —

— — Similar. Proof struck in silver 5000   —   —

— — Similar. Proof struck in gold .... *Unique*

6571 — Martlet below king 500   1500   —

6572 — Annulet below king 450   1200   —

6572A— Nimbus around St Patrick 2500   —   —

— — Similar. Proof struck in silver 15000

6572B— Annulets and martlet below king 450   1300   —

Armstrong and Legge's regal coinage, 1680-84

6574

6574 Halfpenny. Laur. and draped bust r. ℞ Crowned harp. Large lettering.

1680 pellets in legend 95   300   1000

1680 Similar. Proof struck in silver 5000   —   —

1680 Similar. GARTIA error 300   750   —

1680 crosses in legend on *obv*. 250   550   —

1681 100   325   1200

1682 .... *very rare* 125   400   —

Many legend varieties and errors exist for all dates

	F	VF	EF
	£	£	£

6575

6575 **Halfpenny.** Similar, but small lettering.

	F	VF	EF
1681	*Extremely rare*		
1681 Similar. Struck in silver...	900	3000	—
1682	125	400	1000
1683	125	400	1000
1683 MAG BR FRA larger than the rest of the legend	135	475	—
1684	150	550	—

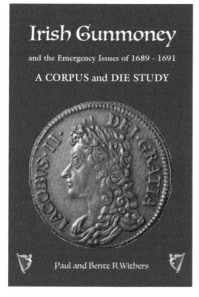

JAMES II, 1685-1691

In 1685 James II transferred the unexpired patent for minting halfpence to Sir John Knox, the Lord Mayor of Dublin, and these were issued until 1688. James fled from England to France in that year and the crown was offered to his daughter, Mary and her husband, William of Orange. After drumming up Catholic support on the continent, James landed in Ireland in March 1689 to continue the struggle. Having insufficient funds to prosecute the war, a plan was devised to issue official base metal token coins which would be exchanged for sterling silver after the war was won, and a nominal month as well as the year was inscribed on them so that they could be redeemed in stages over a period of time. The coins were made of brass or latten from old cannon, bells and other scrap metal and were called 'Brass Money', though they later became known as 'Gunmoney' coins.

The first issue consisted of halfcrowns, shillings and sixpences, but in 1690, as stocks of metal ran down, the sizes of halfcrowns and shillings were reduced and the old halfcrowns were restruck as crowns. This means that on many pieces the intended design is compromised by the undertype. Unlike the lower denominations the crowns are not dated by month as well as year. Later that year, crowns, groats, pence and halfpence were also struck in pewter and most had a plug of copper alloy through them to distinguish the genuine pieces from counterfeits which might be cast in lead. The Gunmoney coins became increasingly unpopular, and as soon as William III seized the Dublin mint, after the Battle of the Boyne, the coins were reduced to their intrinsic value; in 1691 they were demonetized. It is for this reason that they are relatively common today.

The gunmoney coins were struck in Dublin and later also in Limerick. There are some portrait types which some authorities have allocated to Limerick. It is unknown when the Limerick mint began functioning, but Fr Gerard Rice (*SNC* Sept 1989) states that of the two coining presses in use in Dublin, named the 'James' and the 'Duchess', the 'Duchess' press was sent to Limerick in March 1689/90. Coins continued to be struck at Limerick until October, 1690. Limerick continued to hold out for James well into 1691 and the mint there struck halfpennies, small size on freshly prepared blanks, and large size overstruck on large Gunmoney shillings.

Regular coinage

	F	VF	EF
	£	£	£

6576

6576   Halfpenny. Laur. draped bust left. ℞ Crowned harp.

	F	VF	EF
1685 Die axis 0° or 180°	90	295	800
1685 Struck in silver	*Extremely rare*		
1686 Die axis 0, 180° or other	90	295	800
1686 Struck in silver	*Extremely rare*		
1687	*Extremely rare*		
1688	120	400	—

	F	*VF*	*EF*
	£	£	£

CIVIL WAR COINAGE, 1689-91

'Gunmoney' coinage, 1689-90

Struck in *Dublin* unless otherwise noted

6577

6577 Crown (overstruck on large size Gunmoney halfcrown) 1690.
King on horse l., horse's mane visible on the full length of the neck,
legend commences to r. of head 175   500   1000

6577A

6577A — Similar, but legend commences to l. of head, small lettering,
different shields 225   525   1100

6578

6578 — Similar, portrait of different style, horse's mane only visible at the top of neck,
and tail with loop-like curl at top. Rev. legend split **VICT/ ORE**   90   175   575
6578A — Similar, rev. legend is split **VICTO/ RE**   165   300   725
6578B — Similar, reads **RIX** for **REX**   295   575   1000
6578C — Similar, **RIX** and * stop after **CHRIS** ....   *Extremely rare*

There are many varieties of reverse, including three different shapes of shield, mis-spellings, variant
punctuation or abbreviation mark, some of which mule with one or more of the three main obverse types
mentioned above, as well as die axis variations.

For strikings in other metals, gold, silver, copper and pewter, see number **6585**

F	VF	EF
£	£	£

Note: *the following coins are unusual in that they have the* **month** *as well as the year of issue. At this period the New Year commenced on March 25th, hence January 1689 followed December 1689, and coins dated March 1689 and March 1690 were issued in the same month. The abbreviations used are shown in parentheses.*

6579C

Limerick bust

6579 Halfcrown. *Large size.* Laur. and draped bust left. Ɍ Crown over
sceptres dividing *J R*, XXX above, month of issue below. Date at 12 o'clock.

		F	VF	EF
A	1689 July (*July*) large garnished *J R* No stops by date	70	175	500
A2	— — smaller and less garnished *J R*	150	300	750
B	— August (*Aug Aug: Augt:*)..	50	150	400
B2	— — No stop after II...	50	150	400
B3	— — No stop after II, OB over BV..	50	150	400
B4	— — (*Aug:*) Struck in silver	*Extremely rare*		
B5	— — (*Augt:*) Date at 6 o'clock	175	400	1100
C	— September (*Sepr Sepr:*)	50	150	400
C2	— — No stop after II...	50	150	400
C3	— — No stop after II, stop after GRATIA	50	150	400
C4	— — No stops on obverse	80	175	450
C5	— — Stop after BR entered over an A	80	175	450
C6	— — Struck in silver	*Extremely rare*		
D	— October (*Oct: Octr. OCT OCT. OCTr. OCTR.*)	50	150	400
D2	— — No stop after II...	50	150	400
D3	— — Stop after GRATIA..	50	150	400
D4	— — DFI for DEI...	50	150	400
D5	— — No stop after MAG	50	150	400
D6	— — (*Oct:*) Struck in silver	*Extremely rare*		
D7	— — (8BER)	100	275	625
E	— November (*Nov:*)	50	150	400
E2	— — (*Nov:*) No stop after DEI	50	150	400
E3	— — (*Nov:*) No stop after II	50	150	400
E4	— — (*Nov:*) No stops on obverse	50	150	400
E5	— — (*Nov:*) No stop after HIB	50	150	400
E6	— — (*Nov:*) No stop after date	50	150	400
E7	— — (*Nov:*) Struck in silver..	*Extremely rare*		
F	— December (*Dec. Dec:*)	50	150	400
F2	— — No stop after II	50	150	400
G	— January (*Jan Jan. Jan:*)	50	150	400
G2	— — DFI for DEI...	50	150	400

		F	VF	EF
		£	£	£
6579	**Halfcrown.** *Large size.*			
G3	— — No stop after II	50	150	400
G4	— — (*Jan:*) Struck in silver	*Extremely rare*		
H	— February (*Feb Feb. Feb:*)	50	150	400
H2	— — No stops either side of II	50	150	400
H3	— — Stop after GRATIA	50	150	400
H4	— — Stop before DEI	50	150	400
H5	— — (*Feb:*) Struck in silver	*Extremely rare*		
I	— March (*Mar Mar. Mar:*)	50	150	400
I2	— — Stop after GRATIA	50	150	400
I3	— — (*Mar. Mar:*) Struck in silver	*Extremely rare*		
J	1690 March (*Mar:*)	60	160	425
J2	— — Stop after GRATIA	60	160	425
J3	— — (*Mar:*) MAO error for MAG	115	300	700
J4	— — (*Mar:*) Struck in silver	*Extremely rare*		
K	— — 'Limerick' bust	75	200	525
L	— April (*Apr. Apr:*)	50	150	400
L2	— — (*Apr.*) Struck in silver	*Extremely rare*		
L3	— — (*Apr.*) Struck in gold	*Extremely rare*		
L4	— — (*Apr.*) Struck in copper	*Extremely rare*		
M	— — 'Limerick' bust	75	200	525
M2	— — No stops either side of II	75	200	525
N	— May (*May May:*) 'Limerick' bust	40	125	350

6580B

Limerick bust

6580	**Halfcrown.** *Small size.* Laur. head left, otherwise similar.			
A	1690 April (*Apr:*)	150	350	825
B	— May (*May May. may*)	50	140	425
B2	— — Stop after GRATIA	60	160	425
B3	— — Stop before DEI and after GRATIA	60	160	425
B4	— — Stops before IACOBVS and DEI and after GRATIA	60	160	425
B5	— — No obverse punctuation	60	160	425
B6	— — No wreath ties	60	160	425
B7	— — (*may*) Variety with ∗ stops	150	350	850
B8	— — (*May*) Struck in pewter	*Extremely rare*		
B9	— — (*May May.*) Struck in silver	*Extremely rare*		
B10	— — (*May*) Struck in gold	*Extremely rare*		
C	— — (*May May.*) Struck in Limerick, wider, flatter bust	85	200	650
D	— June (*June June.*) Struck in Limerick	50	150	425
D2	— — Error *Jnue.*	100	350	800
E	— July (*July*) Struck in Limerick	60	165	475

		F	VF	EF
		£	£	£
6580	**Halfcrown.** *Small size.*			
F	— August (*Aug:*) Struck in Limerick	75	250	700
G	— October (*Oct:*) Struck in Limerick	200	500	—

6581B   6581E3

		F	VF	EF
6581	**Shilling.** *Large size.* Similar, but XII above crown.			
A	1689 July (*July July.*)	40	85	325
A2	— — No stops on *obv.*	70	150	400
A3	— — Stop after GRATIA	70	150	400
A4	— — No stop after DEI	70	150	400
B	— August (*Aug Aug. Aug: Augt Augt. Augt:*)	40	75	285
B2	— — Stop after GRATIA	40	75	285
B3	— — (*Augt Augt:*) Struck in silver	900	2250	—
C	— September (*Sepr Sepr. Sepr: Sept Sept.*)	40	80	285
C2	— — Stop after GRATIA	40	80	285
C3	— — Stop after GRATIA, no stop after DEI	40	80	285
C4	— — (*Sepr:*) Struck in silver	*Extremely rare*		
D	— October (*Oct Oct: Octr Octr. OCT OCT. OCTr. OCTR.*)	40	80	265
D2	— — No stops on *obv.*	65	150	350
D3	— — No stops on I I For H	65	150	350
D4	— — FI for of ET on *rev.*	100	200	600
D4	— — FT for of ET on *rev.*	100	200	600
D5	— — (*8BER 8BER. 8BrE.*)	115	225	650
E	— November (*Nov. Nov: NOV novr: *)	40	75	285
E2	— — (*9 9r*)	75	175	425
E3	— — (*9r*) Small castle between pellets under bust	675	1500	2500
E4	— — (*9r*) Similar, but no pellets by castle	625	1250	2250
F	— December (*Dec Dec. Dec:*)	40	80	250
F2	— — No stops on *obv.*	40	80	250
F3	— — DFI for DEI	40	80	250
F4	— — ERA for FRA	40	80	250
F5	— — (*10r*)	65	150	350
G	— January (*Jan Jan. Jan:*)	40	80	265
G2	— — Reversed 'a' in *Jan*	125	250	700
G3	— — Reversed 'a' in *Jan* Struck in silver	1500	2500	4000
G4	— — No stops on *rev.*, EI for ET	75	165	350
G5	— — (*Jan:*) Struck in silver	1500	2500	—
H	— February (*Feb Feb. Feb:*)	40	80	275
H2	— — ERA for FRA	40	80	275
H3	— — (*Feb:*) Struck in silver	*Extremely rare*		
I	— March (*Mar Mar. Mar:*)	50	100	295

		F	VF	EF
		£	£	£
6581	**Shilling.** *Large size.*			
J	1690 March (*Mar Mar. Mar:*)	50	100	295
J2	— — No stops on *rev.*	45	100	325
J3	— — FT for ET..	45	100	325
J4	— — (*Mar. Mar:*) Struck in silver	1500	2500	4500
J5	— — FT for ET, in silver	*Extremely rare*		
J6	— — (*Mar.*) Struck in gold	*Extremely rare*		
K	— April (*Apr. Apr:*)	50	100	295
K2	— — No stop after II	50	100	295
K3	— — (*Apr.*) Struck in silver	*Extremely rare*		
K4	— — (*Apr*) Struck in gold	*Extremely rare*		

6582D

Limerick bust

6582	**Shilling.** *Small size.* Stops can vary, either cinquefoils or pellets.			
A	1690 April (*apr*) pellet stops	60	125	300
A2	— — — Cinquefoil stops on *obv.*	50	125	300
A2	— — — Cinquefoil stops both sides	50	125	300
B	— May (*May May. may MAY*) pellet stops...........................	40	100	250
B2	— — (*MAY*) Cinquefoil stops on *obv.*	50	110	300
B3	— — (*May.*) Variety reading GRATA	85	200	450
B4	— — (MAY) ERA for FRA	75	175	400
B5	— — (*May*) Struck in silver	800	1100	2250
B6	— — (*May May.*) Struck in gold	*Extremely rare*		
C	— — (*may*) Date at 10 o'clock, stops at value........................	700	1750	5000
D	— — (*May*) Struck in Limerick	80	180	400
E	— June (*June June.*)	50	125	300
E2	— — (*June.*) with a pewter plug	*Extremely rare*		
E3	— — (*June June.*) Struck in silver	*Extremely rare*		
E4	— — (*June*) Struck in gold	*Extremely rare*		
E5	— — (*June*) Struck in copper	*Extremely rare*		
F	— — (*June June.*) Struck in Limerick	50	125	300
F2	— — Stop before DEI	50	125	300
F3	— — Stop after GRATIA..	50	125	300
F4	— — (*Junc*) Struck on a thin flan	100	275	625
G	— September (*Sep:*) Struck in Limerick	350	850	—

	F	VF	EF
	£	£	£

6583H

6583 Sixpence. Laur. and draped bust l. ℞ VI above crown and sceptres.

		F	VF	EF
A	1689 June (*June June.*)	45	110	300
A2	— — Stop after GRATIA	45	110	300
B	— July (*July July.*)	45	110	300
B2	— — No stop after DEI	45	110	300
B3	— — Stop after GRATIA	45	110	300
B4	— — Error reading GRAIIA	45	110	300
B5	— — (*July*) Struck in silver	*Extremely rare*		
C	— August (*Aug Aug Aug: Augt.*)	50	125	300
C2	— — FR instead of FRA	85	200	575
C3	— — (*Aug*) Struck in silver	*Extremely rare*		
D	— September (*Sepr Sepr:*)	60	150	350
D2	— — No stop after DEI	60	150	350
D3	— — (*Sepr*) Struck in silver	1500	—	—
D4	— — (*7ber*)	125	325	825
F	1689 November (*Nov Nov. Nov:*)	45	110	300
F2	— — Portrait with wreath ties	95	225	600
F3	— — No stop after before or after HIB	45	110	300
G	— December (*Dec Dec. Dec:*)	45	110	300
G2	— — Struck in gold	*Extremely rare*		
H	— January (*Jan Jan. Jan:*)	45	110	300
H2	— — No stop after DEI	45	110	300
H3	— — (*Jan*) ERA for FRA	70	165	400
H4	— — (*Jan.*) RE.X error and 9 over 6 in date	95	225	595
H5	— — (*Jan*) no stops on *rev.*	60	150	375
H6	— — (*Jan Jan. Jan:*) Struck in silver	900	1500	4000
H7	— — (*Jan*) Struck over James II half guinea	*Extremely rare*		
I	— February (*Feb. Feb:*)	50	125	350
I 2	— — (*Feb. Feb:*) Struck in silver	900	1500	4000
I 3	— — (*Feb.*) Struck in gold	*Extremely rare*		
J	— May (*May. May:*) Believed to have been struck at Limerick	65	150	450

	F	VF	EF
	£	£	£

Emergency 'Pewter Money' of 1689-90

6584

6584   Crown. Type as 'Gunmoney' crown but finer work. Edge inscribed:
MELIORIS TESSERA FATI ANNO REGNI SEXTO. Copper alloy plug
through flan 1250   3750 10000

6585   Later off-metal strikes. *Not* from the same dies as the original pewter pieces.
℞ TRIVMPHO Struck in gold .... *Extremely rare*
℞ TRIVMPHO Struck in silver 3500   9000 15000
℞ TRIUMPHO Struck in gold .... *Extremely rare*
℞ TRIUMPHO Struck in silver .... *Extremely rare*
℞ TRIUMPHO Struck in copper .... *Extremely rare*
℞ TRIUMPHO Struck in pewter without brass plug................. *Extremely rare*

6586

6586   Pattern groat. As 'gunmoney' sixpence. ℞ II either side of crowned
harp. 1689 1500   3000   —
Struck from obverse dies later used for sixpences in June and July, this must date
from the very beginning of the gunmoney coinage.

6588   6589

6587   Penny. Type I. As large 'gunmoney' shilling. ℞ Crowned harp,
date 1689 above. Copper alloy plug through flan 1250   3500   —
6588 — — 1690. Copper alloy plug through flan............................ 850   1850   —
6589 — Type II. Smaller laur. head l., 1ᴰ behind. ℞ Harp dividing
date 1690. Copper alloy plug through flan 900   3500   —

	F £	VF £	EF £

6591

6591A silver

6590 **Halfpenny.** Type I. Bust with short hair l. ℞ Date over crowned
harp, 1689. Copper alloy plug through flan 750 2750 5500
6591 — — 1690. Copper alloy plug through flan 300 850 2250
6591A — — 1690. Struck in silver, milled edge 500 950 3500
6591B — — 1690. Struck over France Louis XIV 5 sols, plain edge . 850 2950 —

6592

6593

6592 **Halfpenny.** Type II. Smaller laur. head l., leaf below. ℞ Crown
divides date, 16 90. Copper alloy plug through flan 300 650 2000
6592A — quatrefoil below. Copper alloy plug through flan .... *Extremely rare*

6592A

6592A — — Date above crown. Copper alloy plug through flan .... *Extremely rare*

Limerick besieged 1690-91

6594

6595

6594 **Halfpenny.** Large size, overstruck on large size gunmoney shillings.
Laur. and draped bust l. ℞ Hibernia seated l., holding
cross, reversed И in HIBERИIA 1691 .... 45 200 450
6595 — Small size, struck on virgin flans (and not on small gunmoney
shillings as previously believed). Similar 110 350 675
6596 — Normal N in HIBERNIA 200 450 875

	F	VF	EF
	£	£	£

WILLIAM AND MARY, 1689-1694
WILLIAM III (alone), 1694-1702

The regular issue of Dublin halfpence was continued between 1692 and 1694 for the two rulers, and both their heads are displayed on the coinage. After Mary's death halfpence for William alone were struck in 1696.

William and Mary, 1689-94

6597

		F	VF	EF
		£	£	£
6597	**Halfpenny.** Conjoined busts r. ℞ Crowned harp			
	1692 GRATIA	50	175	650
	1692 error, unbarred As in GRΛTIΛ	75	30725	950
	1693	35	125	550
	1693 plain edge	45	175	650
	1693 similar. Struck in silver	*Extremely rare*		
	1694	45	175	650

6598   6599

William III, 1694-1702

6598	**Halfpenny.** Laur. and draped bust r., GRA ℞ Crowned harp, BR legend, 1696	75	325	1000
	1696 GWLIELMVS error	175	500	—
	1696 Struck in silver	*Extremely rare*		
	1696 Struck in silver gilt	1500	2000	—
6589A	— ℞ BRI legend	85	350	1000
	— — Struck in silver	1500	3500	—
6599	— Similar, but cruder undraped bust, GRATIA 1696	325	800	—
	1696 Struck in silver	*Extremely rare*		

GEORGE I, 1714-1727

No copper coins had been struck for Ireland since 1696, so by 1720 the dearth of small change has become acute. In 1722 a patent for coining copper cons for Ireland and for the American Colonies was granted to William Wood, a London merchant, who had the coins struck at his Bristol foundry. The coins were to be struck at the rate of 2s 6d worth to the pound, though this was substantially lighter than the contemporary English coppers. The Irish parliament was aggrieved at the circumstances under which the patent was granted and government officials were instructed not to accept them; and a general boycott of the coins was urged by Dean Swift in his scathing 'Drapier's Letters' which alleged that Wood was attempting to defraud the public. It became obvious that the coins were unacceptable in Ireland, so in 1724 Wood was forced to stop production, and he surrendered the patent the following year in exchange for a pension of £3,000 a year. The coins were recalled from Ireland and shipped out to America where they circulated alongside Wood's *Rosa Americana* coins. No official coinage was undertaken to replace Wood's Irish coinage, as the London mint ceased production of copper coin between 1724 and 1729.

William Wood's coinage, 1722-24

	F	VF	EF
	£	£	£

6600

6600	**Halfpenny.** Type I. Laur. bust r. ℞ Hibernia seated facing, looking		
	left, holding harp on left. 1722 110	350	1200
	1722 Proof .... *Extremely rare*		
	1722 Proof in silver .... *Extremely rare*		

6601

6601	— Type II. ℞ Hibernia seated l. leaning on harp and holding branch.		
	1722 65	225	750
	1722 Proof .... *Extremely rare*		
	1722 with second 2 inverted 150	450	1250
	1723 45	150	500
	1723 Proof .... *Extremely rare*		
	1723 Proof in silver .... *Extremely rare*		
	1723 3 over 2 55	200	575

	F	VF	EF
	£	£	£
6601 — Type II continued.			
1723 *Obv*. Rs altered from Bs	50	175	550
1723 star after HIBERNIA	*Extremely rare*		
1723 No stop after date	45	160	500
1724 *Rev*. legend divided	50	175	550
1724 *Rev*. legend continuous	65	250	750
1724 — Proof in silver	*Extremely rare*		

6602

6603

6602 **Farthing.** Type I. Laur. bust r., D : G : REX ℞ As 6600. Die axis 0°

1722	450	1500	4000
6603 — Type II. Similar. ℞ As 6601. Die axis 180° 1723	90	550	1500
6603A — — 1723 no colon before REX	150	600	2250

6604

6604 — Type III. Similar, but reads DEI · GRATIA · REX

1723	45	150	525
1723 Proof	*Extremely rare*		
1723 Proof in silver	*Extremely rare*		
1724	60	175	650
1724 Proof in silver	*Extremely rare*		
1724 no stop after date	90	225	725

GEORGE II, 1727-1760

Owing to the shortage of small change, tokens again appeared in Dublin in 1728, and substantial numbers were issued in Ulster between 1734 and 1736. In 1736 a new coinage of halfpence was put in hand at the London mint, which continued in most years until 1755, and to allay further public outcry it was directed that any profit accruing from the coinage should be credited to the public revenue of Ireland. Farthings were also coined in 1737-38 and 1744. In 1760 another issue of George II halfpence and farthings was minted for Ireland but owing to the king's death they were not sent to Ireland. They finally arrived in 1762.

Young Head coinage, 1736-55

6605

	F	VF	EF
	£	£	£

6605 Halfpenny. Type I. Laur. bust l., GEORGIUS R Crowned harp. Small lettering.

	F	VF	EF
1736	25	95	385
1736 Proof		FDC	1100
1736 Proof in silver		*Extremely rare*	
1737	20	75	385
1737 Proof		FDC	1100
1738	20	75	385
1738 8 over 7 in date			
1741			

6606

6606 Halfpenny. Type II. Similar, but large lettering.

	F	VF	EF
1741	20	75	385
1742	20	75	385
1743	25	95	425
1744	25	95	425
1744 4 over 3	25	95	475
1746	25	95	385

	F £	VF £	EF £

6607

6607 — Type III. Similar, but **GEORGIVS**

1747	20	75	385
1747 **V** over **U** in **GEORGIVS**	*Extremely rare*		
1748	20	75	385
1749	20	75	385
1750	20	75	385
1751	20	75	385
1752	20	75	385
1752 Proof	*Extremely rare*		
1753	25	85	385

1755 Royal Mint records show **no** issue for this date. All specimens are counterfeit.

6608

6609

6608 **Farthing.** Type I. As 6605, small lettering.

1737	30	100	400
1737 Proof (2 obverse dies)		FDC	900
1737 Proof in silver	*Extremely rare*		
1738	25	85	350

6609 — Type II. As 6606, large lettering.

1744	25	85	350
1744 Obverse with tall letters			

Old Head coinage, 1760. Not issued in Ireland until 1762.

6610

6611

6610	**Halfpenny.** As 6609, but older features. 1760.	15	70	350
	1760 Proof	*Extremely rare*		
6611	**Farthing.** Similar. 1760	15	60	335

GEORGE III, 1760-1820

Probably as a result of the delay in sending the 1760 copper coins to Ireland, a brief issue of tokens, the 'Voce Populi' series, was produced in Dublin to supply the need for small change, and in the North, others, following the pattern of the earlier promissory tokens, were made for McMinn, McCully and others. New Irish coppers were minted at London in 1766 and 1769 and again in 1775-6 and 1781-2, but supplementing these were large quantities of light-weight counterfeits, manufactured mainly in Birmingham.

The scarce 'Northumberland shillings' of 1763, named after the Earl of Northumberland who famously distributed £100 worth to the populace of Dublin on his appointment as Lord Lieutenant, were not a specifically Irish coin and many more than the 2,000 in £100 were struck at London. Otherwise, virtually no silver coin was struck at London between 1758 and 1804 (apart form a large issue of shillings and sixpences in 1787). Gold had become the standard of currency, and silver coins became progressively scarcer and what was in circulation was badly worn. In Ireland these worn coins continued to circulate as a token currency, the thin discs being stamped with the names or initials of traders through whose hands they passed.

In 1804 the Bank of Ireland had quantities of Spanish and Spanish-American 8 *reales* or 'dollars' restruck as Six Shilling Bank Tokens (the Bank of England had similar coins struck into Five Shilling tokens, for in Ireland silver coin was still at a premium). These were produced by revolutionary steam-powered coining-presses at Matthew Boulton's private mint at Soho, near Birmingham. In the following years 10 pence and 5 pence Bank Tokens were also minted for Ireland, and 30 pence tokens were struck in 1808. In 1813 another issue of 10 pence tokens were struck at the London Mint's new premises on Tower Hill which had been fitted up with Boulton & Watt's steam-powered minting presses.

A great many new copper and some lead tokens were circulating in Ireland between 1789 and 1804, mainly issued by the mining companies and Dublin traders, but in 1805 the Soho Mint struck large quantities of heavy-weight copper pennies, halfpennies and farthings, and today these are perhaps the commonest of the older Irish coins still surviving. The precision striking and the engrailed edges made them difficult to counterfeit; they were the last official copper issue until 1822, but further tokens made their appearance in order to satisfy the public demand.

After the attempted French expeditions of 1796 and 1797 had failed and the Wolde Tone rising of '98 was crushed, the establishments agreed on a merger of the two realms and the English and Irish parliaments approved the Act of Union in May 1800. This is reflected in the changed inscriptions on the gold coinage of 1801 and the new silver coinage of 1816 when M. B. ET H. REX ('King of Great Britain and Ireland') became BRITANNIARUM REX ('King of the Britains')

'London' coinage, 1766-82

	F £	VF £	EF £

6612

6612 Halfpenny. Type I. Laur. bust with short hair. ℞ Crowned harp.

	F	VF	EF
1766	15	75	325
1766 Proof		*FDC*	1100
1769	15	75	325

6613

6613 — Type II. Similar, but taller head of better style. 1769 .... | 20 | 85 | 400 |

6614

6614 — Type III. Laur. bust with long hair.

	F	VF	EF
1774 Pattern	*Extremely rare*		
1775	25	90	375
1775 5 over 4 in date			
1775 Proofs, copper, bronzed copper and plated copper	*Extremely rare*		
1775 Proof on thick flan, struck *en medaille*	*Extremely rare*		
1776	30	95	525
1781	15	75	275
1781 Proof	*Extremely rare*		
1782	15	75	325
1782 8 over 7 in date			
1782 struck with upright die axis, *en medaille*	25	115	395
1782 Proof..	*Extremely rare*		

Note: Counterfeits exist of most dates, including 1783, some being of quite good workmanship.

Bank of Ireland coinage, 1804-13

6615

	F £	VF £	EF £
6615 Six Shillings. Laur. and draped bust r. ℞ Hibernia std. l. with harp.			
1804 *Obv.* top leaf points to upright of E in DEI	125	350	750
1804 — Proof in copper		FDC	2000
1804 — Proof in copper gilt		FDC	2250
1804 — Proof in silver gilt		FDC	4000
1804 — No stops in CHK on truncation	135	400	875
1804 — — Proof in copper		FDC	1750
1804 — No stop after REX	135	400	875
1804 — — Proof in copper		FDC	1650
1804 *Obv.* top leaf points to right side of E in DEI	125	350	875
1804 — Proof		FDC	2000
1804 — Proof in copper		FDC	1250
1804 — Proof in copper gilt		FDC	2250
1804 — Proof in silver gilt		FDC	4000

6616   6616A

	F	VF	EF
6616 Thirty Pence. Laur., drp. and cuirassed bust. 1808. ℞ Hibernia, as above, **XXX PENCE IRISH** below	45	95	325
6616A— — Top of harp points to O in **TOKEN**	75	150	400

6617   6618

	F £	VF £	EF £

6617 Ten Pence. Type I. Obv. similar. ℞ Inscription across field.

1805	15	30	75
1806 Obv. front leaf of wreath under D of DEI	10	25	65
1806 Obv. front leaf of wreath under E of DEI	20	35	85

6618 — Type II. Laur. head r. ℞ Inscription in wreath, 1813

	10	25	75
1813 Proof		*FDC*	650

6619

6619 Five Pence. As 6617.

1805	10	25	65
1806	15	30	75

Note: The bank tokens were much counterfeited, probably mostly in Birmingham. They were copied in base metal and silvered.

Soho (Birmingham) coinage, 1805-6

6620

6620 Penny. Laur. and draped bust r. ℞ Crowned harp.

1805	15	50	225
1805 Proof		*FDC*	525
1805 Proof in bronzed copper		*FDC*	575

		F	VF	EF
		£	£	£

6620 gilt

6620	1805 Proof in gilt copper			FDC	950
	1805 Proof in silver			FDC	4250
	1805 Proof in gold			FDC	17500
	1805 *reverse* muled with English penny *obverse*			FDC	4000

6621   6621 gilt

6621	**Halfpenny.** Similar, 1805	10	20	85
	1805 Proof		FDC	350
	1805 Proof in bronzed copper		FDC	395
	1805 Proof in bronzed copper, plain edge		FDC	350
	1805 Proof in gilt copper		FDC	650
	1805 Proof in gilt copper, thick flan		*Extremely rare*	
	1805 Proof in silver		FDC	3000
	1805 Proof in gold		*Extremely rare*	
	1805 Proof in gold, plain edge		*Extremely rare*	

6622

6622	**Farthing.** Similar, 1806	5	15	50
	1806 Proof		FDC	300
	1806 Proof in bronzed copper		FDC	300
	1806 Proof in bronzed copper, no stop after date		FDC	300
	1806 Proof in gilt copper		FDC	425
	1806 Proof in gilt copper, thin flan, no stop after date		FDC	500
	1806 Proof in gilt copper, plain edge		FDC	425
	1806 Proof in silver, plain edge		FDC	2000
	1806 Proof in gold		*Extremely rare*	

GEORGE IV, 1820-1830

Although a formal union of the two countries took place in 1800, the two exchequers were not merged until 1817. In 1821 the two currencies were amalgamated, which meant that the shilling in Ireland was exactly the same value as the same coin in England. One further issue of copper was made specifically for Ireland in 1822 and 1823 but Irish coinage was formally withdrawn in 1826; thenceforth the imperial coinage was the only regal one current in Ireland for more than a century.

6623

	F £	VF £	EF £
6623 **Penny.** laur. and draped bust l. R Crowned harp.			
1822	15	85	275
1822 Proof		*FDC*	800
1822 Proof in bronzed copper..		*FDC*	900
1822 Proof on a thick flan		*Extremely rare*	
1823	15	85	300
1823 Proof		*FDC*	975
1823 Proof in bronzed copper		*FDC*	1000

6624

6625B

	F £	VF £	EF £
6624 **Halfpenny.** Similar.			
1822	10	35	100
1822 Proof		*FDC*	600
1822 Proof in bronzed copper		*FDC*	650
1823	10	35	110
1823 Proof		*FDC*	650
6625A Farthing. Similar. 1822 Proof only		*FDC*	3750
6625B — 1822 Proof only, thin flan, struck *en medaille*		*FDC*	5500

MODERN IRISH COINAGE FROM 1928

The struggle to have the Act of Union repealed, so valiantly conducted by Daniel O'Connell and others who followed him, was carried on for over a century. The Home Rule Bill which was placed on the statute book in 1914 was suspended during the Great War and was then superseded by the Government of Ireland Act of 1920. This led to the setting up of the Irish Free State, *Saorstát Éireann*, but in the North six of the nine counties of Ulster retained their links with the British crown and became a constituent part of the 'United Kingdom of Great Britain and Northern Ireland'.

The new Irish government decided to institute a coinage quite distinct from the United Kingdom coinage, which continued to circulate throughout Ireland, and in 1926 an advisory committee was appointed under the chairmanship of W. B. Yeats, the poet. The committee invited a number of artists to submit designs and those who competed consisted of three Irishmen, Jerome Connor, Albert Power and Oliver Sheppard, Paul Manship from America, Percy Metcalfe from England, Carl Milles of Sweden and Publio Morbiducci of Italy. The harp was chosen for the obverse type, the symbol used on Irish coins since its introduction under Henry VIII. The reverse designs were to represent the fauna of the Irish countryside, the animals chosen being the horse, salmon, bull, wolfhound, hare, chicken, pig and the woodcock. Many masterpieces were produced but Metcalfe's set was outstanding artistically and his designs were also technically suited to modern coin production processes. The new Irish coinage set an extremely high standard for coinage design and how successful it was is evidenced by the fact that the designs were retained virtually unchanged for forty years.

The new coins were made at the Royal Mint in London in 1928. The three highest denominations, the halfcrown, florin and shilling, we made of 0.750 silver alloyed with 0.250 copper. This produced a whiter metal that discoloured less with wear than the 0.500 silver-copper alloy used for UK coinage, though it was more expensive to produce. The sixpence and threepence were made a larger size proportionally by striking them in pure nickel, a metal that stands up well to wear. The penny, halfpenny and farthing were made of bronze, an alloy of 0.955 copper, 0.030 tin and 0.015 zinc. Six thousand specimen sets of the coinage were specially prepared with 'proof' surfaces and about 4000 of these were sold to the general public in presentation cases.

In June 1937 a new constitution declared the Free State a sovereign republic with the name 'Éire' and this name appeared on the next coins to be issued in 1939. For technical reasons minor modifications were made to the design of the harp and also to the reverses of the halfcrown and the penny. In 1942 pure nickel for the sixpence and threepence was abandoned in favour of cupro-nickel alloy, 0.750 copper and 0.250 nickel. By 1943 the rising price of silver made it uneconomic to mint coins of 0.750 silver, so no shillings were minted that year and of the halfcrowns and florins minted very few went into circulation. No further coins of these denominations were produced until after the 1950 Coinage Act which specified the same cupro-nickel alloy for these coins as was being used for the sixpence and threepence.

The fiftieth anniversary of the 'Easter Rising' of 1916 was commemorated with a special issue of 0.833 silver ten shilling pieces. These bear the bust of Pádraig H. Pearse on one side and on the reverse a copy of the statue, engraved by Oliver Sheppard, of Cúchulainn, the legendary hero of the *Táin Bó Cúailnge*, which now stands in the Post Office at Dublin. The coin did not prove popular with the public as an additional high denomination, and over half the issue was recalled and melted down. The last pre-decimal coins were issued dated 1968 and the first decimal denominations were dated 1969. Ireland changed to Euro Currency with other participating member states on January 1st 2002.

IRISH FREE STATE

SILVER

6625

	F £	VF £	EF £	UNC £
6625 **Halfcrown.** SAORSTÁT ÉIREANN Harp. ℞ Horse standing l.				
1928 Mintage 2,160,000	10	25	50	75
1928 Proof. Mintage 6,001 *FDC* £100				
1930 Mintage 352,000	25	95	425	650
1930 Proof *FDC* £2000				
1931 Mintage 160,000	20	85	350	525
1931 Proof *FDC* £1750				
1933 Mintage 336,000	28	100	350	675
1933 Proof *FDC* £2000				
1934 Mintage 480,000	15	50	175	350
1934 Proof *FDC* £1650				
1937 Mintage 40,000 (Beware of recent counterfeits)	95	375	950	2250
1937 Proof *FDC* £2750				

6626

	F £	VF £	EF £	UNC £
6626 **Florin.** SAORSTÁT ÉIREANN Harp. ℞ Salmon r.				
1928 Mintage 2,025,000	3	5	20	50
1928 Proof. Mintage 6,001 *FDC* £85				
1930 Mintage 330,000	6	25	125	550
1930 Proof *Extremely rare*				
1931 Mintage 200,000	6	28	250	600
1931 Proof *FDC* £1500				
1933 Mintage 300,000	6	25	200	550
1933 Proof *FDC* £1500				

		F	VF	EF	UNC
		£	£	£	£
6626	1934 Mintage 150,000	15	125	475	1100
	1934 Proof *FDC* £2850				
	1935 Mintage 390,000	6	20	90	300
	1935 Proof *FDC* £1500				
	1937 Mintage 150,000	7	30	175	500
	1937 Proof *FDC* £1500				

6627

6627 **Shilling. SAORSTÁT ÉIREANN** Harp. ℞ Bull butting r.

		F	VF	EF	UNC
	1928 Mintage 2,700,000	3	10	20	40
	1928 Proof. Mintage 6,001 *FDC* £60				
	1930 Mintage 460,000	10	40	225	550
	1930 Proof *FDC* £1250				
	1931 Mintage 400,000	8	20	100	375
	1931 Proof *FDC* £1250				
	1933 Mintage	8	20	110	385
	1933 Proof *FDC* £1250				
	1935 Mintage 400,000	7	15	65	175
	1935 Proof *FDC* £1250				
	1937 Mintage 100,000	30	100	450	1250
	1937 Proof *FDC* £1750				

NICKEL

6628

6628 **Sixpence. SAORSTÁT ÉIREANN** Harp. ℞ Wolfhound standing l.

		F	VF	EF	UNC
	1928 Mintage 3.201,480	1	7	15	35
	1928 Proof. Mintage 6,001 *FDC* £55				
	1934 Mintage 600,000	1	8	20	100
	1934 Proof *FDC* £1000				
	1935 Mintage 520,000	2	9	30	175
	1935 Proof *FDC* £1000				

6629

	F £	VF £	EF £	UNC £

6629 Threepence. saorstát éireann Harp. ℞ Hare seated l.

1928 Mintage 1,500,000 .... 1 4 10 25
1928 Proof. Mintage 6,001 *FDC* £35
1933 Mintage 320,000 .... 8 20 90 350
1933 Proof *FDC* £1150
1934 Mintage 800,000 .... 2 8 20 80
1934 Proof *FDC* £1000
1935 Mintage 240,000 .... 2 7 40 200
1935 proof *FDC* £1000

BRONZE

6630

6630 Penny. saorstát éireann Harp. ℞ Hen and chicks l.

1928 Mintage 9,000,000 .... 1 4 10 35
1928 Proof. Mintage 6,001 *FDC* £75
1931 Mintage 2,400,000 .... 1 8 30 110
1931 Proof *FDC* £1500
1933 Mintage 1,680,000 .... 3 12 60 225
1933 Proof *FDC* £1000
1935 Mintage 5,472,000 .... 1 4 20 65
1935 Proof *FDC* £1000
1937 Mintage 5,400,000 .... 1 4 30 100
1937 Proof *FDC* £1000

6631

6631 Halfpenny. saorstát éireann Harp. ℞ Pig and piglets l.

1928 Mintage 2,880,000 .... 1 4 10 35
1928 Proof. Mintage 6,001 *FDC* £50

			F	*VF*	*EF*	*UNC*
			£	£	£	£
6631	1933 Mintage 720,000		10	30	125	575
	1933 Proof *FDC* £850					
	1935 Mintage 960,000		5	18	75	285
	1935 Proof *FDC* £850					
	1937 Mintage 960,000		2	6	17	65
	1937 Proof *FDC* £850					

6632

6632 **Farthing.** SAORSTÁT ÉIREANN Harp. ℞ Woodcock flying l.

			F	*VF*	*EF*	*UNC*
	1928 Mintage 300,000		2	4	8	20
	1928 Proof. Mintage 6,001 *FDC* £30					
	1930 Mintage 288,000		2	5	10	30
	1930 Proof *FDC* £650					
	1931 Mintage 192,000		3	8	15	40
	1931 Proof *FDC* £650					
	1932 Mintage 192,000		4	10	20	50
	1932 Proof *FDC* £650					
	1933 Mintage 480,000		2	5	10	30
	1933 Proof *FDC* £650					
	1935 Mintage 192,00		4	15	30	60
	1935 Proof *FDC* £650					
	1936 Mintage 192,000		5	18	35	70
	1936 Proof *FDC* £650					
	1937 Mintage 480,000		2	5	10	30
	1937 Proof *FDC* £600					
PS1	Proof Set 1928. Halfcrown to farthing. 8 coins.				*FDC* £525	

ÉIRE

SILVER

6633

6633 **Halfcrown.** Type as 6625, but reading ÉIRE and minor alterations
to design and lettering

			F	*VF*	*EF*	*UNC*
	1938			*unique*		
	1939 Mintage 888,000		8	15	35	100
	1939 Proof *FDC* £1450					

		F £	VF £	EF £	UNC £
6633	1940 Mintage 752,000	8	15	40	110
	1940 Proof *FDC* £1500				
	1941 Mintage 320,000	10	20	50	135
	1941 Proof *FDC* £1500				
	1942 Mintage 285,600	8	15	30	95
	1943*	250	500	1500	3500

* Beware of recent counterfeits

6634

6634 Florin. Type as 6626, but **ÉIRE**

		F	VF	EF	UNC
	1939 Mintage 1,080,000	4	12	25	70
	1939 Proof *FDC* £1000				
	1940 Mintage 670,000	6	15	35	90
	1940 Proof *FDC* £1000				
	1941 Mintage 400,000	7	25	40	100
	1941 Proof *FDC* £1000				
	1942 Mintage 109,000	8	15	35	80
	1942 Proof *FDC* £1000				
	1943 (Beware of recent counterfeits)	6000	12500	20000	35000

6635

6635 Shilling. Type as 6627, but **ÉIRE**

		F	VF	EF	UNC
	1939 Mintage 1,140,000	4	8	20	60
	1939 Proof *FDC* £800				
	1940 Mintage 580,000	3	9	20	50
	1940 Proof *FDC* £850				
	1941 Mintage 300,000	5	12	30	60
	1941 Proof *FDC* £850				
	1942 Mintage 286,000	3	8	18	48
	1942 Proof *FDC* £800				

NICKEL

6636

		F	VF	EF	UNC
		£	£	£	£
6636	**Sixpence.** Type as 6628, but ÉIRE				
	1939 Mintage 876,000	1	4	12	65
	1939 Proof *FDC* £750				
	1940 Mintage 1,120,000	1	3	8	60
	1940 Proof *FDC* £800				
6637	**Threepence.** Type as 6629, but ÉIRE				
	1939 Mintage 64,000	5	10	70	285
	1939 Proof *FDC* £750				
	1940 Mintage 720,000	2	8	20	70
	1940 Proof *FDC* £650				

CUPRO-NICKEL

6638

		F	VF	EF	UNC
6638	**Halfcrown.** Type as 6633, except for change of metal				
	1951 Mintage 800,000	2	4	18	65
	1951 Proof *FDC* £1250				
	1954 Mintage 400,000	2	4	20	80
	1954 Proof *FDC* £1250				
	1955 Mintage 1,080,000	2	4	12	35
	1955 Proof *FDC* £1350				
	1959 Mintage 1,600,000	2	4	10	35
	1959 Proof *FDC* £1350				
	1961 Mintage 1,600,000	2	4	20	45
	1961 Proof *FDC* £1150				
	1962 Mintage 3,200,000	1	3	5	30
	1962 Proof *FDC* £1150				
	1963 Mintage 2,400,000	1	2	5	20
	1963 Proof *FDC* £1150				
	1964 Mintage 3,200,000	1	3	6	20
	1964 Proof *FDC* £1150				

		F	VF	EF	UNC
		£	£	£	£
6638	1966 Mintage 700,000	3	5	12	25
	1966 Proof *FDC* £1000				
	1967 Mintage	2	4	8	10
	1967 Proof *FDC* £1000				
6638A	1961 Similar, but muled with *rev.* of 6625 (1928-37), oval letter O in legend,				
	larger PM in exergue, larger base to 2 in value	35	125	500	1250

6639   6640

		F	VF	EF	UNC
6639	**Florin.** Type as 6634, except for change of metal				
	1951 Mintage 1,000,000	—	3	12	40
	1951 Proof *FDC* £900				
	1954 Mintage 1,000,000	—	3	10	40
	1954 Proof *FDC* £900				
	1955 Mintage 1,000,000	—	2	7	40
	1955 Proof *FDC* £900				
	1959 Mintage 2,000,000	—	2	7	40
	1959 Proof *FDC* £1000				
	1961 Mintage 2,000,000	—	3	7	65
	1961 Proof *FDC* £850				
	1962 Mintage 2,400,000	—	2	7	25
	1962 Proof *FDC* £850				
	1963 Mintage 3,000,000	—	2	7	25
	1963 Proof *FDC* £800				
	1964 Mintage 4,000,000	—	2	7	20
	1964 Proof *FDC* £800				
	1965 Mintage 2,000,000	—	2	6	20
	1965 Proof *FDC* £800				
	1966 Mintage 3,625,000	—	2	5	15
	1966 Proof *FDC* £750				
	1968 Mintage 1,000,000	—	2	5	15
	1968 Proof *FDC* £750				
6640	**Shilling.** Type as 6635, except for change of metal				
	1951 Mintage 2,000,000	1	3	7	25
	1951 Proof *FDC* £800				
	1954 Mintage 3,000,000	—	2	7	25
	1954 Proof *FDC* £800				
	1955 Mintage 1,000,000	—	2	7	26
	1955 Proof *FDC* £800				
	1959 Mintage 2,000,000	1	4	10	38
	1962 Mintage 4,000,000	—	2	4	15
	1962 Proof *FDC* £650				

				F	VF	EF	UNC
				£	£	£	£
6640	1963	Mintage 4,000,000		—	2	4	8
	1963	Proof *FDC* £650					
	1964	Mintage 4,000,000		—	1	3	4
	1964	Proof *FDC* £650					
	1966	Mintage 3,000,000		—	1	3	4
	1966	Proof *FDC* £600					
	1968	Mintage 4,000,000		—	—	3	4
	1968	Proof *FDC* £600					

6641   6642

6641	**Sixpence.** Type as 6636, except for change of metal					
	1942	Mintage 1.320.000	1	3	10	65
	1942	Proof *FDC* £800				
	1945	Mintage 400,000	5	10	50	150
	1945	Proof *FDC* £800				
	1946	Mintage 720,000	8	25	135	500
	1946	Proof *FDC* £800				
	1947	Mintage 800,000	2	8	35	125
	1947	Proof *FDC* £800				
	1948	Mintage 800,000	2	5	12	60
	1948	Proof *FDC* £800				
	1949	Mintage 600,000	2	6	12	55
	1949	Proof *FDC* £800				
	1950	Mintage 800,000	3	12	35	150
	1950	Proof *FDC* £1950				
	1952	Mintage 800,000	1	3	8	30
	1952	Proof *FDC* £800				
	1953	Mintage 800,000	1	3	9	40
	1953	Proof *FDC* £800				
	1955	Mintage 600,000	1	3	8	30
	1955	Proof *FDC* £800				
	1956	Mintage 600,000	1	3	7	30
	1956	Proof *FDC* £800				
	1958	Mintage 600,000	2	7	15	80
	1958	Proof *FDC* £1000				
	1959	Mintage 2,000,000	—	1	5	28
	1959	Proof *FDC* £800				
	1960	Mintage 2,020,000	—	1	5	20
	1960	Proof *FDC* £800				
	1961	Mintage 3,000,000	—	1	5	16
	1961	Proof *FDC* £650				
	1962	Mintage 4,000,000	1	5	10	70
	1962	Proof *FDC* £650				

		F	VF	EF	UNC
		£	£	£	£
6641	1963 Mintage 4,000,000	—	1	2	6
	1963 Proof *FDC* £650				
	1964 Mintage 4,000,000	—	1	2	5
	1964 Proof *FDC* £550				
	1966 Mintage 2,000,000	—	1	2	4
	1966 Proof *FDC* £550				
	1967 Mintage 4,000,000	—	—	1	2
	1967 Proof *FDC* £550				
	1968 Mintage 4,000,000	—	—	1	2
	1968 Proof *FDC* £550				
	1969 Mintage 2,000,000	—	—	1	2
	1969 Proof *FDC* £500				
6642	**Threepence.** Type as 6637, except for change of metal				
	1942 Mintage 4,000,000	—	3	8	50
	1942 Proof *FDC* £1000				
	1943 Mintage 1,360,000	2	6	20	100
	1943 Proof *FDC* £900				
	1946 Mintage 800,000	2	7	12	60
	1946 Proof *FDC* £1000				
	1948 Mintage 1,600,000	2	5	35	125
	1948 Proof *FDC* £900				
	1949 Mintage 1,200,000	—	2	6	40
	1949 Proof *FDC* £900				
	1950 Mintage 1,600,000	—	2	6	30
	1950 Proof *FDC* £1150				
	1953 Mintage 1,600,000	—	1	5	18
	1953 Proof *FDC* £900				
	1956 Mintage 1,200,000	—	1	4	15
	1956 Proof *FDC* £900				
	1961 Mintage 2,400,000	—	—	2	6
	1961 Proof *FDC* £700				
	1962 Mintage 3,200,000	—	—	2	12
	1962 Proof *FDC* £700				
	1963 Mintage 4,000,000	—	—	2	12
	1963 Proof *FDC* £550				
	1964 Mintage 6,000,000	—	—	2	4
	1964 Proof *FDC* £550				
	1965 Mintage 3,600,000	—	—	2	3
	1965 Proof *FDC* £550				
	1966 Mintage 4,000,000	—	—	2	3
	1966 Proof *FDC* £550				
	1967 Mintage 2,400,000	—	—	2	3
	1967 Proof *FDC* £550				
	1968 Mintage 4,000,000	—	—	2	3
	1968 Proof *FDC* £550				

	F £	VF £	EF £	UNC £

BRONZE

6643

6643 **Penny.** Type as 6630, but **éIRe**

		F £	VF £	EF £	UNC £
1938	only two specimens known *FDC* £35,000				
1940	Mintage 312,000	10	50	250	750
1940	Proof *FDC* £1750				
1941	Mintage 4,680,000	1	4	12	45
1941	Proof *FDC* £750				
1942	Mintage 17,580,000	—	2	6	25
1942	Proof *FDC* £750				
1943	Mintage 3,360,000	—	2	10	50
1943	Proof *FDC* £750				
1946	Mintage 4,800,000	—	2	5	25
1946	Proof *FDC* £750				
1948	Mintage 4,800,000	—	2	5	25
1948	Proof *FDC* £750				
1949	Mintage 4,080,000	—	2	5	25
1949	Proof *FDC* £650				
1950	Mintage 2,400,000	—	2	7	30
1950	Proof *FDC* £700				
1952	Mintage 2,400,000	—	1	3	10
1952	Proof *FDC* £700				
1962	Mintage 1,200,000	—	1	3	10
1962	Proof *FDC* £500				
1963	Mintage 9,600,000	—	—	2	12
1963	Proof *FDC* £500				
1964	Mintage 6,000,000	—	—	2	4
1964	Proof *FDC* £1250				
1965	Mintage 11,160,000	—	—	2	3
1965	Proof *FDC* £600				
1966	Mintage 6,000,000	—	—	2	3
1966	Proof *FDC* £500				
1967	Mintage 2,400,000	—	—	2	3
1967	Proof *FDC* £500				
1968	Mintage 9,000,000	—	—	1	2
1968	Proof or Specimen *FDC Extremely rare*				

6643A Penny, similar, body of chick nearest hen's leg omitted.

		F £	VF £	EF £	UNC £
1942		3	8	28	80
1968		—	4	15	30

6644

		F	VF	EF	UNC
		£	£	£	£
6644	**Halfpenny.** Type as 6631, but **ÉIRE**				
	1939 Mintage 240,000	3	20	75	250
	1939 Proof *FDC* £1150				
	1940 Mintage 1,680,000	5	30	95	350
	1940 Proof *FDC* £700				
	1941 Mintage 2,400,000	1	5	12	50
	1941 Proof *FDC* £600				
	1942 Mintage 6,931.200	—	2	8	20
	1943 Mintage 2,668,800	2	4	10	40
	1943 Proof *FDC* £600				
	1946 Mintage 720,000	3	8	30	125
	1946 Proof *FDC* £600				
	1949 Mintage 1,344,000	2	5	9	30
	1949 Proof *FDC* £800				
	1953 Mintage 2,400,000	—	1	3	6
	1953 Proof *FDC* £1000				
	1964 Mintage 2,160,000	—	—	1	3
	1964 Proof *FDC* £500				
	1965 Mintage 1,440,000	—	—	3	4
	1965 Proof *FDC* £500				
	1966 Mintage 1,680,000	—	—	1	3
	1966 Proof *FDC* £500				
	1967 Mintage 1,200,000	—	–	1	3
	1967 Proof *FDC* £500				

6645

6645	**Farthing.** Type a 6632, but **ÉIRE**				
	1939 Mintage 768,000	—	3	8	15
	1939 Proof *FDC* £400				
	1940 Mintage 192,000	1	4	12	40
	1940 Proof *FDC* £400				
	1941 Mintage 480,000	—	2	5	15
	1941* Proof *FDC* £400				
	1943 Mintage 480,000	—	2	4	15
	* Beware modern forgery with fault in feathers of wings.				

		F	VF	EF	UNC
		£	£	£	£
6645	1943 Proof *FDC* £400				
	1944 Mintage 480,000	—	2	6	25
	1944 Proof *FDC* £400				
	1946 Mintage 480,000	—	1	5	15
	1946 Proof *FDC* £400				
	1949 Mintage 192,000	1	2	8	25
	1949 Proof *FDC* £400				
	1953 Mintage 192,000	–	—	1	2
	1953 Proof *FDC* £400				
	1959 Mintage 192,000	—	—	1	2
	1959 Proof *FDC* £400				
	1966 Mintage 96,000	—	1	4	8

Easter Rising commemorative issue, 1966 (Sterling silver 0.925)

6646

6646	**Ten Shillings.** Bust r. of Patrick Pearse. ℞ The statue of Cúchulainn by Oliver Sheppard. *Edge:* éɪʀɪ́ amaċ na cásca 1916 (The Easter Rising 1916) Mintage 2,000,000	3	8	20	30
	— Similar. Proof. Mintage 20,000 FDC £30				
	— Similar. *Edge* error nacásca or nasca	35	75	125	

DECIMAL COINAGE

6701

6701A

		EF	UNC	Proof
		£	£	£
6701	**One pound.** Cupro-nickel. Harp. ℞ Stag stg. l.			
	Issued 1990 - 2000.	—	*from* 5	30
6701A	— Millennium commemorative. 2000. Harp as above. ℞ Boat.	—	5	
	— Piedfort proof. Mintage 90,000..................................			40
6701B	— United Nations 50 years anniversary, proof.			165

6702

6702   Fifty pence. Cupro-nickel. Harp. ℞ Woodcock flying l.
Issued 1970-1988, 1996-2000..   *from* 2

6702A — Dublin 988 - 1988 commemorative. ℞ Dates at sides of shield.   5   40

6703

6703   Twenty pence. Brass. Harp. ℞ Horse stg. l.
Issued 1986, 1988, 1992, 1994, 1995, 1996, 1998, 1999, 2000. .   *from* 2

6703A — Trial pieces only, 1985........................ *VF* £2500   *EF* £4500   *Unc* —

6703

6704   Ten Pence. Cupro-nickel. Large size. Harp. ℞ Salmon r.
Issued 1969, 1971, 1973, 1974, 1975, 1976, 1978, 1980, 1982, 1985.*from* 3
— 1986, only available in specimen sets...................................   250

6705

6705   Ten Pence. Cupro-nickel. Small size. Harp. ℞ Salmon l.
Issued 1993 - 2000 inclusive...   *from* 2
A small quantity dated 1992 were issued for vending machine testing purposes,
but the new coins were not put into circulation until the following year.
(Spink sale 206, lot 986)...   *FDC* £3500

6706

6706   Five pence. Cupro-nickel. Large size. Harp. ℞ Bull r.
Issued 1969, 1970, 1971, 1974, 1975, 1976, 1978, 1980, 1982,
1985, 1986, 1990. ....   *from* 2

6707

6707   Five pence. Cupro-nickel. Small size. Harp. ℞ Bull l.
Issued 1992, 1993, 1994, 1995, 1996, 1998, 2000. ....   *from* 2

6708

6708   Two pence. Bronze. Harp.
Issued 1971, 1975, 1976, 1978, 1979, 1980, 1982, 1985, 1986,
1988, 1990, 1992, 1995, 1996, 1998, 2000. ....   *from* 1

6709

6709   One penny. Bronze. Harp.
Issued 1971, 1974, 1975, 1976, 1978, 1979, 1980, 1982, 1985,
1986, 1988, 1990, 1992, 1993, 1994, 1995, 1996, 1998, 2000. ..   *from* 1

6710

6710   Half penny. Bronze. Harp.
Issued 1971, 1975, 1976, 1978, 1980, 1982. ....   *from* 1
— 1985. Majority melted down.   400
— 1986. Only issued in specimen sets.   110

EURO COINAGE

Ireland adopted the Euro currency in 2002 and issued coins
in denominations from 1 Cent to 2 Euro, as above.

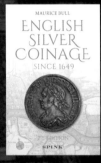

THE ISLANDS

Jersey

Guernsey

Man

Lundy

INTRODUCTION TO COINS OF THE ISLANDS

The coinages of the smaller islands of the British Isles and the Channel Islands add an interesting dimension to those of Great Britain and Ireland. The Channel Islands were at one time part of the dukedom of Normandy and their allegiance to the English throne dates to the time of William the Conqueror. Due to their short distance from the coast of France their small change was reckoned in French 'doubles' or 'sous'. Man, with its own variant Celtic tongue, Manx, came within the orbit of the Norsemen, then the lords of the Western Isles, was disputed by the kings of Scotland and England, was granted to the earls of Derby and eventually sold back to the British crown in the eighteenth century. Today its coinage contributes to the revenue from its tourist trade.

LATIN AND OTHER LEGENDS

QVOCVNQVE IECERIS (or GESSERIS) STABIT (However you throw it stands). Earl of Derby copper coins of the Isle of Man.
SANS CHANGER (Changeless). Earl of Derby copper coins of the Isle of Man.
S BALLIVIE INSVLE DE GERNEREVE (Seal of the Bailiwick of the Island of Guernsey). Appears on 7221, 7225 and 7226.

SELECT BIBLIOGRAPHY

CHANNEL ISLANDS

LOWSLEY, Lt.-Col. B. *The Coinages of the Channel Islands*. 1897.

MARSHAL-FRASER, Lt.-Col. W. *The Coinages of the Channel Islands*. 1949.

PRIDMORE, F. *The Coins of the British Commonwealth of Nations*. Part 1, European Territories. 1960.

ISLE OF MAN

ALLEN, M. 'The Malew (2011) hoard and the currency of the Isle of Man in the 1280s', *BNJ* 87, 2017.

BORNHOLDT, K. 'Myth or Mint? The evidence for a Viking-Age coinage from the Isle of Man', in P.J. Davey (ed.), *Recent Archaeological Research on the Isle of Man,* British Archaeological Reports British Series 278, 1999.

BORNHOLDT COLLINS, K. 'Coinage', in S. Duffy and H. Mytum (eds), *A New History of the Isle of Man. Volume 3: Medieval Period, 1000–1406*. 2015.

CLAY, C. 'On the Brass, Copper and other Currency of the Isle of Man'. *Proc. Manchester Num. Soc.*, Pts. I-V, 1864-7.

CUBBON, A.M. 'A remarkable decade of Manx coin hoards, 1972–1982', *Proceedings of the Isle of Man Natural History and Antiquarian Society* 11, no. 1, 1997–9.

DOLLEY, M. 'Hiberno-Manx Coinage, *c*.1025-35'. *NC*, 1976.

LISTER, M. *Manx Money*. 1947.

NELSON, P. 'Coinage of the Isle of Man'. *NC*, 1899.

— 'Contemporary Forgeries of the Isle of Man Coinage of 1733'. *SNC*, 1901.

PRIDMORE, F. *The Coins of the British Commonwealth of Nations*. Part 1, European Territories. 1960.

STEWART, I. 'An eighteenth-century Manx find of early Scottish sterlings', *BNJ* 33, 1964.

LUNDY

MORRIESON, Lt.-Col. H.W. 'The Coinage of Lundy 1645-6'. *BNJ* XIX, 1927/8.

JERSEY

The Channel Islands off the French coast have been in the possession of the British Crown since the English kings held the Dukedom of Normandy. Jersey, the largest island in the Channel Island group, changed from French to English currency in 1834. As the pound was then equivalent to 26 French *livres* of 20 *sous* each, and a *sous* was held equal to one halfpenny, it followed that the Jersey penny or *piece de deux sous* should be one thirteenth of a shilling. The first copper coinage did not appear until 1841, and was struck at the Royal Mint in London. A change to a bronze coinage was made in 1866, and in 1877 the values were altered to the more convenient one twelfth, one twenty-fourth, and one forty-eighth of a shilling. Unlike the coins of neighbouring Guernsey, the Jersey coins have always borne the portrait of the reigning monarch.

After the War, in 1949, an issue of pennies commemorating the liberation of the island from German occupation carries the inscription LIBERATED 1945. The name STATES OF JERSEY was replaced by ISLAND OF JERSEY on the Liberation issue, and was changed to BAILIWICK OF JERSEY on the 1957 pennies.

In 1960 a penny was issued commemorating the tercentenary of the Restoration, and a crown, threepence and penny dated 1066-1966 commemorate the accession of William, Duke of Normandy, to the throne of England. Decimal coinage was introduced in 1968.

VICTORIA 1837-1901

COPPER

7001

	VF £	EF £	B.Unc. £
7001 One thirteenth of a shilling. Young head, date below.			
R Arms of Jersey			
1841 Mintage 116,480	8	70	395
1841 Proof *FDC* £500			
1844 Mintage 27.040	8	70	395
1844 Proof *FDC* £525			
1851 Mintage 160,000	8	80	325
1851 Proof *FDC* £550			
1858 Mintage 173,333	8	70	275
1858 Proof *FDC* £525			
1861 Mintage 173,333	8	80	295
1861 Proof *FDC* £550			
1865 Proof only *FDC* £950			

7002

7003

	F £	VF £	EF £	B.Unc. £
7002 One twenty-sixth of a shilling. Similar to 7001.				
1841 Mintage 232,960		8	50	250
1841 Proof *FDC* £600				
1844 Mintage 232,960		8	50	275
1851 Mintage 160,000		8	50	250
1858 Mintage 173,333		8	50	250
1858 Proof *FDC* £500				
1861 Mintage 173,333		8	50	200
1861 Proof *FDC* £600				
7003 One fifty-second of a shilling. Similar to 7001.				
1841 (last 1 of date over 0) Mintage 116,480	10	40	150	385
1841 Proof *FDC* £1000				
1861 Proof in copper *FDC* £1250				
1861 Proof in bronze *Extremely rare*				

BRONZE

First issue, with 'square' shield. Similar types.

7004 One thirteenth of a shilling				
1866 Mintage 173,333		8	40	145
1866 Proof *FDC* £400				
1866 no L.C.W. on truncation. Pr. 9B. Proof only *FDC* £400				
1870 Mintage 160,000		8	40	145
1870 Proof *FDC* £500				
1871 Mintage 160,000		8	40	145
1871 Proof *FDC* £500				

7005

7005 One twenty-sixth of a shilling				
1866 Mintage 173,333		7	40	165
1866 Proof *FDC* £450				
1870 Mintage 160,000		7	40	165
1870 Proof *FDC* £525				
1871 Mintage 160,000		7	40	165
1871 Proof *FDC* £525				

Second issue, with 'spade' shield. Larger diameter and increased weight.

7006

	VF	EF	B.Unc.
	£	£	£

7006 One twelfth of a shilling
  1877 Proof only *FDC* £500
  1877 Proof in nickel £3000
  1877 Trial specimen struck on thick flan £2500

1877H Mintage 240,000	3	15	100

  1877H Proof *FDC* £600
  1877H Proof in nickel £3000

1881 Mintage 75,153	3	15	70
1888 Mintage 180,000	3	15	60
1894 Mintage 180,000	3	15	60

  1894 Proof *FDC* £500

7007

7007 One twenty-fourth of a shilling
  1877 Proof only *FDC* £350

1877H Mintage 336,000	3	15	50

  1877H Proof *FDC* £500

| 1888 Mintage 120,000 | 3 | 15 | 50 |
| 1894 Mintage 120,000 | 3 | 15 | 50 |

  1894 Proof *FDC* £400

7008

7008 One forty-eighth of a shilling
  1877 Proof only *FDC* £350

1877H Mintage 288,000	15	90	250

  1877H Proof *FDC* £600

EDWARD VII 1901-1910

BRONZE

	VF £	EF £	B.Unc. £

7009

7009 One twelfth of a shilling

1909 Mintage 180,000	3	18	125

7010

7010 One twenty-fourth of a shilling

1909 Mintage 120,000	4	18	110
1909 Matt proof *FDC* £875			

GEORGE V 1910-1936

BRONZE

First issue, 'spade' shield as before

7011

7011 One twelfth of a shilling

1911 Mintage 204,000	—	10	60
1913 Mintage 204,000	—	10	60
1923 Mintage 204,000	—	10	60

7012 One twenty-fourth of a shilling

1911 Mintage 72,000	—	10	45
1913 Mintage 72,000	—	10	45
1923 Mintage 72,000	—	10	45

Second issue, 'square' shield, scrolls above and below

	VF £	*EF* £	*B.Unc.* £

7013

7013 **One twelfth of a shilling**

	VF £	*EF* £	*B.Unc.* £
1923 Mintage 301,200	3	10	60
1926 Mintage 82,800	3	10	50

7014 **One twenty-fourth of a shilling**

1923 Mintage 72,000	3	10	45
1923 Proof *FDC* £350			
1926 Mintage 120,000	3	12	50
1926 Proof *FDC* £350			

Third issue, type as before, but without scrolls

7015

7015 **One twelfth of a shilling**

1931 Mintage 204,000	—	7	25
1931 Proof *FDC* £575			
1933 Mintage 204,000	—	7	25
1933 Proof *FDC* £575			
1935 Mintage 204,000	—	7	25
1935 Proof *FDC* £575			

7016

	EF £	B.Unc. £
7016 One twenty-fourth of a shilling		
1931 Mintage 72,000	8	25
1931 Proof *FDC* £350		
1933 Mintage 72,000	8	25
1933 Proof *FDC* £350		
1935 Mintage 72,000	8	25
1935 Proof *FDC* £350		

GEORGE VI 1936-1952

First issue

7017

7017 One twelfth of a shilling		
1937 Mintage 204,000	6	15
1937 Proof *FDC* £350		
1946 Mintage 204,000	5	12
1946 Proof *FDC* £350		
1947 Mintage 444,000	5	12
1947 Proof *FDC* £350		

| | EF | B.Unc. |
| | £ | £ |

7018   One twenty-fourth of a shilling

1937   Mintage 72,000   6   18

1937   Proof *FDC* £400

1946   Mintage 72,000   6   18

1946   Proof *FDC* £400

1947   Mintage 72,000   6   18

1947   Proof *FDC* £400

Second ('Liberation') issue

7019

7019   One twelfth of a shilling. Dated 1945. Issued in 1949, 1950 and 1952

1945   Mintage 1,200,000   4   10

1945   Proof *FDC* £300

ELIZABETH II 1952-present

CUPRO-NICKEL

7020

7020   Five shillings, 1966. William I commemorative, 1066-1966

1966   5   10

1966   Proof *FDC* £15

NICKEL BRASS

EF B.Unc.
£   £

7021   7022
7021A

7021 One fourth of a shilling (threepence). Round flan, 1957   3   8
— 1957 Proof *FDC* £15
— 1960 Proof only *FDC* £80
7021A— Dodecagonal flan, 1964   3   8
— 1964 Proof *FDC* £80
7022 — William I commemorative, 1066-1966   3   8
— 1966 Proof *FDC* £10

BRONZE

7023   7024

7023 One twelfth of a shilling. 'Liberation' issue dated 1945 (issued in 1954)
1945   2   8
1945 Bronze proof *FDC* £325
7024 — Normal issue, without 'LIBERATED 1945'
1957   2   7
1957 Proof *FDC* £20
1964   2   7
1964 Proof *FDC* £10

	EF	B.Unc.
	£	£

7025

7025 — Restoration Tercentenary commemorative, with dates 1660-1960

1960   2   7

1960 Proof *FDC* £10

7025A— Mule with obv. as 7023. Proof only *FDC* £200

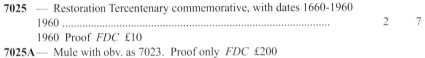

7026

7026 — William I commemorative, 1066-1966

1966   2   7

1966 Proof *FDC* £10

PROOF AND SPECIMEN SETS

	No. of coins in set	FDC £
7160 1957 double set, fourth and twelfth shilling	(4)	30
7161 1960 double set, fourth and twelfth shilling	(4)	15
7162 1964 double set, fourth and twelfth shilling	(4)	12
7163 1966 double set, fourth and twelfth shilling	(4)	8
7164 1966 double set, two crowns	(2)	10

GUERNSEY

Guernsey, the other large island in the Channel Islands group, officially retained French denominations as its legal money of account until 1921. The unit of local coinage was the Double, derived from the French *double tournois*, a small seventeenth century copper coin. Prior to 1921 twelve eight-doubles went to the 'Guernsey shilling', but twenty-one of these were equated with the pound sterling. It can be said that the double was worth approximately half a farthing – 8 doubles being of equivalent value to the old British penny.

The first Guernsey coins were copper four doubles and one doubles made in 1830 at Boulton and Watt's Soho Mint; an eight doubles was issued in 1834 and a two doubles in 1858. A change to a lighter bronze coinage was made in 1864. The designs were maintained practically unchanged until 1956, when a Guernsey lily was used as an emblem on the eight and four doubles, and a new threepenny denomination was introduced, depicting the Guernsey cow. The two doubles was last minted in 1929, and the one double in 1938.

In 1935, 500 proof-like eight doubles, dated 1934, were issued to commemorate both the Silver Jubilee of George V and the centenary of the institution of the coinage.

A square ten shilling piece was issued in 1966 to celebrate the 9th centenary of the Battle of Hastings. It depicts William the Conqueror on the reverse. Decimal coinage was introduced in 1971.

WILLIAM IV 1830-1837
COPPER

7200

7201

7202

	F	VF	EF	BU	Proof FDC
		£	£	£	
7200 Eight doubles. Arms of Guernsey etc. ℞ Value and date					
1834 Mintage 221,760	—	12	65	400	65
7201 Four doubles. Similar.					
1830 Mintage 655,200	—	10	50	300	48.
7202 One double. Similar.					
1830 Mintage 1,648,640 total	—	4	25	100	25
1830 Stop before date	20	75	350	—	—

VICTORIA 1837-1901

COPPER

7205

		VF	*EF*	*BU*	*Proof FDC*
		£	£	£	£
7203	**Eight doubles.** Type as before. Mintage 111,469				
	1858 five berries on left branch	12	65	350	650
	1858 four berries on left branch	12	65	350	—
7204	**Four doubles.** Similar. 1858 Mintage 114,060	12	65	350	—
7205	**Two doubles.** Similar. 1858 Mintage 56,128	18	75	400	—

BRONZE

H = Struck by R. Heaton & Sons, Birmingham (later The Mint, Birmingham, Ltd.)

7206

7206	**Eight doubles**				
	1864 (5 *obv*., 2 *rev*. dies) Mintage 184,736	15	60	200	—
	1864 Three stalks to spray	20	85	250	—
	1868 (5 *obv*. dies) Mintage 54,720	20	85	180	—
	1874 (4 *obv*., 2 *rev*. dies) Mintage 73,248	20	85	180	—
	1885H Mintage 69,696	—	15	85	300
	1889H Mintage 215,620	—	15	70	—
	1893H large or small lettering on *rev*. Mintage 117,600	—	15	70	—

	F	*VF*	*EF*	*BU*	*Proof* *FDC*
	£	£	£	£	£

7207

7207 Four doubles

	F	VF	EF	BU	Proof FDC
1864 Single stalk to sprig of laurel. Mintage 212,976	—	6	60	285	—
1864 Three stalks to sprig of laurel	—	6	60	285	—
1868 Mintage 57,696	—	6	60	285	—
1874 Mintage 69,216	—	5	50	270	—
1885H Mintage 69,696	—	—	10	50	375
1889H Mintage 103,744	—	—	8	40	450
1893H Mintage 52,224	—	—	10	50	—

7208

7208 Two doubles

	F	VF	EF	BU	Proof FDC
1868 Single stalk to sprig of laurel. Mintage 35,136	5	30	120	275	—
1868 Three stalks to sprig of laurel	5	30	120	275	—
1874 Wide or narrow date. Mintage 45,216	4	25	100	250	—
1885H Mintage 76,800	—	—	20	40	150
1889H Mintage 35,616	—	—	25	45	—
1899H Mintage 35,636	—	—	25	45	—

7209

7209 One double

	F	VF	EF	BU	Proof FDC
1868 Four leaves. Mintage 64,368	5	30	100	250	—
1868 Date altered from 1830 (1868/30)	5	30	100	250	—
1885H Three leaves. Mintage 76,800	—	—	3	15	10
1889H Mintage 112,016	—	—	3	10	—
1893H Mintage 56,016	—	—	3	15	—
1899H Mintage 56,000	—	—	3	15	—

EDWARD VII 1901-1910

BRONZE

7210

			Proof
	EF	*BU*	*FDC*
	£	£	£
7210 **Eight doubles**			
1902H Mintage 235,200	15	40	—
1903H Mintage 117,600	15	40	—
1910H Mintage 91,467	15	40	—

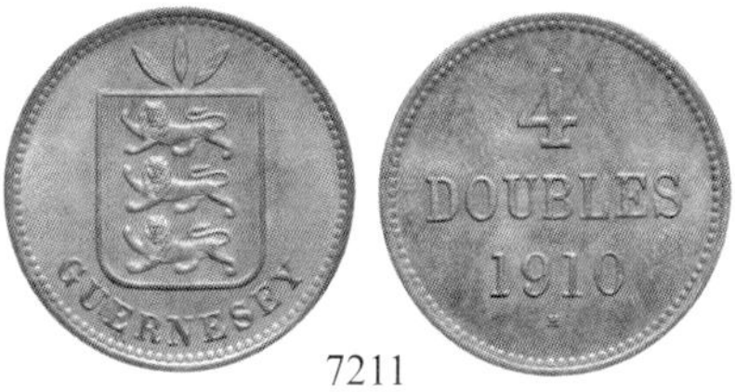

7211

7211 **Four doubles**			
1902H Mintage 104,534	10	30	—
1903H Mintage 52,267	10	30	—
1906H Mintage 52,266	10	30	—
1908H Mintage 25,760	12	40	—
1910H Mintage 52,267	10	30	—

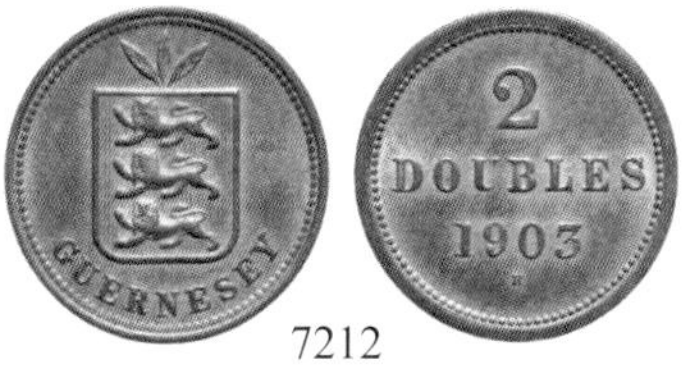

7212 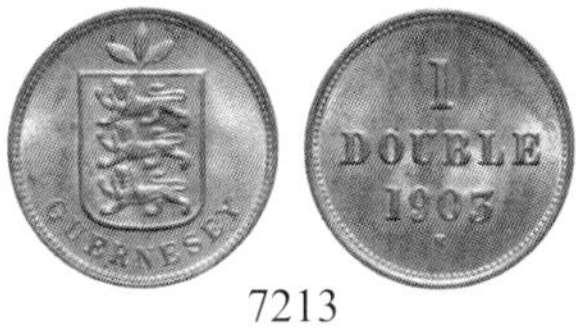   7213

7212 **Two doubles**			
1902H Mintage 17,818	20	45	—
1903H Mintage 17,818	20	45	—
1906H Mintage 17,820	20	45	—
1908H Mintage 17,780	20	45	—
7213 **One double**			
1902H Mintage 84,000	4	15	—
1903H Mintage 112,000	3	12	—

GEORGE V 1910-1936

BRONZE

7214

				Proof
	VF	EF	BU	FDC
	£	£	£	£
7214 Eight doubles. Three leaves above shield				
1911H Mintage 78,400...	5	40	100	—

7214A

7214A— Redesigned shield.				
1914H Mintage 156,800	—	8	25	—
1918H Mintage 156,800	—	8	25	—
1920H Mintage 156,800	—	7	20	—
1934H Mintage 123,600	—	7	20	125

	F £	VF £	EF £	BU £	*Proof* FDC £

7215A

7215 **Four doubles.** Three leaves above shield.

1911H Mintage 52,267 .... — 3 10 40 —

7215A— Redesigned shield.

1914H Mintage 209,067 .... — — 8 35 —

1918H Mintage 156,800 .... — — 8 35 —

1920H Mintage 156,800 .... — — 8 35 —

7216   7216A

7216 **Two doubles.** Three leaves above shield.

1911H Mintage 28,509 .... 4 10 40 100 —

7216A— Redesigned shield.

1914H Mintage 28,509 .... 4 10 40 100 —

1917H Mintage 14,524 .... 15 40 90 300 —

1918H Mintage 57,018 .... — 5 20 50 —

1920H Mintage 57,018 .... — 5 20 50 —

1929H Mintage 79,100 .... — — 6 15 —

7217   7217A

7217 **One Double.** Three leaves above shield.

1911H Mintage 67,200 .... — — 6 20 —

7217A— Redesigned shield.

1914H Mintage 44,800 .... — — 10 25 —

1929H Mintage 79,100 .... — — 4 15 —

1933H Mintage 96,000 .... — — 3 12 —

GEORGE VI 1936-1952

BRONZE

	Proof	
EF	*BU*	*FDC*
£	£	£

7218

7218 Eight doubles. Type as before.

1938H Mintage 120,000	8	20	—
1945H Mintage 192,000	5	15	—
1947H Mintage 240,000	5	15	—
1949H Mintage 230,000	5	15	—

7219

7220

7219 Four doubles. Type as before.

1945H Mintage 96,000	4	15	—
1949H Mintage 19,200	5	25	—

7220 One double. Type as before.

1938H Mintage 96,000	4	15	—

ELIZABETH II 1952-present

CUPRO-NICKEL

7221

7221 Threepence. ℞ Guernsey cow.

1956 Mintage over 500,000	—	5	1£
1959 increased weight. Mintage 480,000	—	5	1£
1966 Proof only. Mintage 10,000			1(

Battle of Hastings commemorative

7223

		Proof
	BU	*FDC*
	£	£

7223 **Ten shillings.** ℞ Bust of William the Conqueror.

1966 Mintage 300,000 .... 5 15

BRONZE

7225

7225 **Eight doubles.** Guernsey lily.

1956 Mintage 480,000	7	15
1959 Mintage 480,000	7	—
1966 Proof only. Mintage 10,000		10

7226

7226 **Four doubles.**

| 1956 Mintage 240,000 .... | 6 | 15 |
| 1966 Prof only. Mintage 10,000.. | | 10 |

PROOF SETS
Issued in official case

		No. of coins	*FDC*
		in set	£
7320	1956 Double set, threepence, 8 and 4 doubles	(6)	35
7321	1966 Ten shillings, threepence, 8 and 4 doubles	(4)	15

ISLE OF MAN

Man is situated in the Irish Sea, and was at one time an independent Viking kingdon, although suzerainty of the island has been claimed at various periods by the kings of Norway, Scotland, and England. In 1406 the island was granted with sovereign rights to Sir John Stanley, and the Earls of Derby held the island, first as 'Kings' and later as 'Lords' of Man. The island was inherited by James Murray, the second Duke of Atholl, in 1736, who sold it to the British Crown in 1765 for the sum of £70,000. Man still has its own parliament, the Tynwald, and passes its own laws.

Irish, Scottish and English coins circulated freely in the island and although coins from an early 11th century Hiberno-Manx mint are now known, a distinct Manx minor coinage was not introduced until 1709. These pennies and halfpennies were cast in moulds, and have the Earl's motto, **SANS CHANGER**. together with the Stanley crest, an eagle clutching a child upon the Cap of Maintenance. The reverses of most Manx coins bear the Triune, or 'three legs' with the motto **QVOCVNQVE JECERIS STABIT** (Whichever way you throw it, it will stand). In 1733 a second issue of coins appeared which were die-struck, not cast.

The first coins issued under the British Crown were made at the Mint in London in 1786, but the 1798 and 1813 issues were made by Matthew Boulton at the Soho Mint, Birmingham, and in style resemble the English 'cartwheels'. In 1840 the older Manx coins were demonetized as until the 1839 coinage, fourteen Manx pennies were equal to the English shilling. The new pennies at twelve to the shilling caused serious rioting. The island's coinage was allowed to lapse until the 200th anniversary of the Revestment of the Manx crown rights to the British Crown which was marked in 1965 by a gold coin set issue. This was followed by the issue of a crown piece depicting a Manx cat in 1970. A year later, decimal currency was introduced.

HIBERNO-MANX ISSUE *c.*1025

7400

7400 **Penny.** SIHTRIC SILKBEARD, King of Dublin and Overlord of Man (c.1014-35). Blundered copy of an English Long Cross penny of Æthelred II. Legend mostly upright strokes, quatrefoil of pellets at beginning of legend and behind head. ℞ Long cross with pellet in each quarter copying the Irish coins of the moneyer Feremin of Dublin. .... *Extremely rare*

JAMES STANLEY, TENTH EARL OF DERBY

First issue		F £	VF £	EF £

7401

		F	VF	EF
7401	**Penny.** 1709, cast. The Stanley crest, eagle and child on cap of maintenance. ℞ Triskelis (triune)	90	200	700

7402

		F	VF	EF
7402	**Halfpenny.** 1709, cast. Similar..	100	250	750

RICHARD MAGUIRE / JOSIAH POOLE ISSUE

First issue

	F £	VF £	EF £

7403   7404

| **7403** | **Shilling.** 1723. The Stanley crest, eagle and child on cap of maintenance. ℞ Triskelis (triune) | 2500 | 4000 | 7500 |
| **7404** | **Sixpence.** 1723. Similar | 1500 | 2500 | 5500 |

7405   7406

| **7405** | **Penny.** 1723. Similar | 1000 | 2000 | 4500 |
| **7406** | **Halfpenny.** 1723. Similar | 1000 | 2000 | 2400 |

Notes: Richard Maguire, a Dublin banker, and Josiah Poole, a wealthy Liverpool merchant, leased the customs of the Isle of Man from James Stanley, Tenth Earl of Derby, in March 1721, for the sum of £1,050 a year. It soon became apparent that it was going to be difficult to transact everyday business due to the dire shortage of coinage in circulation. Single sample coins of halfpenny and penny dated 1721, based on the 1709 design, were prepared by the two men and they approached James Stanley for official approval to strike up a quantity of the coins, but he refused. By 1723 the situation became so serious that Maguire and Poole acquired another pair of dies, probably from William Wood, and, unofficially, the coins were manufactured locally, almost certainly by the Wilks family at Ballasalla, who later assisted Samuel Topping and Amos Dyall with the production of the 1733 coinage in Castle Rushen. It would appear that, to save money, the halfpenny and penny dies were re-used to strike up the silver sixpence and shilling coins.

Second issue

7407

| **7407** | **Halfcrown.** 1725. Similar | *Extremely rare* |

Notes: In 1725 Maguire and Poole coined a halfcrown but, according to contemporary official Manx Government papers, 'they were almost instantly suppressed by the Legislature of the Isle'. Consequently, very few examples have survived.

An example in the British Museum coin collection is over-struck on a 1696 William III halfcrown.

Two different electrotype copies by Ready, British Museum, exist of this coin, weighing 13 grams and 17 grams respectively. A genuine 1725 halfcrown weighs approximately 14.50 grams.

JAMES STANLEY, TENTH EARL OF DERBY

Second issue

<table>
<tr><td></td><td>F
£</td><td>VF
£</td><td>EF
£</td></tr>
</table>

			F	VF	EF
7408	**Penny.** 1733. Similar to above, I D J between legs		45	150	800
	a — Struck in silver		400	700	1500
7409	**Halfpenny.** 1733. Similar but I D ½		75	200	800
	a — Struck in silver		300	500	800

Notes: The official 1733 coin issue, consisting of £300 in pence and £200 in halfpence, were struck by William Wood's successors, Amos Topping and Samuel Dyall, in Castle Rushen, Castletown. There are a number of different types of contemporary forgeries ofthe halfpenny and penny, in brass and copper, produced in Birmingham, and Rush and Skerries, Ireland. Modern forgeries of the 1733 coinage, including the silver pieces, were produced during the late 1960's and early 1970's by a jewellery firm for a collector in Rochdale, Lancashire.

JAMES MURRAY, SECOND DUKE OF ATHOLL

		F	VF	EF
7410	**Penny.** 1758. AD monogram surmounted by ducal coronet			
	R Triskelis (triune)	25	75	450
	a — — Struck in silver (Mintage 47)	500	900	2250

	F £	VF £	EF £

7411 Halfpenny. 1758. Similar 35   100   500

Notes: The 1758 coin issue, consisting of £250 in pence and £150 in halfpence, were struck by John Florry, a factor, of Easy Row, Birmingham. The original invoice exists in archives and states the mintage of the silver pennies as forty-seven – the number of pieces Florry could make from approximately £5 worth of silver (18 ounces at 6/- an ounce - £5. 8s). Around 1780 Florry was approached, unofficially, by a number of Manx businessmen to re-strike quantities of both the copper coins, which he did, although the dies had deteriorated over the years.

There are a number of different contemporary forgeries of the penny, the majority of which were again produced in either Birmingham or Rush and Skerries, Ireland. The most interesting of these used a set of dies the forgers made, struck over worn Irish halfpennies of George II and George III. On some of these pieces the underlying wording and date can still be made out, with the latest date of the host coin found so far being 1769.

GEORGE III 1760-1820

First issue. London

7413 Penny. 1786. Laureate bust right. ℞ Triskelis (triune) 25   65   400
    a — — Plain edge proof on thick flan. *FDC* £1500

7414 Halfpenny. 1786. Similar 20   50   300
    a — — Plain edge proof on thick flan. *FDC* £2000

	F £	VF £	EF £

Second issue. Soho 'cartwheel' coinage

7415

7415	**Penny.** 1798. Laureate bust right. ℞ Triskelis (triune)	50	90	550

    a — Proof *FDC* £700
    b — Bronzed proof *FDC* £800
    c — Gilt proof on ordinary flan. *FDC* £4000
    d — Gilt proof on thin flan. A later restrike *FDC* £3750
    e — Proof in silver on thin flan. A later restrike *FDC* £7500

	1813	25	60	450

    f — Proof *FDC* £700
    g — Bronzed proof *FDC* £800
    h — Gilt proof *FDC* £5000

7416

7416	**Halfpenny.** 1798. Similar	15	50	350

    a — Proof *FDC* £450
    b — Bronzed proof *FDC* £500
    c — Gilt proof *FDC* £3750

	1813	15	50	350

    d — Proof *FDC* £450
    e — Bronzed proof *FDC* £500
    f — Gilt proof *FDC* £5000

	F	VF	EF
	£	£	£

VICTORIA 1837-1901

7417

7417 Penny. 1839. Bust left. ℞ Triskelis (triune) 20 50 200
  a — 1839 Bronzed proof *FDC* £850
  b — 1841 Bronzed proof *FDC* £5000
  c — 1859 Bronzed proof *FDC* £4500

7418

7418 Halfpenny. 1839. Similar 15 35 175
  a — 1839 Bronzed proof *FDC* £500
  b — 1841 Bronzed proof *FDC* £5000
  c — 1860 Bronzed proof *FDC* £3000
  d — 1860 Bronzed proof with a streak of gold *FDC* £4000

7419

7419 Farthing. 1839. Similar 15 30 150
  a — — Bronzed proof *FDC* £500
  b — 1841 Bronzed proof *FDC* £5000
  c — 1860 Bronzed proof *FDC* £3000
  d — 1860 Bronzed proof with a streak of gold *FDC* £4000
  e — 1864 Bronzed proof *FDC* £5000

ELIZABETH II 1952 - present

GOLD

7420

7421   7422

Bicentenary issue	BU	Proof
	£	£
7420 **Five pounds.** 1965. ℞ Triskeles on shield within wreath	1875	2000
7421 **One pound.** 1965. Similar	375	400
7422 **Half pound.** 1965. Similar	200	225

CUPRO-NICKEL

First cat crown

7423

	UNC
7423 **Crown.** 1970. ℞ Manx cat	£3
a — — Silver proof in case *FDC* £25	

SPECIMEN SETS

3 coins issued in official case	*FDC* £
7770 1965 Gold £5, £1, £½	2750

now

LUNDY ISLAND

Lundy, an impregnable cliff-girt island in the Bristol Channel, was once noted as a pirate stronghold; today it is a favourite day sea excursion for summer visitors to North Devon. The island has had some celebrated owners, the most recent being Martin Coles Harman, who issued his own stamps and coins in 1929. On being prosecuted for contravention of the 1870 Coinage Act, Mr Harman defended his sovereign right to do so before the Devonshire Quarter Sessions on the grounds that Lundy was outside the Realm of England. His appeal to the King's Bench against a fine of £5 was dismissed.

The coins, called 'puffins' and 'half puffins', depict the seabird for which lundy is famous, and they have around the edge the inscription LUNDY LIGHTS AND LEADS.

MARTIN COLES HARMAN

BRONZE

7850   7851

		EF	BU
		£	£
7850	**Puffin.** 1929	5	15
7851	**Half puffin.** 1929	5	15

Note: Sets of Lundy Island 'coins' manufactured in 1965 are not listed as they were a purely private speculative issue of no numismatic significance.

ANGLO-GALLIC COINS

INTRODUCTION

Anglo-Gallic coins are those struck in Normandy, Aquitaine, Poitou, Ponthieu, and other parts of France by the kings and princes of England between 1154 and 1453 when the kings of England had interests in their various capacities as duke, or prince of Aquitaine, earl of Poitou, or count of this, that, or the other. It all began when Henry, Duke of Normandy, Count of Anjou, Maine and Touraine, married Eleanor of Aquitaine, and thus became Duke of Aquitaine and Count of Poitou. Even a century later, Edward I was probably more French than English. The king and queen of France were his uncle and aunt and he was as at home in Aquitaine, or the French court, as he was in England.

Although one might conclude that the coins were struck as a result of conquest, for the majority of these pieces this is not true. Indeed, it is best not to think of the protagonists as being either French, or English, for France, as we now know it, did not then exist. The rulers of the time were members of the same family who were constantly jostling for power, not for their country, but for themselves. At any one time, military or logistical superiority re-sulted in one faction or the other being in the ascendant. Eventually, however, geography took control and the English faction were expelled from France, even though some might argue that their claim to the crown of France at that time was then more valid than it had ever been !

No English coins were struck by the Black Prince, nor did Richard I strike English coins in his own name, so those collectors that want a representative coin of either have need of an Anglo-Gallic piece.

The coins were minted to the standards prevailing in France, not the sterling standard of England. They do not resemble the English coins of those kings in whose names they were struck, but French feudal and regal types of the time and sometimes other coins circulating in the Low Countries and Burgundy. There is one exception to this, which is the sterling. A silver coin, the sterling was not only a coin, but a money of account against which everything else was measured and compared.

Unlike English silver coins, which, with few exceptions were maintained at sterling fine-ness, small denomination continental coins were often debased. At the time of issue they would have had a good silver appearance, but after some use and handling, their colour would change to black, hence their name of 'black money'. They were hastily produced in large numbers and in consequence poorly struck. At the time they were the common circulating medium and became very worn. There were frequent re-coinages when they were first into the melting pot. Surviving examples are therefore now rare and most examples are low grade.

Although the black coins and the small billon coins up until Edward III are prosaic at best, the larger silver coins are quite unlike anything in the English series and the gold is ex-citing, even if their gothic style is perhaps a little overdone, they are certainly impressive, and the symbolism in the designs of the gold and silver coins is redolent of the age of chivalry and the feudal system.

The last of the feudal coins bear the name Henricus, but are not attributable with certainty to a particular Henry, IV - VI. The Aquitanian coinage continued until the loss of Bordeaux in 1453.

Henry V laid claim to the French throne in 1415. On his second invasion, in 1417, he captured Caen and established a mint there, followed by another in Rouen in 1419. During the reigns of Henry V and VI coins were minted to the same standards as the French royal issues.

NOTE ON VALUES

In order to value Anglo-Gallic coins properly, it is critical to understand that workmanship (die quality, flan size/shape and strike) can vary considerably throughout the series. Generally speaking, coins up until the time of Edward II are relatively well made. The silver and black coins of Edward III and Bergerac are often of indifferent workmanship, quickly made and poorly struck on small and/or irregular flans. Silver coins from the Black Prince to the end of the series are once again relatively well made, although black coins continue to be problematic. Coins are priced based on the workmanship that is expected for the period. In any event, well struck coins on large round flans will command a premium to the quoted prices, especially if they date to the period 1340-1361.

It is also important to realize that there are three overlapping markets for Anglo-Gallic coins: the UK in pounds sterling, France in euros and the US in dollars. As a result currency exchange rates can play a larger role in price fluctuations for this series than the others covered in this book. Finally, the competition for some pieces, particularly rare ones, can vary from one market to another, especially in auction venues.

SELECT BIBLIOGRAPHY

AINSLIE, G R. *Illustrations of the Anglo-French coinage.* London, 1830.

BROOKE, G C. *English Coins.* London, 1955.

DUCAREL, Andrew C. *A Series of above two hundred Anglo-Gallic or Norman and Aquitain Coins of the Antient Kings of England.* London, 1757.

DUPLESSY, J. *Les Monnaies Françaises Royales de Hugues Capet à Louis XVI,* 1. Paris, 1999.

— *Les monnaies Françaises Féodales,* 1. Paris, 2004.

— *Les monnaies Françaises Féodales,* 2. Paris, 2010.

ELIAS, E R Duncan, *The Anglo-Gallic Coins.* London/Paris, 1984.

ENGEL, Arthur & SERRURE, Raymond, *Traité de Numismatique du Moyen Age.* 3 vols., Paris 1891-1905, repr. Bologna, 1964.

FINN, P and WOODHEAD, P. *The Jonkheer E R Duncan Elias collection of Anglo-Gallic, English and French Medieval coins.* Spink Auction Catalogue no. 77, London, 1990.

HEWLETT, Lionel M. *Anglo-Gallic Coins.* London, 1920.

POEY d'AVANT, Faustin. *Monnaies feodales de France.* Paris, 1860, repr. Graz, 1961.

RECHENBACH, Mary C. *The Gascon Money of Edward III. A Study in Monetary History.* Unpublished PhD dissertation, University of Maryland, USA, 1975

RUDING, Rogers. *Annals of the Coinage of Great Britain and its Dependencies,* 3rd edition, London, 1840.

SNELLING, Thomas. *A View of the Coins struck by English Princes in France.* London, 1769.

WITHERS, Paul & Bente R and FORD, Steve D. *Anglo-Gallic Coins.* Llanfyllin, 2015.

ANGLO-GALLIC MINTS

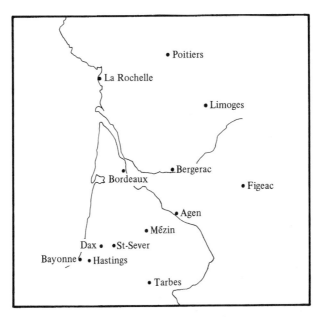

The Anglo-Gascon mints (1338–72).

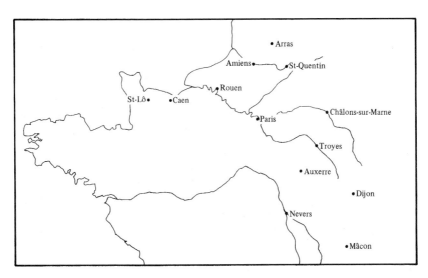

The royal French mints of Henry V and Henry VI

HENRY II, 1152-68. HENRY III, 1216-72

It is not certain whether the coins in the name of Henry were struck by Henry II or Henry III. The evidence is conflicting. However, it is likely that 8001 and 8002 were struck by Henry II.

Henry, great grand-son of William the Conqueror, duke of Normandy and count of Anjou etc., married Eleanor of Aquitaine in 1152, thereby becoming duke of Aquitaine and count of Poitou. In 1154 he became king of England. In 1168 Henry relinquished his French titles to his son Richard, who in in 1169 did homage for them to Louis VII of France. In 1185 Richard was forced to surrender his titles to his mother, who ruled when he was absent.

	F £	VF £
AQUITAINE		

8001   8002   8003

		F	VF
8001	**Denier.** ✠ (h)ENRICVS REX ℞ o ✠ o AQVI TANI o € o	80	200
8002	**Obole.** Types similar to above.	600	1500
8003	— Obv. similar to above. ℞ ɱ above REX cross below.	125	300

RICHARD COEUR DE LION
Duke of Aquitaine 1172-85, king of England 1189-99

AQUITAINE

8004   8005   8006

8004	**Denier.** RICA RDVS, ✠ above, ω below. ℞ ✠ AGVITANIE	*from* 75	150
8005	**Obole.** Types similar to above.	*from* 90	200
8006	**Denier.** Similar, ɱ above, ✠ below.	100	200
8007	**Obole.** Types similar to above.	400	800

POITOU

8008   8009

8008	**Denier.** ✠ RICARDVS REX ℞ PIC TAVIE NSIS	*from* 75	175
8009	**Obole.** Types similar to above.	*from* 100	250

There are many minor varieties known of all of the above 8004-8009, except 8007.

	F £	VF £

ISSOUDUN

8010

8010	**Denier.** • RICARD' REX R ✠ EXOLDVNI	900	1750

ELEANOR, wife of Henry II, mother of Richard

AQUITAINE

8011

8012

8011	**Denier.** ✠ DVCISIT R ✠ AQVITANIE or AGVITANIE	150	300
8012	**Obole.** Types similar to above.	750	1750

PRINCE EDWARD, duke of Aquitaine 1252-72, son of Henry III

AQUITAINE

8013

8014

8013	**Denier.** + EDVVARD' FILI R + h REGIS ANGLIE	75	175
8014	**Obole.** Types similar to above.	100	250

There are many varieties of both of the above.

EDWARD I, 1272-1307

AQUITAINE

8015

8016

8017

8015	**Denier.** + EDVVARDVS REX R + DVX AQVITANIE	200	400
8016	**Obole.** Types similar to above.	300	600
8017	**Denier.** + EDVARDVS R ANG R DVX AQI TBV RDB	250	600

	F £	VF £

8018   8020

8018 **Denier.** + EDWARDVS REX, AGL below lion. ℞ DVX AQIT BVRD,
      Є in one angle of cross.   *from* 60   150
8019 **Obole.** Types as above.   125   275
8020 **Denier.** Similar to 8018, but, Є and crescent in two angles. *from* 80   175
8021 **Obole.** Types as above.   150   325

PONTHIEU

8022   8023

8022 **Denier.** +EDOARDVS REX ℞ ꟽONETA PONTI   350   700
8023 **Obole.** Types similar to above.   400   800

EDWARD II, 1307-27

AQUITAINE
Silver

8024

8024 **Gros Turonus Regem.** + EDWAR o DVS o REX in inner circle, BΩDICTV
      SIT etc. in outer. ℞ TVRONVS RЄGꞴꟽ around chatel tournois.   3000 6500

8025   8026

8025 **Maille Blanche.** Types similar to above. + ЄD: RIX: AΩGLIЄ
      ℞ + DVX: AQITAΩIЄ   2500 5500
8026 **Maille Blanche Hibernie.** Types similar to above.
      + ЄD': RЄX AΩGLIЄ ℞ + DΩS: hIBЄRΩIЄ   75   175

	fair	*F*	*VF*
		£	£

Black coins

8027

8027 **Double à la couronne.** + EDV VARDVS REX Large crown.
R ꟿOꟿETA DVPLEX Processional cross.   500 1000 2500
Modern cast fakes are known.

8028   8029

8028 **Denier au léopard.** + ЄD' RЄX: AꟿGLIЄ Lion left above a line;
ꟿ B below. R + DVX: AQITAꟿIЄ Cross within inner circle,
a crown in one quarter.   *from* 40   75   150

8029 **Obole au léopard.** Similar types.   *from* 50   100   200

8030

8030 **Denier à l' couronne.** + EDWARDVS REX, in centre, AGI'; crown above; Є below.
R DVX AQIT BVRD, Є in one angle of cross.   250   500 1250

8031   8032

8031 **Denier au léopard.** +°EDꞈ REX°AꟿGLIE Cross within inner circle.
R +DVX: AQITAꟿIЄ Lion left above line, G below.   250   500 1250

8032 **Obole au léopard.** Similar types.   250   500 1250

8033   8034

8033 **Denier au léopard.** + ЄDWARDVS RЄX Lion left, cross
above and below. R Legend around short cross, G in one angle of rev.
                                                         from 50   100   200

8034 **Obole au léopard.** Similar types.   *extremely rare*

AQUITAINE
Gold

EDWARD III, 1327-62, 1372-77

VF
£

EF
£

8035

8035   **Ecu.** King enthroned holding shield. ℞ Ornamented cross.   3000   7500

8036

8036   **Florin.** + DVX: AQITAΩIԐ Fleur-de-lis. ℞ S IOHANNԐS B
St. John the Baptist.   8000   20,000
Found with initial mark crown, crowned head (sometimes over crown), and none.
Issued in 1344 at 3.50g, 1353 at 3.14g, 1354 at 2.92g.

8037

8037   **Léopard. 1st issue.** + ԐDVVARDVS♣ DԐI♣ GRA♣ AGLI♣ FRAΩCIԐ♣ RԐX♣
Crowned lion left. ℞ Cross fleury with lions in angles, no inner circle.
70 grains (4.54gm).   *extremely rare*

8038   8039

8038   **— 2nd issue.** + ԐDVVARDVS: DԐI: GRA: AΩGLI: FRAΩCIԐ: RԐX Crowned
lion left. ℞ Cross fleury with lions in angles, within circle.   6250   13,500
65 grains (4.21gm). There are many varieties of this type.

8039   **— 3rd issue.** + ԐDVVARDVS: DԐI: GRA: AΩGLI: FRAΩCIԐ: RԐX Crowned
lion left. A mullet ★ in one spandrel. ℞ Cross fleury with lions in angles,
within circle. 56 grains (3.63gm). Several varieties.   5250   12,500

8040   **— 4th issue.** English title only. + ԐDVVARDVS: DԐI: GRA: AΩGLIԐ: RԐX
Crowned lion left. ℞ As last. 56 grains (3.63gm).   12,500   27,500

	VF	*EF*
	£	£

8042

8041 **Léopard, 4th issue.** English and Aquitanian titles. + ƎDVVARDVS: RƎX:
AᑎGLIƎ: DᑎS: AQITAᑎIƎ   12,500   27,500

8042 — — English, Aquitanian and Irish titles. + ƎDVVARDVS: D: G: RƎX:
AᑎGLIƎ: DᑎS: AQITAᑎIƎ: z: hYB. Several varieties.   12,500   27,500

8043

8043 **Guyennois. 1st type.** Bordeaux. King standing facing, lion either
side within inner circle. R Cross fleury with lions and lis in alternate
angles. B in centre.   25,000   55,000

From this issue onwards, coins were struck at various mints. Bordeaux uses a letter B in the centre of
its reverse as its mark. Figeac mint uses F at the end of the obverse legend, whilst Limoges, Poitiers and
La Rochelle have L, P and R respectively to the right of the arch; or in the case of the coins of La
Rochelle, it may be between the king's legs. Coins without mint mark also occur. There are many minor
legend variations.

8044   8045

8044 — **2nd type.** Bordeaux. King advancing right, lions below his feet.
R Cross fleury with lions and lis in alternate angles.   15,000   35,000

8045 — **3rd type.** R Cross fleury with lions and lis in alternate angles,
within tressure of arches.   *from* 6250   12,500
Figeac, Limoges, Poitiers, La Rochelle, no mint mark.

Silver

There were many changes of coinage during the long reign of Edward III, due to economic and political circumstances. Most silver types were rapidly debased by reducing weight, fineness or both.

F   VF
£   £

8046

8046   **Gros au 3 fleurs-de-lis.** Cross within inner circle, inward pointing lis in 2nd and third quarter. R Chatel with annulet-topped towers and lis in centre, lion left below, arches containing lis around.   *extremely rare*

8047   8048

8047   **Sterling.** Crowned bust 3/4 left, lion left below. R Cross, crowns in angles. Many varieties of punctuation.   125   300
8048   **Demi-sterling.** Types as last.   175   450

8049   8050

8049   **Gros aquitanique.** Cross within inner circle. R Chatel aquitanique, lion left above. Many varieties.   *from*   500   1250
8050   **Blanc au léopard.** Cross within inner circle, a lis in one quarter. R Crown above lion left. Many sub-types with the following marks below the lion: mullet, cross, pellet, crescent, rosette, trefoil, I, m.   *from*   125   350
    Some are struck on small, light-weight flans. They vary in weight from 0.69 to 2.47 grams and size from 18 to 25 mm.. Nearly all are of poor quality.

8051

8051   **Gros with M.** Cross within inner circle. R Crowned M, legend around, border of arches containing leaves.   *extremely rare*

F   VF
£   £

8052   8053

8052 Gros tournois. Cross cutting inner and outer legends. ℞ Chatel
tournois containing pellet-in-annulet.   400   800
8053 Gros à la couronne. Cross cutting inner legend only. ℞ Crown.   *extremely rare*

8054   8055

8054 Gros tournois à la couronne. Cross cutting inner and outer legends.
℞ Chatel tournois containing a crown.   1000   2500
8055 Gros au léopard. Cross, each arms terminating in a crown, cutting
inner and outer legends. ℞ Crowned lion std. left, head front.   2500   6000

8056   8057

8056 Gros à la fleur de lis. Cross within inner circle. ℞ Fleur de lis.   3000   7000
8057 Gros au léopard passant. Cross cutting inner legend only. ℞ Lion
walking left.   1200   3000

8058   8059

8058 Gros aquitanique. Cross within inner circle. ℞ Chatel aquitanique.   300   700
8059 Gros à la couronne. Cross within inner circle. ℞ Crown.
Several varieties with annulets in or at the sides of the crown. *from* 300   750

F   VF
£   £

8060   8061

8060   **Gros tournois.** Cross within inner circle. ℞ Chatel tournois containing
symbol between pellets or annulets, lion left above.   *from* 250   600
There are varieties of central symbol in the castle: annulet, cross, crescent, crescent over
cross, mascle, lozenge, pellet in annulet.
There are many minor varieties. Usually badly produced on small, irregular flans.
8061   **Gros tournois.** Cross cutting inner and outer legends. ℞ Chatel tournois.
There are many varieties due to privy marks and punctuation.   *from* 350   750

8062   8063

8062   **Gros tournois.** Cross cutting inner legend. ℞ Chatel tournois.   1000   2500
8063   **Gros à la porte.** Cross within inner circle. ℞ Chatel aquitanique,
gateway below. Many varieties of symbol in or around the gateway. *from* 300   700

8064   8064A

8064   **Gros aquitanique.** Cross within inner circle, lis in one quarter. ℞ Chatel
aquitanique, lion left below (within legend or cutting it).   *from* 750   1750
Nearly always struck on small irregular flans of poor quality silver.
8064A **Blanc auc quadrilobes.** Cross with quatrefoils in two angles. ℞ Crown
above and below inscription   *extremely rare*

8065   8066

8065   **Gros au léopard couchant.** Cross. ℞ Lion std. left.   2000   500⊄
8066   **Gros au léopard couchant.** Similar, but latin cross cutting inner circle at its foot.
℞ Lion std. left, two line inscription below.   *extremely rare*

	F £	VF £

8067

8068

8067   Gros à la couronne. Cross calvary within inner circle, its foot
breaking both legends. R Crown.   550   1350
There are many varieties due to privy marks and punctuation.

8068   Gros tournois à la couronne. Cross within inner circle.
R Chatel tournois containing crown, lion left above.   800   1750

8069

8070

8069   Double sterling. Bordeaux. Long cross, three pellets and crown in alternate
quarters. R CIVITAS BVRDЄGALЄ Crowned male bust left.   1500   4000

8070   Sterling. Bordeaux. Long cross, three pellets and crown in angles.
R CIVITAS BVRDЄGALЄ Crowned lion's head facing.   1250   2750

8071   — Dax. DVX AQITAΩIЄ Crowned lion's head.   R CIVITAS ACΩSIS
Cross with crowns and three pellets in angles.   1250   2750

8072

8072   Gros au lion. Cross cutting inner legend. EDOVARDVS REX
R Lion rampant left. Agen, Bordeaux, La Rochelle or no mint name.
                                                              from 1000   2500
Modern cast fakes exist of this type.

8073

8074

8073   Demi gros au lion. Bordeaux or no mint name. As gros.   3000   6000

8074   Demi-gros or Double. Cross within circle. R Lion rampant. La Rochelle.
                                                              extremely rare

F	VF
£	£

8075 **Sterling guyennois.** Type 1. Half-length figure to edge of coin,
dividing legend. ℞ Long cross. Bordeaux.   *extremely rare*

8076

8077

8076 — Type 2. Similar, but half-length figure within inner circle.   *from* 500 1100
Bordeaux, Figeac, La Rochelle, no mint name.
8077 **Gros.** Half-length figure right. ℞ Long cross.   *extremely rare*

8078   8079

8078 **Demi gros.** Types as last.   1500 3500
8079 **Hardi d'argent.** Half-length facing figure. ℞ Long cross, lions and
lis in opposing angles.   *extremely rare*

Black money

Unlike English silver coins which, with few exceptions were maintained at sterling fineness, small denomination continental coins were often debased. At the time of issue they would have had a good silver
appearance, but after some use their colour would change to black, hence their name. They were hastily
produced in large numbers and in consequence poorly struck. At the time they were the common circulating medium and became very worn. There were frequent re-coinages when they were first into the
melting pot. Surviving examples are therefore now rare and most examples are low grade. Doubles,
typically worth two deniers, have the reverse legend MONETA DVPLEX.

8080   8082

	fair	F	VF
	£	£	£

8080 **Double au léopard sous couronne.** + ЄD' RЄX: AΩGLIЄ
Lion left, sometimes with symbol (sexfoil, trefoil, annulet)
below; large crown above. ℞ Short cross, crowns in two angles.
Many varieties.   *from* 40 100 250
8081 — + ЄD' DVX: AQITAΩIЄ Types as above.   100 250 550
8082 **Double au léopard.** Lion left. ℞ Cross, each arm terminating
with a crown.   *extremely rare*

	fair £	F £	VF £

8083   8083A

8083 **Double au léopard.** + €D' R€X: A∩GLI€ Lion left between two
lines, A above, GI or QI below. R + ℿO∩€TA DVPL€X Cross with
crown at end of each arm.   *from* 500   1000   2250

8083A — Lion above AGL I€ R Legend and type as above.   *extremely rare*

8084   8085

8084 **Double à la couronne.** Large crown above A∩GL IE in two lines.
R Processional cross.   750   1500   3250

8085 — Large crown above A∩G LIE in two lines. R Cross fleury. 600   1250   2750

8086   8087

8086 — Large crown inscribed REX. R Processional cross.   *from* 500   1000   2250

8087 **Double.** Legend around AGL€ FRA€ in two lines. R Latin
cross within inner circle.   275   750   1750

8088   8089

8088 **Double à la couronne.** Large crown, R⊖X below. R Cross
within inner circle.   750   1500   3250

8089 **Double guyennois.** Bordeaux. ED': REX: A∩GL: D∩S Crown above
AQVI TA∩€. R + ℿO∩€TA DVPL€X B Processional cross. 750   1500   3250

8090   8091

8090 **Denier au léopard.** + €DVARDVS: R€X Lion left above ANGL
between two lines. With or without symbol below (* ♣ or +)
R +DVX: AQITA∩I€ Cross within inner circle.   *from* 30   75   200

8091 **Obole au léopard.** Similar types.   *extremely rare*

	fair £	F £	VF £

8092

8093

8092 **Denier au léopard.** + ЄD RЄX etc. on obv. or rev. Lion between two lines, letters or symbols above and below. R Cross within inner circle. *from* 60   150   300

8093 **Obole au léopard.** Similar types. *extremely rare*

8094

8095

8094 **Denier au léopard.** Lion left between two lines, quatrefoil or lis below. R Cross within inner circle.   150   375   750

8095 **Denier au léopard.** Lion left, AΩG between two lines below. R Cross within inner circle.   *extremely rare*

8096

8097

8096 **Obole au léopard.** + ЄDVARDVS: RЄX Lion left above a line, AG or AΩG below. R Cross within inner circle.   300   600   1200

8097 — No line, * below lion. R Cross, crown in one angle.   75   150   300

8098

8099

8098 **Denier, lion right.** + ЄD RЄX AΩGLIЄ R + DΩS AQITAΩIЄ Cross within inner circle.   *from* 60   150   300

Bordeaux, Figeac, Limoges, Poitiers, La Rochelle (?), no mintmark.

8099 **Denier, lion left.**   *from* 75   200   400

Agen, Bordeaux, Limoges, Poitiers (?), La Rochelle.

PONTHIEU

8100

8101

	F £	VF £

8100 **Denier.** +ЄDVVARDVS REX. R ᛖONET POTIVI Lion left.   500   125C

8101 **Obole.** Types similar to above.   750   175C

HENRY OF LANCASTER, 1347-61

Cousin of Edward III. Earl of Lancaster; from 1351 Duke of Lancaster

BERGERAC

This coinage was struck in times of war and is hurriedly produced, mostly on small, irregular flans, in consequence of which the outer legends are nearly always illegible or missing.

Coinage as Earl - 'COMES' 1347-51

Silver

	F £	VF £

8102

8103

		F	VF
8102	**Gros à la couronne.** hЄฏ COꟿЄS LAฏCЄ Cross cutting inner legend only. R + DฏS BRAGAIRACI Crown.	*extremely rare*	
8103	**Gros tournois à la couronne.** Cross cutting inner and outer legends. R Chatel tournois contaning crown.	*from* 2500	5500

8104

8105

		F	VF
8104	**Gros au léopard.** Cross cutting inner and outer legends. R Lion std. left.	4000	10,000
8105	**Gros a la fleur de lis.** Cross within inner circle. R Fleur de lis.	4000	9000

8106

8107

		F	VF
8106	**Gros au léopard passant.** Cross cutting inner legend only. R Lion walking left, a line above and below.	4000	10,000
8107	**Gros aquitanique.** Cross within inner circle. R Chatel aquitanique.	2500	6000

F VF
£ £

8108

8109

8108 **Gros à la couronne.** Cross within inner circle. ℞ Crown, with or
without symbols in crown or at side. *from* 1250 3250
8109 **Gros tournois au léopard.** +hЄΩR COꟽ LAΩCAST Cross within inner circle.
℞ Lion above chatel tournois. 1250 3250

8110

8110 **Gros tournois.** hЄΩ COꟽ LA ΩCЄ Cross cutting both inner and
outer legend. ℞ + DΩS BRAGAIRC Chatel tournois. 3000 7000

Black coins

8111

8112

8111 **Double à la couronne.** Legend around crown inscribed COꟽ.
℞ Processional cross, cutting legend and circle at bottom. 3500 7500
8112 **Double.** + h DΩS⠒ BRAGAIRACII Across field LAΩC COꟽЄ.
℞ + ꟽOΩETA⠒ DVPLEX Cross calvary. 2500 6000

8113

8113 **Denier.** + hЄΩRICVS COꟽ Lion left between two lines within
inner circle. ℞ + DΩS* BRAGAIRA Cross within inner circle. 3000 7500

Coinage as Duke - 'DVX' 1351-61
Silver

	F £	VF £

8114

8115

8114   **Gros au léopard couchant.** Cross within inner circle. ℞ Lion
std. left.   4000   10,000
8115   — + ᕮΩ: DΩS BRAGIE Latin cross cutting inner legend.
℞ LAΩCAI IE: DVX in two lines below crowned lion left.   3500   9500

8116

8117

8116   **Gros tournois à la couronne.** + ᕮΩ: DΩS: BRAGIIᕮ Cross within
inner circle. ℞ DVX: LAΩCAIIᕮ Crown in chatel, lion above.   2750   6000
8117   **Sterling.** + hEΩ᛬ DVX᛬ LAΩCAST ℞ DΩS BRA GAI RAC Long cross,
crowns and three pellets in alternate quarters.   2500   7000

8118

8118   **Gros au lion.** ᕮΩO VRI COS DΩS Cross cutting inner legend.
℞ +MOΩET ♣ BRAGII Lion rampant left.   *from*   4000   10,000

Black coins

8119

8120

8119   **Double.** Cross within inner circle. ℞ Lion std. left.   *extremely rare*
8120   **Denier.** Lion stg. left above BRA between two lines. ℞ Cross
within inner circle.   *extremely rare*

EDWARD THE BLACK PRINCE, Prince of Aquitaine 1362-72.

Edward arrived in Bordeaux in July, 1363. In the next nine years some of the most spectacular, interesting and attractive coins were produced.

The pavillon d'or has an unusual feature - four ostrich feathers in the field. These have an interesting story behind them and are the probable origin of the badge of the prince of Wales, which Edward was, as well as being prince of Aquitaine.

John the Blind (1309-1346) was king of Bohemia and count of Luxembourg. He put down several revolts in Bohemia; he fought against Frederik of Austria, the Duke of Brabant, and the Count of Flanders; he conquered the North of Italy and led three campaigns against Lithuania. It was there, possibly, that he contracted the disease which led to his blindness. John's relations with the French were excellent, his sister married Charles IV of France, and his daughter Bonne married Jean le Bon; and his eldest son Charles was married to Blanche of Valois. After the death of his first wife, John himself married a French princess, Beatrix of Bourbon and naturally supported Philip IV against Edward III.

In 1346 the English army commanded by the Black Prince met the French army at Crécy. John, despite his blindness, was there with 500 knights. On being told that the French were suffering heavy losses and that an English victory was certain, John asked his immediate companions to link their horses with his and to ride one last charge. The whole troop, the medieval equivalent of modern suicide bombers, plunged into the fray and, with the exception of just two knights, was slaughtered. Legend relates that the Black Prince was so impressed by the dead hero's actions that he adopted John's ostrich feather crest and his motto "ICH DIEN" as his own.

The name and titles of the prince given on the coins is EDWARDVS PRIMO GENITVS REGIS ANGLIE PRINCEPS AQVITANIE - Edward, first-born of the king of England, Prince of Aquitaine. Obviously, this could not be quoted in full, and had to be abbreviated on even the largest coin. This resulted in an enormous number of varieties.

Mint marks. the first letter of the mint name, usually found at the end of the obverse or reverse legend. Prices are for the most common varieties of the most common mints.

Aquitaine	VF	EF
Gold	£	£

8121   8122

8121	**Léopard.** Crowned lion left. ℞ Cross fleury.	7500	15,000
8122	**Guyennois.** Prince right, lions at his feet. ℞ Cross fleury.	14,000	28,000

8123   8124

8123	**Noble guyennois à la rose (Pavillon d'or).** Prince, holding sword, standing in ornate gothic portico; ostrich feathers in field. ℞ Cross with acorn and oak-leaf terminals, a rosette in centre.	8000	16,000
	No mintmark, Bergerac, Bordeaux, Limoges, Poitiers, La Rochelle.		
8124	**Demi noble.** Similar to 8123. No mintmark.	*extremely rare*	

VF   EF
£   £

Rose in centre,
no. 8123

8125

Ꮛ in centre,
no. 8125

8125 **Noble guyennois à l'E. 1st issue.** Similar, but Ꮛ in centre of cross.
No mintmark, Bordeaux, Figeac, Limoges, Poitiers, La Rochelle.   *from* 7000 14,000
8126 **— 2nd issue.** Similar to last, with punctuation at start of obverse
legend.   *from* 7000 14,000
Bordeaux, Figeac, Limoges, La Rochelle.

8127

8127 **Chaise.** Prince, bearded, with flowers in his hair and holding
sceptre, enthroned facing. ℞ Cross fleury.   *from* 10,000   20,000
No mintmark, Bergerac, Bordeaux, Limoges, Poitiers, La Rochelle.

8128

plain diadem   rosette diadem

8128 **Hardi.** Diademed half-length figure facing. Diadem usually plain, but may
have three roses. ℞ Cross with acorn and oak-leaf terminals.
There are many varieties.   *from* 8000   20,0000
Bordeaux, Limoges, Poitiers, La Rochelle.

Silver   F   VF

8129

8129 **Gros.** Half-length figure right. ℞ Long cross over legend.   *from* 1750   4000
No mintmark, Agen, Bordeaux, Tarbes.

	F	VF
	£	£

8130   8131

8130 **Demi gros.** 1st issue. Types as gros, 8129.   *from* 150   350
No mm., Agen, Bordeaux, Dax (mm. AS), Figeac, Limoges, Poitiers, La Rochelle, Tarbes.

8131 — 2nd issue. Similar, initial mark at start of legends both sides. *from* 125   325
No mm., Agen, Bordeaux, Dax (mm. AS), Figeac, Limoges, Poitiers, La Rochelle, Tarbes.

8132   8133

8132 **Sterling.** 1st issue. Types similar.   *from* 200   500
No mm., Bordeaux, Tarbes (other mints reported but not confirmed).

8133 — 2nd issue. Similar, initial mark at start of legends.   *from* 125   300
No mm., Bordeaux, Dax (mm. AS), Figeac, Limoges, Poitiers, La Rochelle, Tarbes.

8134 Agen    8134 La Rochelle

8134 **Hardi.** Half-length figure facing below gothic arch. ℞ Cross,
lis and lion in alternate quarters. Portraiture style varies greatly,
and there are innumerable varieties of legend and punctuation. *from* 100   250
No mm., Agen, Bordeaux, Figeac, Limoges, Poitiers, Tarbes.

	fair	F	VF
	£	£	£

Black money

8135

8135 **Double guyennois.** Crown above AQVI TAIE, within inner circle.
℞ Processional cross with lis or trefoil terminals.   *from* 300 1000 2000
Agen, Dax, Figeac, Poitiers, La Rochelle, (other mints reported but not confirmed).

8137

8138

		fair £	*F* £	*VF* £
8136	**Denier, lion right.** ℞ + DℿS• AQVITAℿIℬ Short cross.	100	250	500
	Poitiers. (Black prince/Edward III mule)			
8137	— ℞ + PℿPS: AQVITAℿIℬI or similar. Short cross. *from*	75	175	400
	Bordeaux, Figeac, Poitiers, La Rochelle.			
8138	**Denier, lion left.** Similar, but lion faces the other way. *from*	100	300	600
	No mm., Bordeaux, Poitiers (?), La Rochelle, Tarbes.			

8139

8139	**Denier.** Cross within inner circle, lis and lions in alternate angles.			
	℞ Cross within inner circle. *from*	50	150	300
	No mm., Agen, Bordeaux, Dax, Figeac, Limoges, Poitiers, La Rochelle			

RICHARD II, 1377-99

Aquitaine
Gold   *VF*   *EF*

8140

8141

8140	**Hardi.** Crowned half-length figure facing. ℞ Cross with acorn and oak-leaf terminals. No mm. or Bordeaux.	5500	12,500
8141	**Demi hardi.** Crowned bust facing. ℞ Cross with acorn and oak-leaf terminals. No mm. or Bordeaux.	15,000	35,000

Silver   *F*   *VF*

8142

8143

8142	**Double hardi.** Crowned half-length figure facing below gothic arch. ℞ Cross, lis and lions in alternate angles.	2500	6000
8143	**Hardi**. Similar types.	100	250

8144

	fair	F	VF
	£	£	£

Black money

8144   Denier. Cross; lis and lions in alternate angles. ℞ Cross within
inner circle.   60   125   300

HENRY IV, HENRY V, HENRV VI, 1399-1453

The kings of the English have never been imaginative when naming their sons. This means that we are not able to say which monarch(s) struck the last feudal coins of the duchy of Aquitaine.

People have long speculated on the various abbreviations of the king's name, hENRICVS, from ENRICVS to ERIC, and the meaning of the various symbols above the crown and in the legend, but we are still none the wiser as to their meaning, if any.

Gold

8145

8145   Hardi. Crowned half-length figure facing, holding sword; hound and
bear to left and right. ℞ Cross with acorn and oak-leaf terminals.   *extremely rare*

Silver

8146   8147

8146   Double hardi. Crowned half-length figure facing below gothic
arch. ℞ Cross, lis and lions in alternate angles.   1500   3300
8147   Hardi. Similar types. Numerous varieties, with different symbols
above crown and on reverse.   *from* 40   75   175

8148   8149

8148   Double hardi aux genêts. Similar to 8146, with branch of broom in
field either side, and in place of the lis on reverse.   *unique ?*
8149   Hardi aux genêts. Similar types.   *extremely rare*

	fair	F	VF
Black money	£	£	£
8150 **Denier.** Cross within inner circle, lis and lions in alternate angles. ℞ Cross within inner circle.	50	100	250
8151 **Denier au genêt.** Branch of broom. ℞ Cross with lis and lions in angles	150	400	1000

French regal coins

HENRY V, 1413-22

At the beginning of the 15th century France was in disarray, with Charles VI insane and the country split into factions. Henry V tried to intervene by supporting the Armagnacs, but this achieved nothing for him. He tried to resurrect the terms of the Treaty of Bretigny, but this was refused by the French, so Henry invaded France in September 1415, captured Harfleur and won a glorious victory at Agincourt on St. Crispin's day. Henry tried again in the summer of 1417. In September he captured Caen and then battled on for the rest of Normandy.

In August of 1419, Jean sans Peur, duke of Burgundy, was assassinated by the Armagnac faction. Jean's son, Philip the Good, now gave his support to Henry, who as per the Treaty of Bretigny was given the hand of the French king's daughter as well as the succession to the throne on Charles's death, and in the meantime, the regency. This treaty was signed at Troyes on 21st May, 1420.

Henry then went back to England and returned in the summer of 1421. He died at Vincennes on 31 August 1422, a few weeks before Charles VI.

Gold VF EF

| 8152 | **Agnel,** 1st issue. Paschal lamb. ℞ Cross fleury, rosette in centre. | 12,500 | 30,000 |
| 8153 | — 2nd issue. Similar, **h** in centre of reverse. | 12,500 | 30,000 |

| 8154 | **Salut.** The angel Gabriel and the virgin Mary either side of shield. ℞ Latin cross, **h** below. | 20,000 | 45,000 |

Silver   *F*   *VF*

8155    8156

8155   **Guénar.** Shield bearing three lis. ℞ Cross, crowns and lis in alternate angles. Sun below initial cross. Caen.   1500   3500

8156   **Florette,** 1st issue. hԑΩRICVS FRANCORV RԑX Crown above three lis. ℞ Cross fleury, crown and lion in two opposite angles. Rouen.   175   400

8157    8158

8157   — 2nd issue. Similar, but **h** in centre of cross. Rouen.   750   1750

8158   — 3rd issue. Lion rampant either side of crown above three lis. ℞ As last. Rouen, St. Lô.   *from*   175   400

8159    8160

8159   — 4th issue. h RԑX ANGLIԑ Z hԑRԑS FRANCIԑ Types as 8158. Rouen, St. Lô.   *from*   175   400

Rouen - pellet under first letter    St. Lô - pellet under second letter

8160   **Gros au léopard.** Crown above lion left among three lis. ℞ Cross fleury, **h** in centre. Rouen and St. Lô.   *from*   3000   7000

Black money.

8161

8161   **Mansois.** Three fleurs de lis. ℞ ΩOΩ ETA DVP LEX Cross with **h**.   2250   5000

8162

8163

F *VF*
£ £

8162 **Niquet.** Lis above crowned lion. ℞ Cross, **h** in centre. *from* 60 125
Rouen, St. Lô.

The niquet was issued 30 november, 1421, current for 2 deniers tournois. At the time of its production this was practically the only coin in circulation.

8163 **Denier tournois** (demi niquet). Crowned lion. ℞ Cross, **h** in centre.
Rouen, St. Lô. *from* 100 250

The two coins illustrated here are of a different style from the genuine niquet pictured above. They are contemporary forgeries.

HENRY VI

King of England 1422-1461, king of France 1422-1450

When Henry V died, his son, became king of England at the age of nine months. Then, seven weeks later, his grandfather, Charles VI of France also died, and in accordance with the Treaty of Troyes, the infant Henry VI also became king of France.
On his accession under the Treaty of Troyes, Henry VI was acknowledged as King of France by three parts of the country – by Normandy, by the city of Paris, and by those provinces in the north and east which were under the control of Philip the Good, who was a signatory to the Treaty. Close co-operation with Burgundy was therefore maintained.
The regent of France for Henry VI was John, Duke of Bedford, one of the king's uncles. He continued Henry V's policies. He bound England more closely to Burgundy by marrying Philip the Good's sister, and in 1422 he even offered Philip the regency, which Philip declined. Regarding the currency Bedford and Burgundy deliberately adopted the policy of having a stable and uniform coinage.
The history of the provision of coin is an example of satisfactory civil administration by the English which contrasts strongly with the political and military misjudgements which characterize the last days of English government in France.
The mints, with the exception of that of Dijon, were centrally controlled from Paris, where the dies were manufactured. A master general was responsible to the regency council for all the mints. Dijon, being in the duchy of Burgundy and thus under the control of the duke remained autonomous. Twelve mints struck coins in Henry's name.
On 12 December 1422 an order was made that allotted each mint a mark that was to be placed at the start of the obverse and reverse legends.

Amiens		paschal lamb	(1422-35)
Auxerre		mill iron* (also called a cross ancrée)	(1422-35)
Châlons		crescent	(1422-29)
Dijon		vernicle**	(1423-36)

Le Mans	🜚	root (there are several forms of this)	(1425-48)	
Mâcon	♣	trefoil	(1422-35)	Struck silver coins only
Nevers	★	Mullet	(1422-35)	Struck silver coins only
Paris	♕	crown	(1422-36)	
Rouen	🦁	léopard (lion passant)	(1422-49)	
St. Lô	✣	lis	(1422-49)	
St. Quentin	✷	pierced mullet	(1422-35)	
Troyes	❀	rose (there are several forms of this)	(1422-29)	

* the iron part that fixes the rotating mill stone onto the mill machinery.
** the face of Christ allegedly burned onto St Veronica's handkerchief.

Gold

VF £   EF £

8164   8165

8164   **Salut.** Half-length figures of virgin Mary and angel Gabriel, AVɑ
on scroll between; French and English royal arms below. ℞ Latin
cross, **h** below, lis and lion at sides.   *from*   1000   2500
Amiens, Auxerre, Châlons, Dijon, Le Mans, Paris, Rouen, St. Lô, St. Quentin, Troyes.
There are very many varieties.

8165   **Angelot.** Half-length figure angel Gabriel above French and English
royal arms. ℞ Latin cross, lis and lion at sides.   *from*   9000   18,000
Le Mans, Paris, Rouen, St. Lô, Troyes.

Silver

F   VF

8166

8166   **Grand blanc.** h̄ɑRICVS above French and English royal arms.
℞ Latin cross, lis and lion at sides, h̄ɑRICVS on a line below. *from* 100   200
Amiens, Auxerre, Châlons, Dijon, Le Mans, Mâcon, Nevers, Paris, Rouen,
St. Lô, St. Quentin, Troyes. There are very many varieties.
The king's name is abbreviated h̄ɑRICVS on all coins of this denomination.

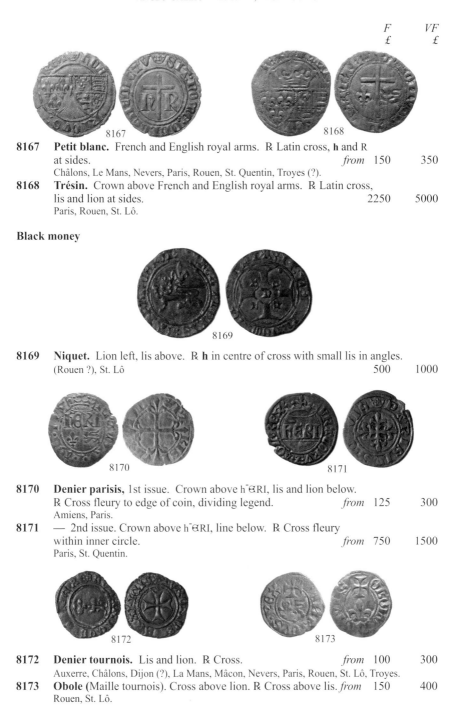

	F £	VF £

8167   Petit blanc. French and English royal arms. ℞ Latin cross, **h** and R
at sides.   *from* 150   350
Châlons, Le Mans, Nevers, Paris, Rouen, St. Quentin, Troyes (?).

8168   Trésin. Crown above French and English royal arms. ℞ Latin cross,
lis and lion at sides.   2250   5000
Paris, Rouen, St. Lô.

Black money

8169

8169   Niquet. Lion left, lis above. ℞ **h** in centre of cross with small lis in angles.
(Rouen ?), St. Lô   500   1000

8170   8171

8170   Denier parisis, 1st issue. Crown above h⁻ᙠRI, lis and lion below.
℞ Cross fleury to edge of coin, dividing legend.   *from* 125   300
Amiens, Paris.

8171   — 2nd issue. Crown above h⁻ᙠRI, line below. ℞ Cross fleury
within inner circle.   *from* 750   1500
Paris, St. Quentin.

8172   8173

8172   Denier tournois. Lis and lion. ℞ Cross.   *from* 100   300
Auxerre, Châlons, Dijon (?), La Mans, Mâcon, Nevers, Paris, Rouen, St. Lô, Troyes.

8173   Obole (Maille tournois). Cross above lion. ℞ Cross above lis. *from* 150   400
Rouen, St. Lô.

286

ALPHABETICAL INDEX OF RULERS

APPENDIX 1 The 2015 version of Ireland, Edward IV.
EDWARD IV, 1461-1483

The accession of Edward IV saw the issue of the coinage ordered in 1460. It was of distinctive type with a large crown on the obverse instead of a royal portrait, and to discourage the export of silver coin it was made to a specific Irish weight standard which was three-quarters that of the English coinage. In view of the events which led to the transfer of sovereignty from the Lancastrians to the Yorkists it is scarcely surprising that the first issue was anonymous. Another innovation was the minting of farthings made of billon (silver heavily debased with copper) in the name of St Patrick, followed in 1463 by a larger coin depicting the Saint's mitred head. A second silver coinage minted at Dublin and Waterford in 1463 was of somewhat similar type to the first except for the addition of the king's name and Irish title on the obverse, **EDWARDVS DEI GRA DNS HYBERN**, and an outer inscription on the reverse, **POSVI DEVM ADIVTOREM MEVM**, 'I have made the Lord my Helper'.

In 1465 the weights of the English silver coins were considerably reduced and it may be about this time that the Dublin mint followed suit by minting a new coinage only two-thirds the weight of the English issue, the earlier crown device being replaced by two Yorkist badges, a rose on one side with a cross superimposed and a sun in splendour on the other. Two years later the Irish money was again devalued, the Irish groat being rated half the English equivalent, but now an eightpenny coin was issued the same size as the English groat.

A stylised royal portrait copied the English groat, but Edward's rose en soleil device supplied a distinctive type for the reverse, the coins being issued from the mints of Dublin and Drogheda and the great fortress at Trim. An interesting base metal farthing of this issue has for its obverse type a shield bearing the fifteenth-century arms of Ireland, three crowns.

No coins were minted in Ireland bearing the name of Henry VI during his brief restoration, 1470-1; the groats that at one time were attributed to this period are now clearly seen to be coins of Henry VII. In 1470 a new coinage giving nominal allegiance to King Edward was instituted which was the same type and almost the weight of his English issues, possibly made with the object of having them available, if necessary, for currency in England, They were minted at Dublin, Waterford, Drogheda and Trim and at temporary mints in the west and south-west of Galway, Limerick and Cork. Only two coins have survived of the Galway mint, and though it is possible that a mint was also opened at Carlingford no coins of this period are now known of that mint. Coins were also minted at Wexford but they are so crude that they are unlikely to be an official issue. About 1472 the coinage was again devalued by reducing the groat to 32 grains, though it is known that some of the 1470 'heavy' issue had been struck at weights below the proper standard. For this reason, and because heavy coins were frequently clipped down to the weights of the later issue, it is sometimes difficult to determine the proper issue of these coins. Some pence of this issue copy coins of York or Durham with a quatrefoil or **D** in the centre of the reverse.

On the coins of this English type, as well as other issues of Edward, an elaborate system of 'privy' marks (private or secret marks) were inserted into the design in order to discourage fraud at the mint and to detect counterfeits. In addition, initial marks or 'mintmarks' denoting the period of issue were usually inserted at the commencement of the inscription and were changed annually or at other intervals.

In 1476 in order to encourage the import of gold coin into Ireland the English noble of ten shillings was rated at 13s 4d Irish and the angel of 6s 8d at 8s 4d, and at the same time foreign gold was made legal tender – ducats, riders, crowns, cruzados and salutes at 5s and Burgundian nobles at 10s.

The last coinage of this reign was confined to the mints of Dublin and Drogheda, and the groats have roses and suns alternating by the king's neck and crown and a large rose in the centre of the reverse cross. The pence of this coinage are of two distinct types, the earlier with a small rose at the centre of the reverse cross and with roses and suns in the angles, the later with a large rose as the groats.

SILVER

I. Anonymous 'Crown' coinage, c.1460-63

F   VF
£   £

6272

6272 **Groat** (45 grs.) *Dublin*. Large crown in tressure of 9 arcs with
pellets at points, no legend. ℞ Mint name, cross and pellets 1000 3000

6272A   6274

6272A— — Crosses in three top angles of tressure 675 2000
6273 — Similar, but 8 arcs to tressure, small sun in each angle 1000 3000
6274 — Similar, but arcs of tressure fleured, suns or rosettes in angles 1100 3250
6275 — — Large rosette in each angle of tressure 1250 3500
6275A— Light issue (c. 35 grs.) As 6272. .... 575 1750

6276   6280

6276 **Penny.** *Dublin*. As groat, 6272 .... 900 3000
6277 — — Crosses in top angles of tressure 900 3000
6278 — — Saltire below crown 1000 3250
6279 — Crown in tressure of 8 arcs 1000 3250
6280 — No tressure 900 3000
6281 *Waterford*. Crown in tressure of fleured arcs 1750 4500
6281A Halfpenny. *Dublin*. Crown in tressure of 7 arcs, pellets in angles. *Extremely rare*

	F	VF
	£	£

II. Named and titled 'Crown' coinage, 1463

Mintmarks: rose *(Dublin)*, cross *(Waterford)*

6282

6284

6282	**Groat.** *Dublin.* King's name and titles, large crown in tressure, small annulets in spandrels. ℞ POSVI etc., cross and pellets. *Mm.* rose	1850	5000
6283	*Waterford.* Similar, but pellets in angles, *mm.* cross	2000	5500
6284	— Annulets in angles of tressure, saltires by crown	2250	6000

6285

6285	**Half groat.** *Dublin.* Pellets in angles of tressure, two saltires over crown	2000	5500
6285A	*Waterford.* Pellels in angles of tresssure	2250	6000
6286	**Penny.** *Dublin.* Inscription around crown, no tressure	1350	3500
6287	*Waterford.* Similar	1500	3750

III. Small Cross on Rose/Radiant Sun coinage, *c.*1464 or 1478 ?

6288

6289

6288	**Groat.** *Dublin.* Large rose, cross at centre, within tressure of five arcs. ℞ POSVI etc., mint name, sun with face	3000	7500
6289	**Penny.** *Dublin.* Similar, but no tressure around rose. ℞ Mint name, a sun with pellet in annulet at centre..	750	2250

V. Heavy 'Cross and Pellets' coinage, 1465

Basically the same type as the English coins of the period. The letter G on some coins is the initial of the mintmaster Germyn Kynch. Extra pellets, annulets, crosses or roses occur in one or more angles of the cross on some coins.

Mintmarks: rose, pierced cross double fitchy

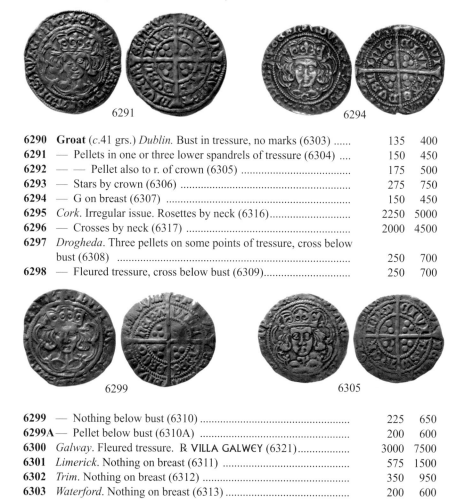

6291   6294

		F	VF
6290	**Groat** (*c*.41 grs.) *Dublin.* Bust in tressure, no marks (6303)	135	400
6291	— Pellets in one or three lower spandrels of tressure (6304)	150	450
6292	— — Pellet also to r. of crown (6305)	175	500
6293	— Stars by crown (6306)	275	750
6294	— G on breast (6307)	150	450
6295	*Cork.* Irregular issue. Rosettes by neck (6316)........................	2250	5000
6296	— Crosses by neck (6317)	2000	4500
6297	*Drogheda.* Three pellets on some points of tressure, cross below bust (6308)	250	700
6298	— Fleured tressure, cross below bust (6309)............................	250	700

6299   6305

		F	VF
6299	— Nothing below bust (6310)	225	650
6299A	— Pellet below bust (6310A)	200	600
6300	*Galway.* Fleured tressure. ℞ VILLA GALWЄY (6321)..................	3000	7500
6301	*Limerick.* Nothing on breast (6311)	575	1500
6302	*Trim.* Nothing on breast (6312)	350	950
6303	*Waterford.* Nothing on breast (6313)	200	600
6304	— Crosses by neck (6314)	225	650
6305	— Annulets by neck. ℞ Crowned leopard's head at end of legend (wt. 45 grs.) (6347)...	525	1350
6306	— V on breast (6314A)...	225	650
6307	— Ƨ on breast, crosses or saltires by neck (6315).....................	275	750

F	*VF*
£	£

6308 **Half groat.** *Dublin*. Pellets over crown and below bust (6318) .. 700 1750
6308A— — Similar, but pellets in each angle of tressure (6319) 725 1750
6309 — Annulets by neck, no pellets (6320) 650 1500
6310 *Trim*. Two small pellets over crown (6322) 1500 3500

6311

6317

6311 **Penny.** *Dublin*. No marks by bust (6323) 60 200
6311A— — Similar, but pellet either side of neck (6324) 70 225
6311B— — Similar, but two pellets below bust 75 250
6311C— — Similar, but saltire either side of neck (6325) 85 275
6312 *Drogheda*. No marks by head 70 225
6313 *Galway*. No marks by head (6327) 900 2750
6314 *Limerick*. No marks by head (6328) 200 650
6315 *Trim*. No marks by head (6328A) 125 450
6316 *Waterford*. No marks by bust 125 450
6316A— Two crosses either side of neck, pellets by crown
         (6326) 125 450
6317 **Halfpenny.** *Dublin*. No marks by head (6329) 475 1250

V. Bust/Rose on Sun coinage, 1467

6318

6318 **Double groat** (45 grs.) *Dublin*. Crowned bust in fleured tressure.
         ℞ Rose at centre of large sun, suns and roses divide legend (6290) 2250 6500
6318A— Similar, but unfleured tressure (6291) 2500 7000

6319

6319 *Drogheda*. As 6318 (6292)... 2750 7500
6320 *Trim*. Two pellets over crown and below bust (6293)................. 3250 9000

6321   6323

		F £	VF £
6321	**Groat.** *Dublin.* As 6318A (6294)	1750	5000
6322	*Drogheda.* Similar (6295)	2000	5500
6323	*Trim.* Pellets over crown and below bust (6296)	2250	6000

6324A   6325

6324	**Half groat.** *Dublin.* As 6318 (6297)	1350	4000
6324A—	Similar, but crosses by neck (6298)	1500	4250
6325	*Drogheda.* As 6319	2000	5500
6326	*Trim.* As 6324 (6299)	1750	5000
6326A—	Similar, but two pellets over crown (6300)	1750	5000
6327	**Penny.** *Dublin.* No tressure (6301)	1500	4500
6328	*Drogheda.* Similar (6302)	1500	4500
6328A	**Halfpenny.** *Dublin.* (Reported, not confirmed).		

Heavy coinage, 1470

6329	**Groat.** *Drogheda.* Full English title, not Irish	*Extremely rare*

VI. Light 'Cross and Pellets' coinage, 1472-78?

As heavy issue, but weight reduced to *c*.32 grains in 1473.

Mintmarks: pierced cross double fitchy, sun, rosette, plain cross, crown, trefoil

6330   6334

6330	**Groat.** *Dublin.* G below bust (for Germyn Lynch)	135	400
6331	— — Similar, but annulets in two spandrels of tressure	150	450
6332	— — — As above, but with crosses by neck	175	550
6333	— — Annulets by neck	175	550
6334	— — Annulets by neck and in two spandrels of tressure	165	500

	F £	VF £

6335

6337

6335 — — Pellets in some spandrels of tressure	175	550
6336 — I on king's breast	350	950
6337 *Cork*. Crude work. No marks by neck (6350)	2000	4500

6338

6341A

6338 — Pellets by neck (6351)..	2000	4500
6339 *Drogheda*. G below bust, annulets in two spandrels of tressure by crown (6337)	175	550
6340 — Similar, but annulets by neck and in two spandrels (6338) ..	225	675
6341 — Trefoil on king's breast (6339)	225	675
6341A— No marks other than G. ℞ Two extra pellets in one quarter (6339A)	185	575

6342

6343

6342 *Limerick*. L on breast, quatrefoils, crosses or saltires by neck (6340)...	450	1100
6343 — Cinquefoils by neck and in two quarters of reverse (6341) ..	475	1250

6345

6344 *Trim*. No letter on breast (6342)	325	900
6345 — — Pellet in some spandrels of tressure and/or over crown (6343)	300	850
6346 — — Pellets by neck (6344)	350	1000
6347 — B on breast (6344A)	475	1350

F   VF
£   £

6350   6351

6348	*Waterford.* No letter on breast, rosettes by neck (6345)	250	650
6349	— — Crosses or saltires by neck (6346)	250	650
6350	— V on breast (6348)	185	575
6351	— G on breast (6349)	150	450

6351A   6352

6351A—	No extra symbols on *obv.* ℞ Saltire in two quarters	250	650
6352	*Wexford.* Very crude. ℞ VILLA WEISFOR	3000	7500

6353   6354

6353	**Half groat.** *Dublin.* No marks by neck..	650	1500
6354	— Annulets by neck	700	1600

6355   6359

6355	*Drogheda.* No marks by neck	1500	3500
6356	*Limerick.* L on king's breast, rosettes or cinquefoils by neck.......	1350	3250
6357	— Similar, no letter on breast	1250	3000
6358	*Waterford.* No marks on breast or neck	1500	3500
6359	*Wexford.* Crude work ℞ VILLA WEISFOR	2500	6000

	F £	VF £

6361

6362

6360	**Penny.** *Dublin.* No marks by neck. ℞ Plain cross	45	175
6361	— — ℞ Quatrefoil in centre of cross	35	150
6361A	— — ℞ Rose in centre of cross	50	200
6361B	— — ℞ D in centre of cross (6361A)	75	275
6362	— Crosses or saltires by neck. ℞ Plain cross	50	200
6363	— — Similar, but with saltire to r. of crown ℞ Plain cross	45	175
6364	— Pellets by neck. ℞ Plain cross	35	150
6365	— — ℞ Quatrefoil in centre of cross	35	150
6365A	— — ℞ Rose in centre of cross	50	200
6365B	— Pellets by crown and neck. ℞ Rose in centre of cross	50	200
6366	— Mullets by neck. ℞ Quatrefoil in centre of cross	45	175
6367	— Mullets by crown ℞ Quatrefoil in centre of cross	45	175
6368	*Cork.* Pellets by crown ℞ Plain cross (6387)	400	1350
6368A	— Unusually large head ℞ Plain cross (6387A)	450	1500
6368B	— Pellets by crown. ℞ Quatrefoil in centre of cross	500	1650

6369

6378

6369	*Drogheda.* No marks by neck. ℞ Plain cross (6368)	50	200
6370	— — ℞ Quatrefoil in centre of cross (6369)	45	175
6370A	— — ℞ Rose in centre of cross	45	175
6371	— Crosses by neck. ℞ Plain cross	45	175
6372	— Pellets by neck. ℞ Plain cross	45	175
6373	— — ℞ Small rose at centre of cross (6370)	50	200
6374	— Pellets by neck and/or crown ℞ Plain cross (6363)	45	175
6375	— Pellets by neck and/or crown ℞ Quatrefoil in centre of cross	45	175
6376	— Pellets and rosettes by neck. ℞ Plain cross (6374)	100	325
6377	— Pellet and rosette by neck, saltire by crown. ℞ Small rose at centre of cross (6375)	135	450
6378	*Limerick.* Rosettes or cinquefoils by neck (6376)	150	525
6378A	— Rosettes by neck. ℞ Two pellets and one rose in two quarters	175	575
6379	— Crosses or saltires by neck ℞ Quatrefoil in centre (6377)	175	575
6380	*Trim.* No marks. ℞ Plain cross (6383)	110	425
6380A	— — ℞ Quatrefoil in centre of cross (6384)	110	425
6381	— Pellets by bust. ℞ Plain cross (6385)	125	450
6381A	— — ℞ Quatrefoil in centre of cross 6386)	125	450

	F £	VF £

6383

6382	*Waterford*. No marks R Plain cross (6378)	110	425
6382A—	— R Quatrefoil in centre of cross	125	450
6383	— Annulets by neck. R Plain cross (6379)	125	450
6383A—	— R Quatrefoil in centre of cross (6379A)	110	425
6384	— Pellets by neck. R Plain cross (6380)	135	500
6384A—	— R Quatrefoil in centre of cross	135	500
6385	— Crosses by neck and crown (6381)	135	500
6386	— Crosses by neck. R Quatrefoil in centre of cross (6382)	110	425

Note: These pennies rarely turn up on a full round flan and are usually clipped as the illustrations on the previous page. A full flan coin is worth considerably more.

| 6387 | **Halfpenny** *Dublin*. Saltires by crown. R Rose at centre of cross | 475 | 1250 |

VII. Bust with suns and Roses/Rose on Cross coinage, *c*.1478-83

Mintmark: rose

6388   6390

6388	**Groat.** *Dublin*. Sun and rose alternating at crown and neck. R POSVI, etc., mint name. large rose at centre of cross................	650	1750
6389	— Similar but rose and sun alternating at crown and neck	650	1750
6390	— — Larger symbols by crown and neck	750	2000

6391

| 6391 | *Drogheda*. As 6388 .... | 600 | 1650 |
| 6392 | — As 6389 .... | 675 | 1850 |

	F	VF
	£	£

6393

6393B

6393 Penny, large rose. *Dublin.* Sun and rose alternating at crown and neck.
R *Large* rose at centre of cross, no marks in angles (6396)   275   800
6393A— Rose and sun alternating at crown and neck (6397)   250   750
6393B— — Similar, but without symbols by crown (6398)   350   950
6394 *Drogheda.* As 6393A R *Large* rose at centre of cross, no marks
in angles   1250   3500

6394A   6395   6396

6394A— Similar, but rose both sides at crown and neck   1350   3750
6395 Penny, small rose. *Dublin.* Sun and rose alternating at crown and neck.
R *Small* rose at centre of cross, rose and 2 suns and sun and 2
roses alternating in angles (6393)   110   300
6396 — Similar, but rose and sun alternating at crown and neck (6394)   100   275

6397   6398

6397 — — Similar, but larger symbols on *obv.* (6395)   125   325
6398 Halfpenny. *Dublin.* Saltires by crown. R Rose at centre of
cross, no marks in angles   475   1250

BILLON AND COPPER

Issues of *c.***1460-61**

6400   6400A   6401

6399 Half farthing, or 'Patrick' (Æ). PA branch TRIK branch, crown
in centre. R Quatrefoil tressure around large cross, no legend ..   1250   3000
6400 PA branch TRIK branch, crown in centre. R Large cross, no legend
(6399)   1000   2500
6400A— Similar, but retrograde inscription (6399A)   1100   2750
6400B— — R P in one angle of cross (6400)   1250   3000

Issue of 1462

6401 Farthing (billon). *Dublin.* Large crown, sun and roses in place of legend.
R Mint name, cross in centre   1250   3000

		F £	VF £

Issue of 1463-65

6402

6404

6402   **Farthing** (Æ). PATRICIVS, mitred Saint's head facing, sun and
       rose. ℞ SALVATOR, cross with rose and sun in alternate angles.
       Several varieties, some with blundered legends   1500   3500
6403   **Half farthing** (Æ). Crown, no legend. ℞ Cross and pellets, no
       legend   1350   3250

Issue of 1467-70?
6404   **Farthing** (Æ). Shield bearing three crowns. ℞ Cross with rose
       over sun at centre   1750   4000

A 'farthing' of brass in the National Museum of Ireland with a facing
bust and cross and pellets on the reverse, with strokes for legend, is
probably a counterfeit of an English halfpenny of Henry VII or Henry
VIII.

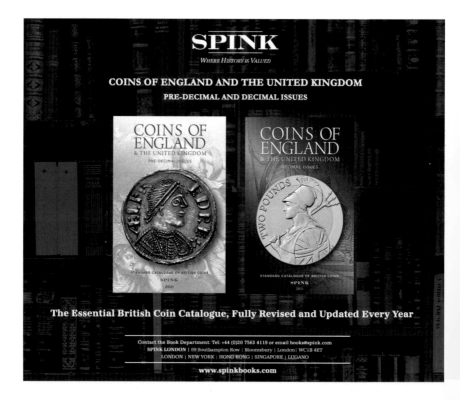

APPENDIX 2 – Table of Concordance for Edward IV and Edward V Ireland

2020	2015	2020	2015	2020	2015	2020	2015
6280	6272	6312A	6308A	6357	6360	6374C	6372
6280A	6272A	6312B	6309	6359	6380A	6374D	6373
6280B	6273	6314	6310	6366	6330	6374I	6376
6280C	6274	6315	6311	6366A	6331	6374J	6377
6280D	6275	6315A	6311A	6366B	6332	6375	6380
6281	6275A	6315B	6311B	6366C	6333	6376	6382A
6282	6276	6315C	6311C	6366D	6334	6376A	6383A
6282A	6277	6316	6312	6366E	6335	6376B	6384A
6282B	6278	6316A	6370A	6366F	6336	6376C	6385
6282C	6279	6317	6313	6367	6339	6376D	6386
6282D	6280	6318	6314	6367A	6340	6377	6387
6283	6281	6319	6315	6367B	6341	6379	6337
6284	6281A	6320	6316	6367C	6341A	6379A	6338
6289	6288	6320A	6316A	6368	6344	6380	6342
6290	6289	6320C	6383	6368A	6345	6380A	6343
6293	6282	6321	6317	6368B	6346	6381	6352
6294	6283	6328	6318	6368C	6347	6382	6356
6294A	6284	6328A	6318A	6369	6348	6382A	6357
6295	6285	6329	6319	6369A	6349	6383	6359
6296	6285A	6330	6320	6369B	6350	6384	6368
6297	6286	6331	6321	6369C	6351	6384A	6368A
6299	6287	6332	6322	6369D	6351A	6384B	6368B
6306	6290	6333	6323	6370	6353	6385	6378
6306A	6291	6334	6324	6370A	6354	6385A	6379
6306B	6292	6334A	6324A	6371	6355	6388	Same
6306C	6293	6335	6325	6372	6358	6388A	6389
6307	6295	6336	6326	6373	6361A	6388B	6390
6307A	6296	6336A	6326A	6373A	6361B	6389	6395
6308	6297	6337	6327	6373B	6362	6389A	6396
6308A	6298	6338	6328	6373C	6363	6389B	6397
6308B	6299	6339	6328A	6373D	6361	6390	6393
6308C	6299A	6347	6399	6373F	6364	6390A	6393A
6309	6301	6347A	6400	6373G	6365	6390B	6393B
6310	6302	6347B	6400A	6373H	6365A	6391	6398
6311	6303	6347C	6400B	6373I	6365B	6392	6391
6311A	6304	6348	6401	6373J	6366	6392A	6392
6311B	6305	6349	6402	6373K	6367	6394	Same
6311C	6306	6350	6403	6374	6369	6394A	Same
6311D	6307	6351	6404	6374A	6370		
6312	6308	6356	6329	6374B	6371		

NOTES

NOTES

NOTES

NOTES

NOTES

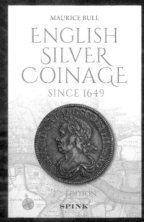